JACK DAVIS

SOME OF MY GOOD STUFF!

Master cartoonist Jack Davis
reveals previously unpublished artwork
and other rarely seen gems from his personal archives.

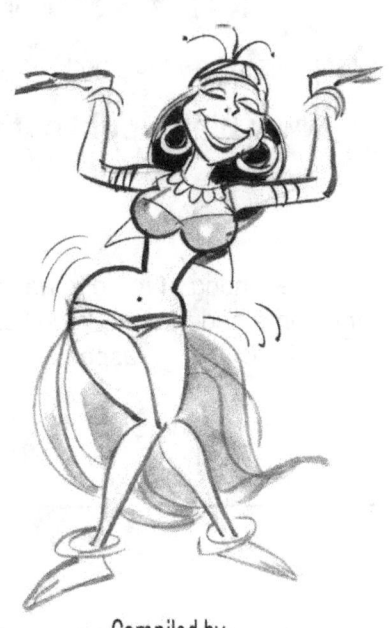

Compiled by

HANK HARRISON

Foreword By Harvey Kurtzman, Stan Lee, Mort Walker and Lynn Johnston

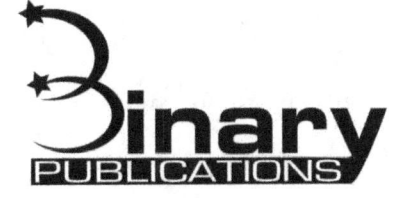

Binary
PUBLICATIONS

Originally Published by Stabur Press.

JACK DAVIS: SOME OF MY GOOD STUFF!
Compiled by Hank Harrison

(c) 2013 by Binary Publications
All rights reserved including rights of reproduction or portions thereof in any form.
Originally published and (c) 1990 by Stabur Press.

ISBN: 978-0-9854807-0-7

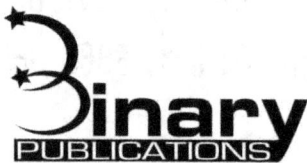

for more information on Binary Publications:

www.binarypublications.com

This edition is a reprinting of the original book released in 1990. The contents are the same and the only modifications are in the reproduction aspects.

Production on the Binary Edition by Dan Royer

Thanks to the many people who made this book possible:

Most importantly, thanks to Jack and Dena Davis for their interest, assistance, and hospitality. All artwork reproduced in this book is from Jack Davis' personal collection.

Thanks to my wife Polly, for her support.

Thanks to Paul Burke for publishing this volume and *The Art of Jack Davis* in 1987.

Thanks to Mom, Dad, Jeff, Scott and Dinah.

Thanks, also, to all the unnamed publishers, editors and art directors who had a part in any of these illustrations.

For
Dena

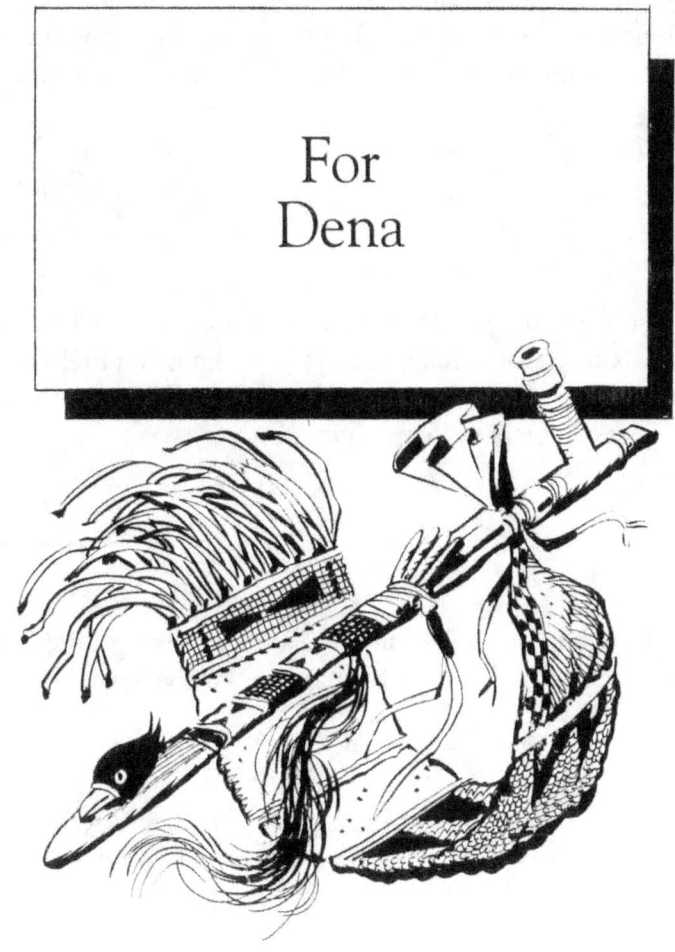

Foreword

Jack is one of my oldest friends. I knew him a-way back before his hair turned to white and mine turned to bald. My wife Adele and I kept a special mint patch out back, just so's Jack could make Juleps when he and his wife Dena visited. He had Dena convinced that their county of White Plains was named after the little white planes that landed there. What a funny guy! At our Halloween party, Jack secretly put pebbles inside the other reveler's hub caps. Can you imagine? I could go on and on, but let me tell you one thing; If everyone was suddenly like Jack, psychiatrists would be out of business tomorrow!

— Harvey Kurtzman
Editor of Mad, Trump & Humbug
To name a few . . .

Jolly Jack Davis is the quintessential cartoonist's cartoonist as well as being the nicest guy you'll ever meet. He's also a walking catastrophe; He draws like a house on fire! His style hits you between the eyes like an explosion, and you can die laughing at his humor! On top of that, his facility makes you choke with envy! Oh, in case I forgot to mention it . . .
I think he's the greatest!

— Stan Lee
Creator of Spiderman & The Hulk

Most cartoonists love their own work but there are a few exceptions: Most of them love Jack Davis' work better. Gee, I wish I could draw like that guy! I'd give my favorite putter just to be able to crosshatch with his skill.

— Mort Walker
Creator of "Beetle Bailey" & "Hi and Lois"

Jack Davis can draw. That's like saying "the sky is blue", but to somebody who has loved and studied his work, this is a statement of sincere admiration. I've learned from him that it's not enough to just draw - but to bring a character to "life". Jack Davis has been one of my most valued and respected instructors!

— Lynn Johnston
Creator of "For Better or for Worse"

Introduction

This book offers a rare look into the working methods and techniques of master illustrator Jack Davis. For this book, I spent a week going through all of the artwork in Jack Davis' archives. I selected what I considered to be prime examples of Davis' art, concentrating on the unusual and spectacular. My preliminary selection represented a fraction of Jack's files. Then Jack and I went through the material I had selected and thinned the stack down even more, with Jack selecting pieces that he especially liked. This is the material you will find in the following pages. Jack said he wanted to show his fans "Some of my good stuff." This is it.

The art runs the gamut from quick pencil sketches to finished color renderings. There are a few rarely seen previously printed pieces but the majority are unpublished gems seen here for the first time. In particular you will see the preliminary drawings which Davis feels reveal the essence of his style. (It is Davis' impression that some of the spontaneity and energy of the original sketch can be lost when it is inked.)

It might be of interest to know how Jack Davis approaches a typical illustration project. Jack first gets the specific details of a job from his agent at Rapp, Inc. He then does a rough layout in pencil or brush & ink and marker on tracing paper which he then photocopies and faxes to his agent. Jack's agent then presents the rough idea to the client. The approved illustration is then returned to Jack with any changes marked. When the approved idea is rendered in its final form, he ships the finished illustration to the client by delivery service. In most cases, after the job is printed, the original art is returned to the artist. Jack retains the original rough drawings. Many of these originals and roughs are in this book. The other art in this volumn consists of finished but unused *Time Magazine* covers, drawings Jack has done for himself, roughs and alternative approaches to projects for *Mad*, *Help!*, *Playboy* and a myriad of roughs for advertising illustrations.

All illustrations are presented without regard to chronology, technique or subject matter. I hope you enjoy this look at some of Jack Davis' good stuff!

Hank Harrison

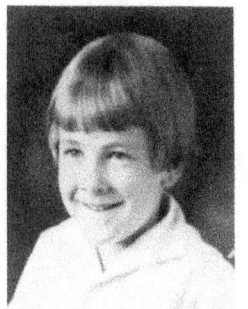

Jack Davis, age 5.

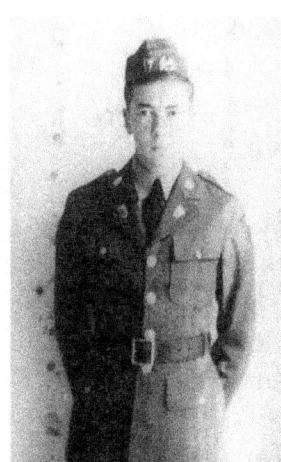

North Fulton High School
R.O.T.C.

Jack Burton Davis, Jr. has always been interested in art. The only child of Jack and Callie Davis, Jack Jr. was born in Atlanta, Georgia on December 2, 1924. He began sketching cartoon characters like *Henry* and *Popeye* from the newspaper comic strips at an early age. By the time he was twelve, Jack had won a cartoon contest in *Tip Top Comics*, and had gag cartoons published in the Georgia Tech humor magazine *The Yellow Jacket*. Through his school years, Jack's art was frequently featured in the school paper and he illustrated the entire 1943 North Fulton High School annual *Hi-Ways*, in which he was described as: "An unusual combination: Artist and Basketball Star. Prevailing Sin: Spelling. Personality in one word: Shy."

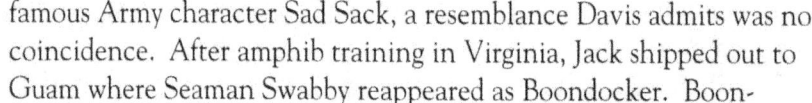

In a Georgia pond, age 8.

Jack enlisted in the Navy after graduation and went to boot camp in Pensacola, Florida where he created Seaman Swabby for the *Gosport Weekly*. Seaman Swabby was highly reminiscent of George Baker's famous Army character Sad Sack, a resemblance Davis admits was no coincidence. After amphib training in Virginia, Jack shipped out to Guam where Seaman Swabby reappeared as Boondocker. Boondocker ran daily in *The Navy News* for the nine months Davis was stationed at Agana Air Base.

After his hitch in the Navy, Davis returned to Georgia where he enrolled at the University of Georgia on the G.I. Bill. Jack was staff artist for the university paper the *Red and Black* and also put out several issues of a slightly risqué off-campus humor magazine called the *Bull Sheet* which was very successful. At the University of Georgia, Jack and pretty coed Dena Roquemore became seriously involved.

In 1947, Davis wrote and illustrated a weekly sports article for the *Atlanta Journal-Constitution* and also covered a sensational murder trial as a courtroom artist. For about a month that same year Jack worked with cartoonist Ed Dodd, creator of *Mark Trail* and a fellow Georgian. Dodd recognized the talent in his assistant and suggested that Davis continue his art training at the *Art Student's League* in New York, but it was two years before opportunity knocked in the

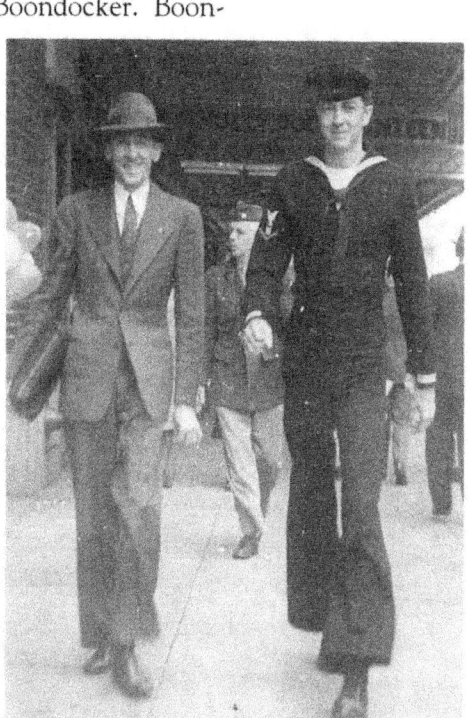

Jack Jr. home on leave in 1944, with Jack Davis Sr.

form of a call from Coca-Cola. They needed illustrations for *Here's How*, a manual for Coca-Cola route drivers. It was Jack's first commercial art assignment, he remembers "...I made enough money with that to buy a car and move to New York." Davis and his fiancee Miss Roquemore agreed he should move to New York to get established, so Jack drove up from Georgia with a portfolio full of samples and great expectations.

When he got to New York, Davis enrolled in the Art Student's League, "I was attending classes at night and looking for work during the day. I had already been around to all of the comic book publishers and newspaper syndicates...I was getting kind of depressed with not having much luck finding work, living on the G.I. Bill and going to school." Then Jack saw a notice on the bulletin board at the Art Student's League that The Herald-Tribune Syndicate

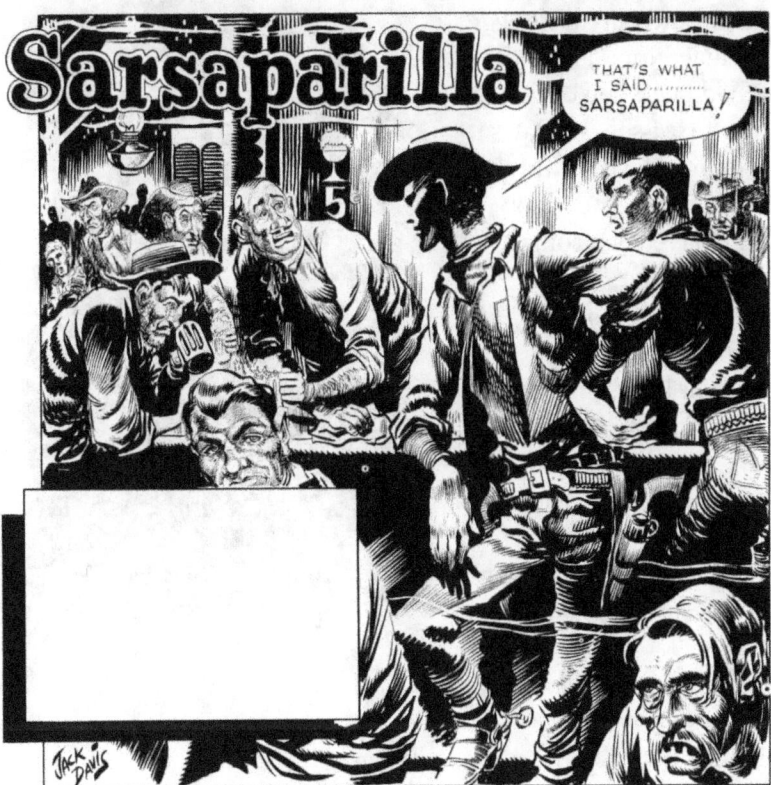

needed an inker for *The Saint* comic strip. Jack remembers; "I went down there with my portfolio, and sure enough they called me back. That was a big break. I was thinking about getting married and those were lean, lean times."

This comic book splash panel from *Sarsaparilla*, ca. 1949, is one of the samples Jack Davis had in his portfolio as he looked for work in New York. This rare pre-E.C. comic art is published here for the first time.

"I stayed with The Saint for about a year. It taught me a lot," Jack adds. But in 1950 the Herald-Tribune closed. A few jobs like *Lucky Star* (a cowboy comic book) came along, but nothing looked very promising.

Then Jack tried one more comic book company. "I took the subway downtown to E.C. after I looked up their address inside one of their comics. They gave me a script right away!" Jack's first work for E.C. ran in 1951. Within months Davis was holding his own with some of the brightest stars in the comic book industry, and soon became one of the most pro- lific: "I would go in about once a week after that to drop off one story and pick up another." Jack Davis had found a home. He stayed at E.C. for six years, doing horror, war, suspense, humor and science fiction comic books. It was a great training ground for the young artist. "I enjoyed the war books and I didn't really mind the horror books. It all came easy."

But by the mid-50's, things began to change. The McCarthy-era comics industry, in response to hysterical accusations that comic books contributed to juvenile

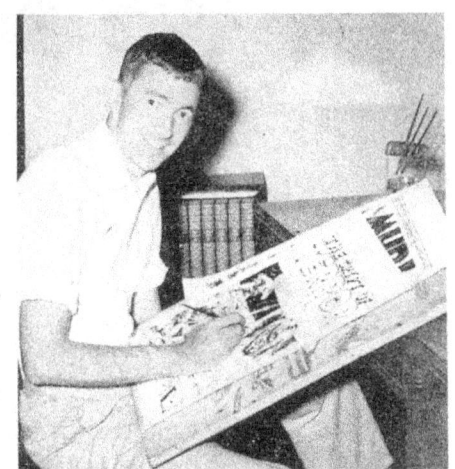

E.C. artist Davis, at the drawing table, 1952.

delinquency, decided that a good offense was the best defense. The Comics Code Authority was instituted to guard against any real or imagined excesses on the part of comic book companies. To avoid this ridiculous self-imposed censorship, Bill Gaines, the far-sighted publisher of E.C. comics, withdrew all of his popular comics from print except one...Mad. Mad was a satirical comic book that had been in existence for 23 issues under the editorship of Harvey Kurtzman. It was decided that E.C. would put all its eggs in one basket and make Mad a real magazine. Jack Davis' humorous illustration style had been one of the hallmarks of the Mad style since the first issue, so Davis joined E.C. publisher Bill Gaines, editor Harvey Kurtzman and fellow artists Will Elder and Wally Wood in this speculative venture. There may have been some anxiety regarding the switch to a new format, but it proved unnecessary. The first issue of Mad sold out. *Mad Magazine* was a hit!

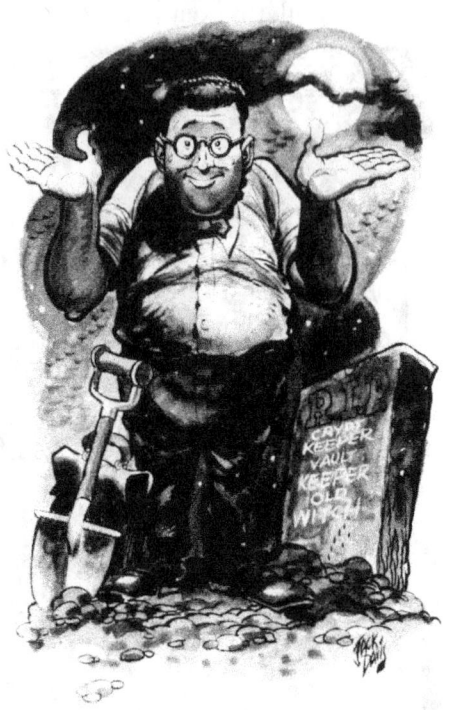

Jack did this painting of Bill Gaines in 1955, when Bill buried his successful line of horror comics.

In 1957, Harvey Kurtzman, Jack Davis and Will Elder left Mad to develop a new slick humor magazine for Playboy publisher Hugh Hefner. The magazine *Trump*, only lasted two issues but it was arguably the most beautiful and expensive satire magazine ever printed. Jack also produced a series of 15 color cartoons for Playboy and later worked on *Little Annie Fanny* with Kurtzman, Elder and Frank Frazetta.

After Trump, the Kurtzman repertory company pooled their resources to produce *Humbug*, another highly creative and critically acclaimed but short-lived satire magazine.

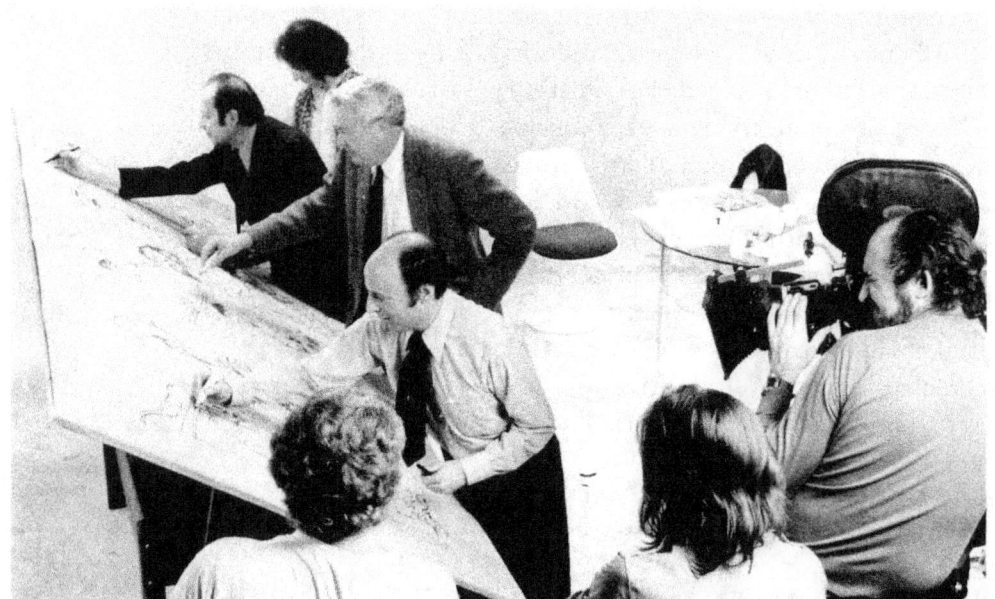

Harvey Kurtzman, Jack Davis and Will Elder working at the same drawing table for a French film crew in the '60s.

The failure of *Humbug* left Davis with no steady outlet for his lightning-fast pen, so the period from 1958 to 1965 became a time of experimentation for the ex-Mad man. Jack, who had always wanted to draw his own syndicated comic strip, made a concerted effort to syndicate *Beauregard*, which featured the exploits of a Confederate soldier in the Civil War. The McClure Newspaper Syndicate, sadly, wasn't able to generate the interest necessary to introduce the new strip. During this same time, Jack worked for Atlas comics, as he'd been doing since E.C. Comics folded and he developed his own humor comic book for Dell comics called *Yak Yak*.

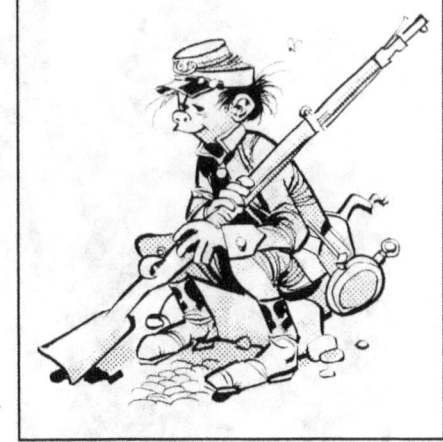

Beauregard in a rare moment of repose.

During the mid-'60s, Davis did several stories for Harvey Kurtzman's *HELP!* magazine, as well as other humor magazines, western magazines, Cavalier magazine, gum cards and greeting cards.

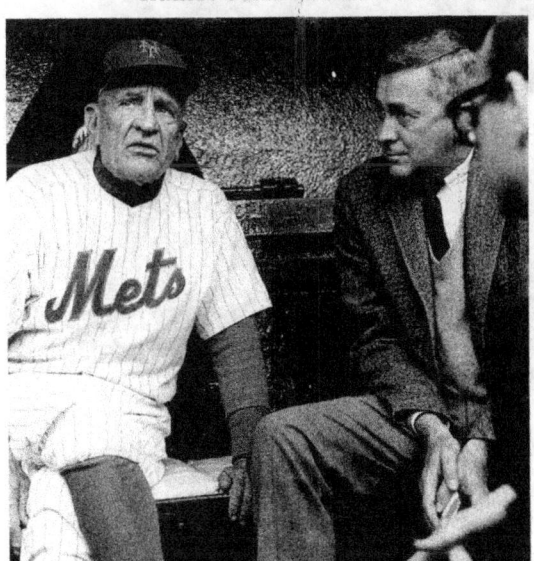

One of Jack's favorite assignments for *Help!*: Interview the Ol' Perfessor, Casey Stengel for the 1963 article, *Jack Davis Meets the Mets*.

Jack's first movie poster was done in 1956, but in 1964, Jack Davis' movie poster for *It's a Mad, Mad, Mad, Mad World* set the style for humorous movie poster design. In all, Davis has illustrated 46 movie posters.

The first Jack Davis record album cover was done in 1957. One year later, he began a long-running association with RCA Records. Since that first record, Davis has illustrated 64 record albums

Jack's first book illustrations appeared in 1956. Since then he has illustrated no fewer than 81 books, many of which have won design awards.

Jack's first advertising art appeared in 1961, but in 1965, with his award-winning series of ads for NBC, Jack not only began a high-profile career in advertising that has kept him in constant demand for 25 years, but has established humorous illustration techniques that are admired and much imitated.

Since the mid-60s, Davis' illustrations have appeared in nearly every major publication in the country: Life, Esquire, Playboy, Sports Illustrated, Money, Fortune, Ladies Home Journal, TV Guide and on many prestigious Time covers.

When Jack returned to Mad Magazine in 1965, he was one of the best known illustrators in the country. Jack is the only member of the original Mad Comics staff to still contribute regularly to Mad Magazine. Since his return to Mad, Davis has participated in most of Bill Gaines' legendary Mad trips, including expeditions to Russia, Africa and Europe.

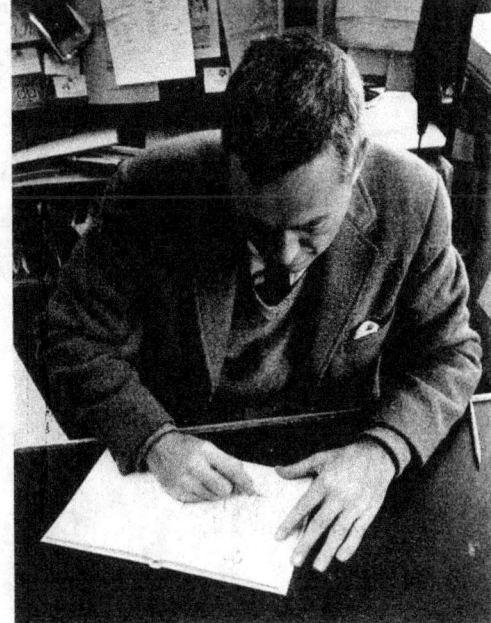

Davis, hard at work on the rough layout for the 1965 Random House children's book *Meet Abraham Lincoln*.

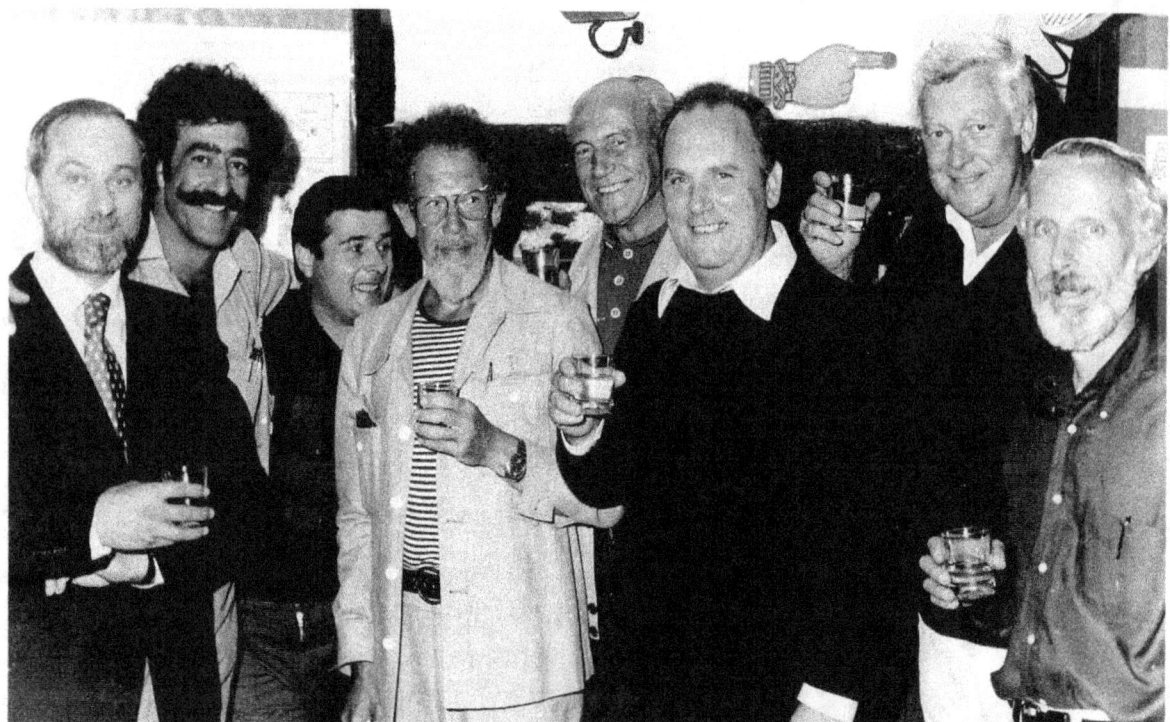

Mad crew at the Cartoon Museum in Italy. Amongst Italian cartoonists are; Sergio Aragones second from left; Al Jaffee fourth from left; Davis second from right and Paul Coker, Jr. far right.

In fact, Jack is one of the reasons Bill Gaines started the trips. In Frank Jacob's excellent biography, *The Mad World of William M. Gaines*, Bill says, "I knew Davis loved to travel, and since he's become eligible he's never missed one. I like having Davis in the magazine, and the trips are a way of keeping him there,

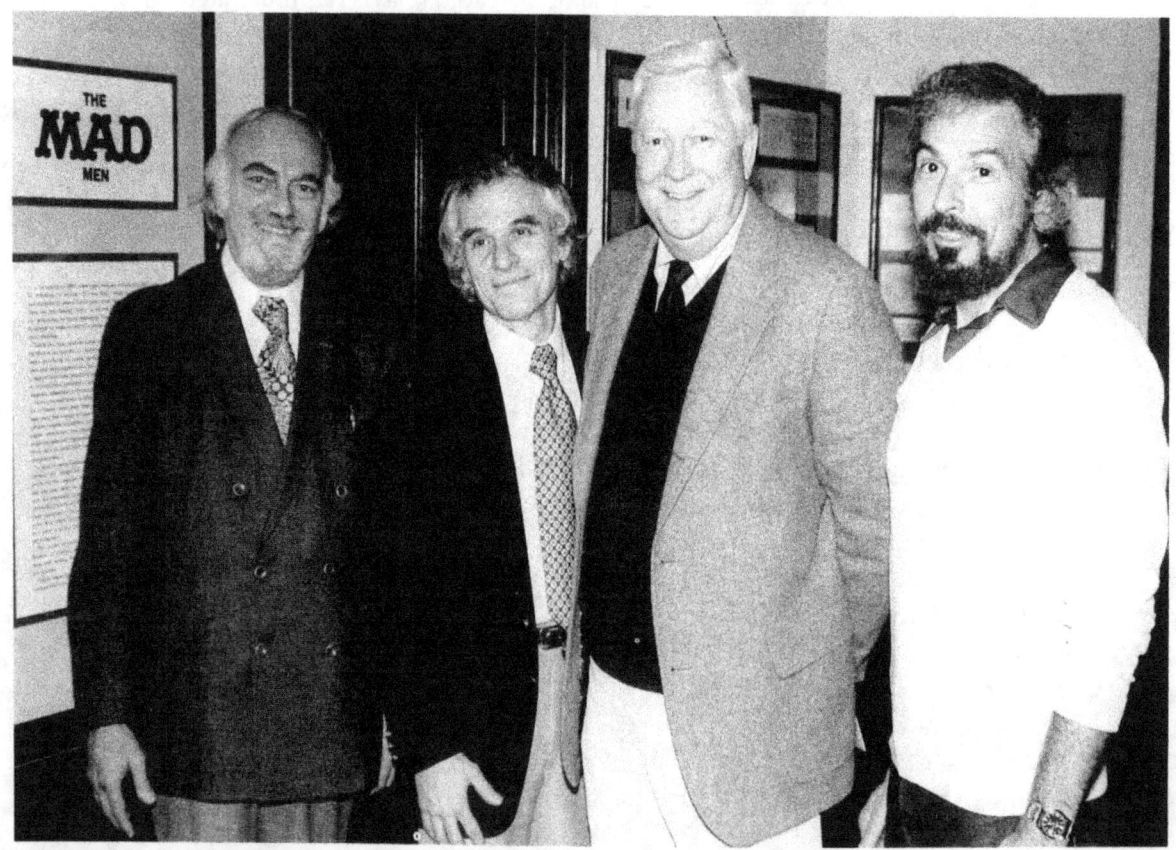

left to right: Mad artists Bob Clarke, Mort Drucker, Jack Davis and editor Nick Meglin.

despite the fact that I know he can make more money elsewhere."

For nearly forty years Jack Davis has produced an astonishing quantity and variety of work, which, along with his inimitable action-packed style and unimpeachable mastery of technique, has made him a true legend among American illustrators.

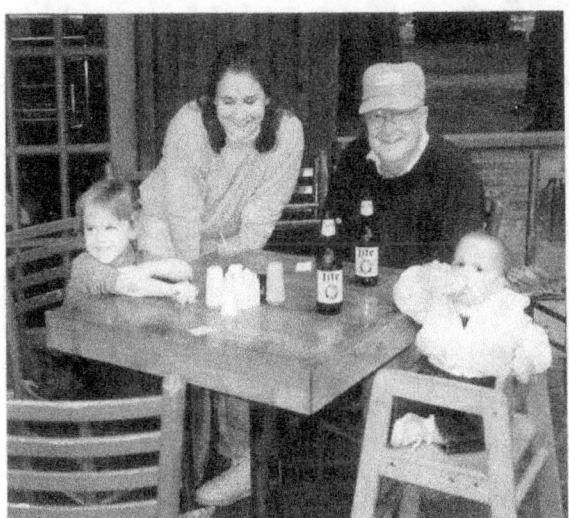

Jack Davis with daughter Katie Davis Lloyd and granddaughters Sara (left) and Molly.

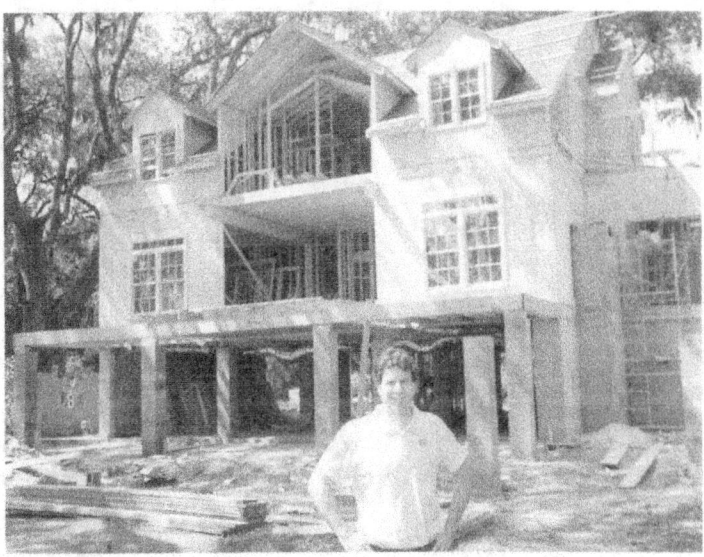

Architect Jack Davis III, in front of the Davis home in Georgia, under construction in 1989.

Jack and Dena Davis were married in 1951. Their two children, Jack III and Katie, live in Georgia. Katie Lloyd is an interior decorator, and Jack III is an architect, both in Atlanta. The Davis' new home in Georgia was designed by their son Jack (see photo).

Jack and Dena's recent move back to Georgia doesn't mean Jack Davis is retiring. He's closer to his grandchildren, but no further away from his drawing board. In an interview in *Atlanta Weekly*, Jack said, "As long as there are people who want my work, I'll do it. Beyond that, I plan to enjoy life, play golf, sit down and have a drink and do what I want to do."

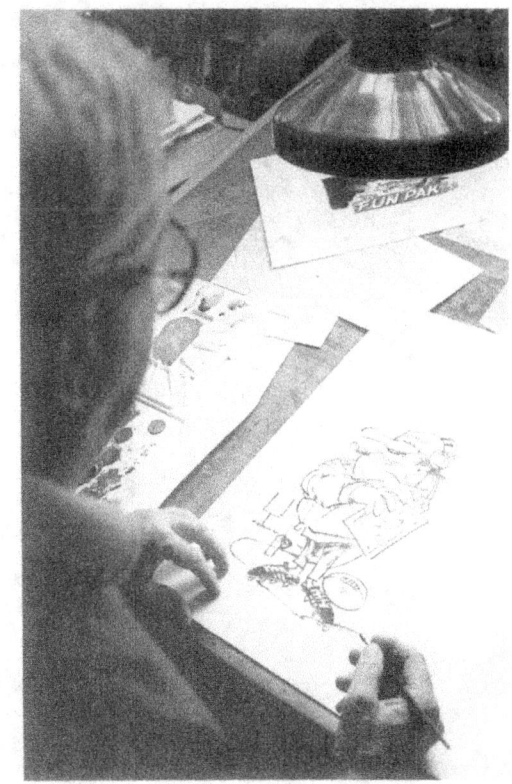

Viking Ship
Pencil on illustration board
Poster design

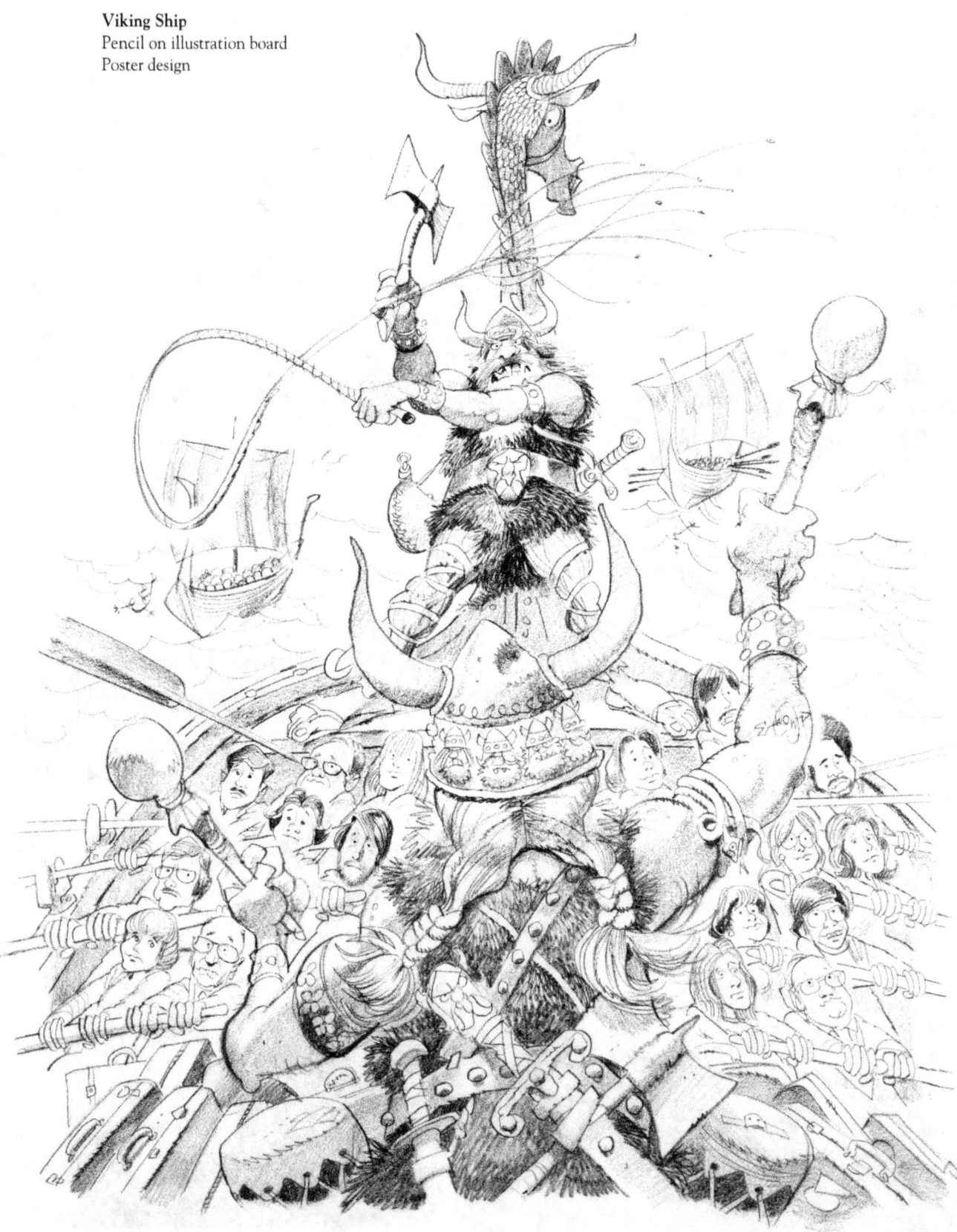

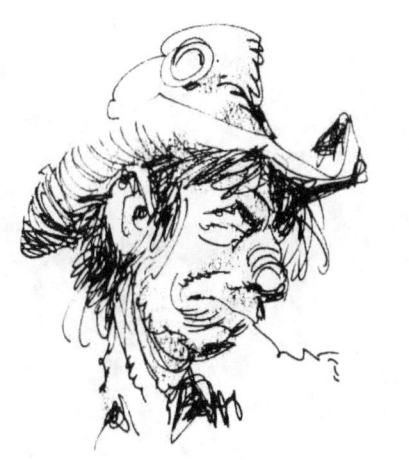

Cowboy
Felt-tip and pencil sketch
on illustration board

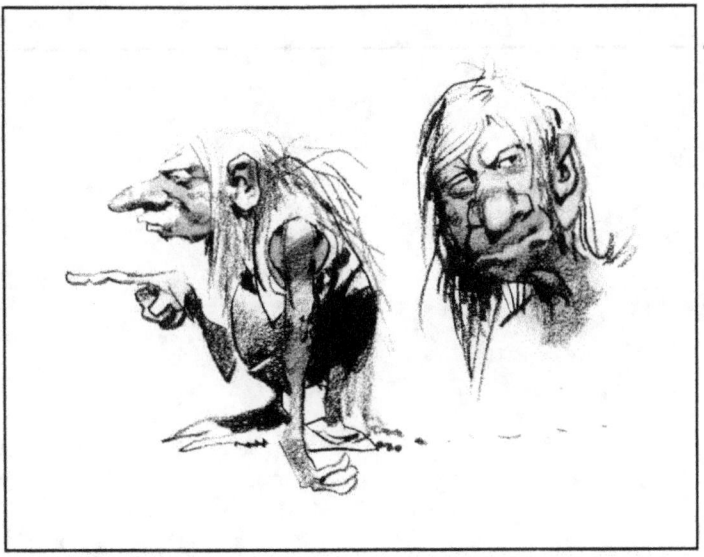

Gnomes
Pencil and watercolor sketch
on illustration board

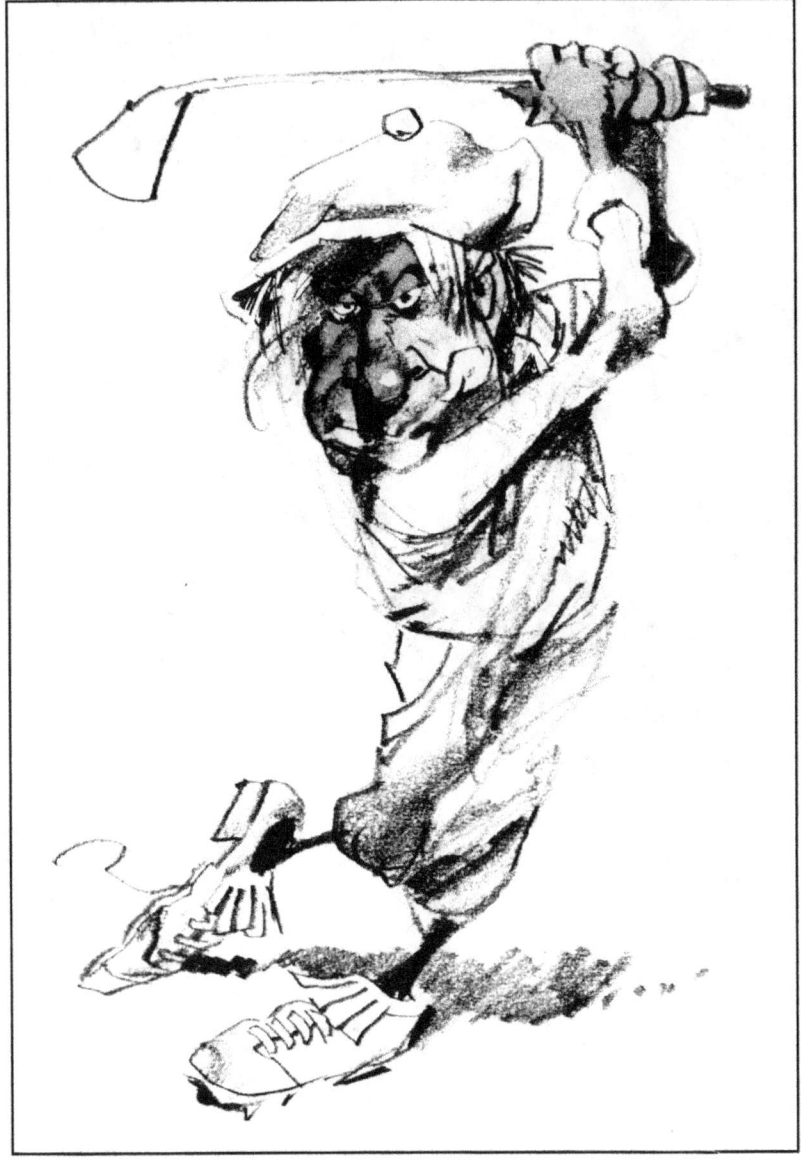

The No-Name Man of the Mountain
Brush & ink on Strathmore
Rough for children's book, 1964

Gnome Golfer
Pencil and watercolor sketch
on illustration board

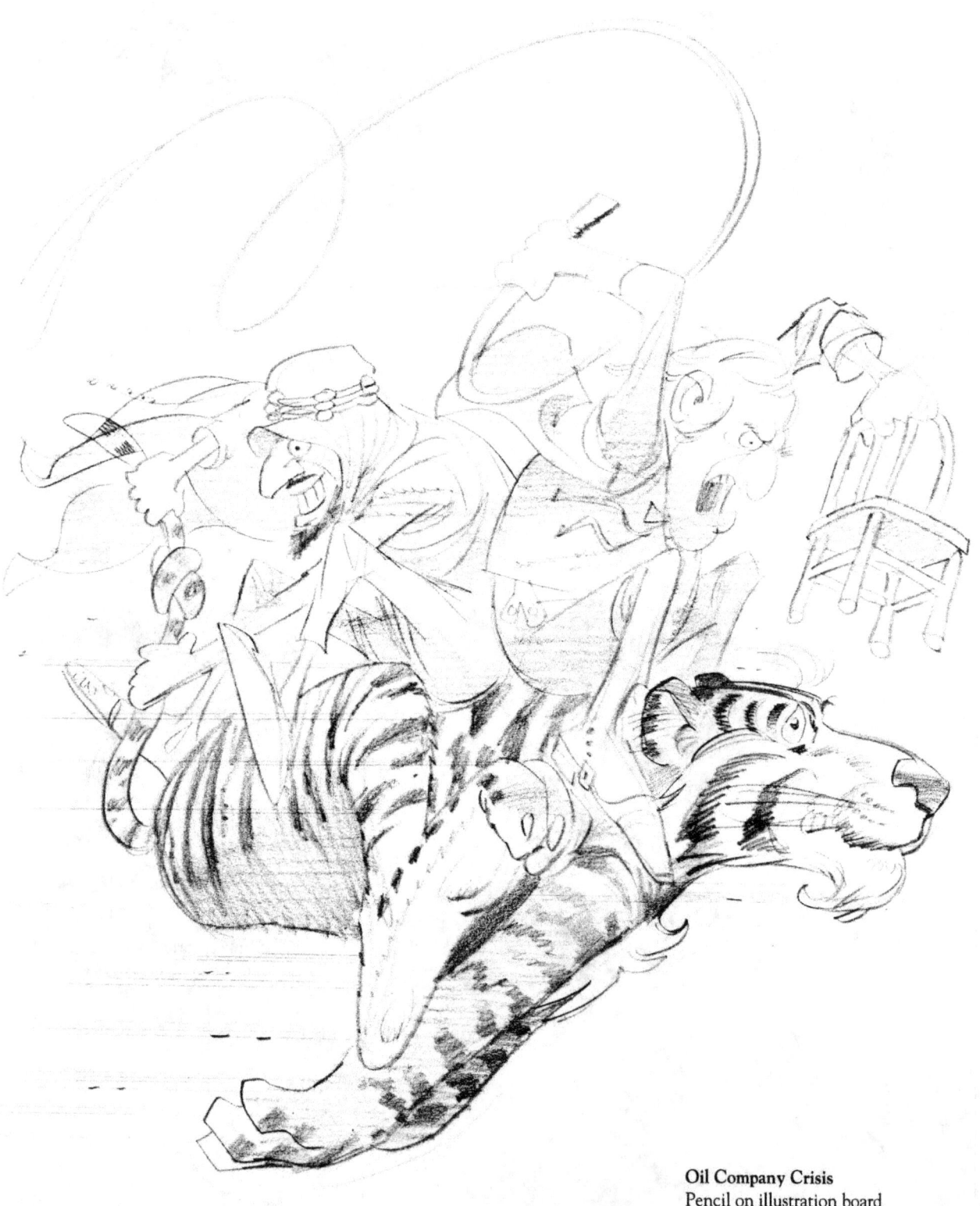

Oil Company Crisis
Pencil on illustration board
Rough for magazine cover

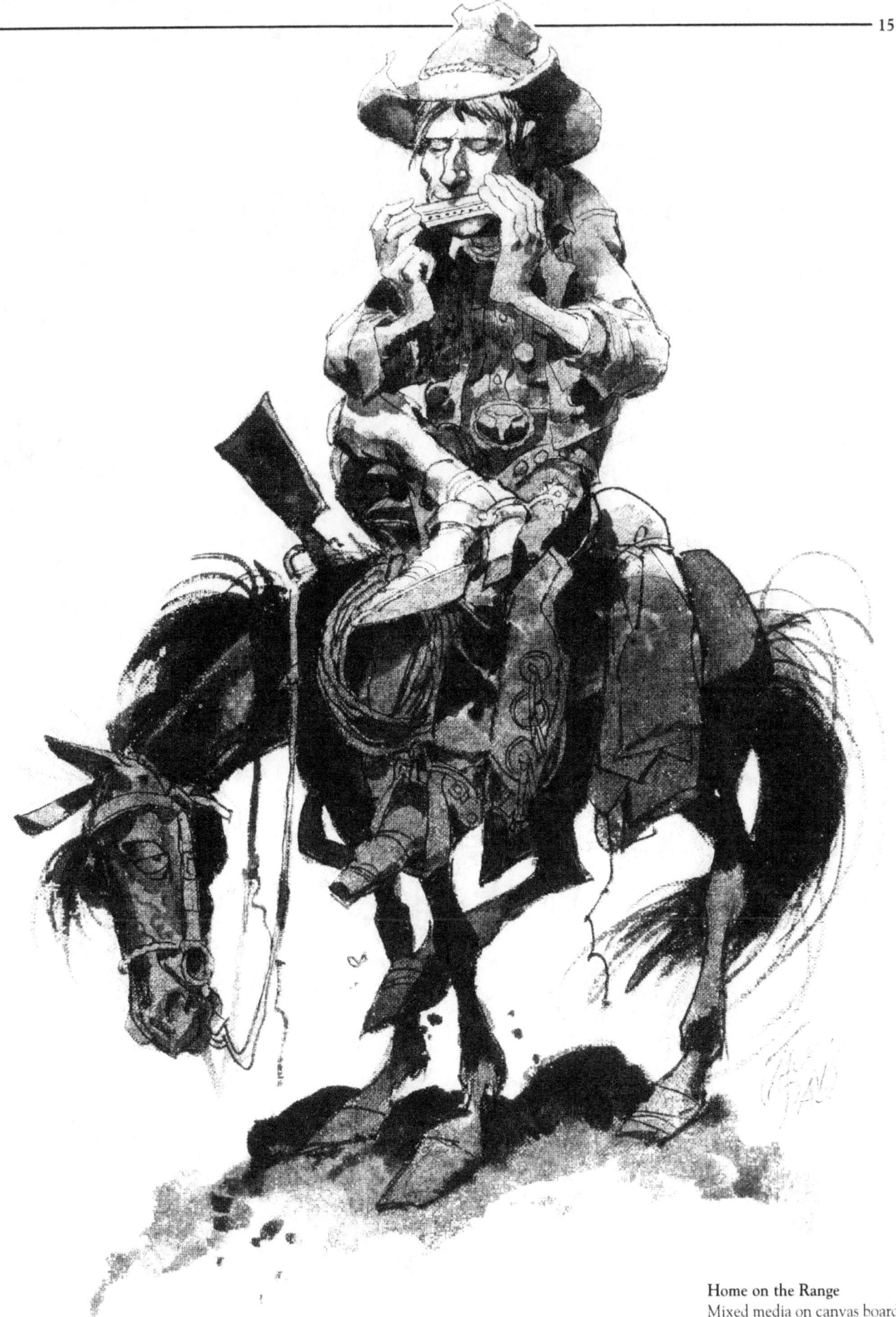

Home on the Range
Mixed media on canvas board

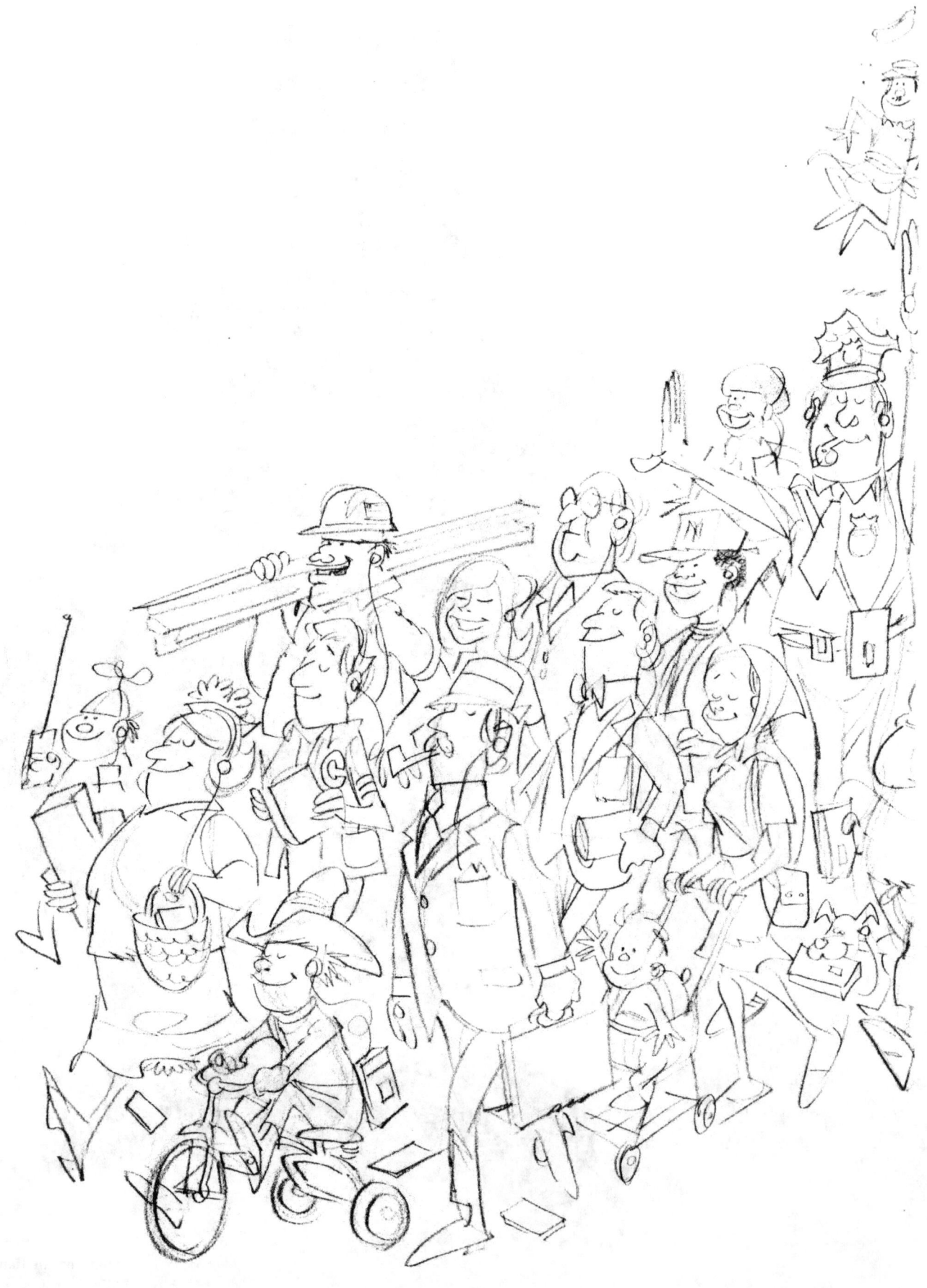

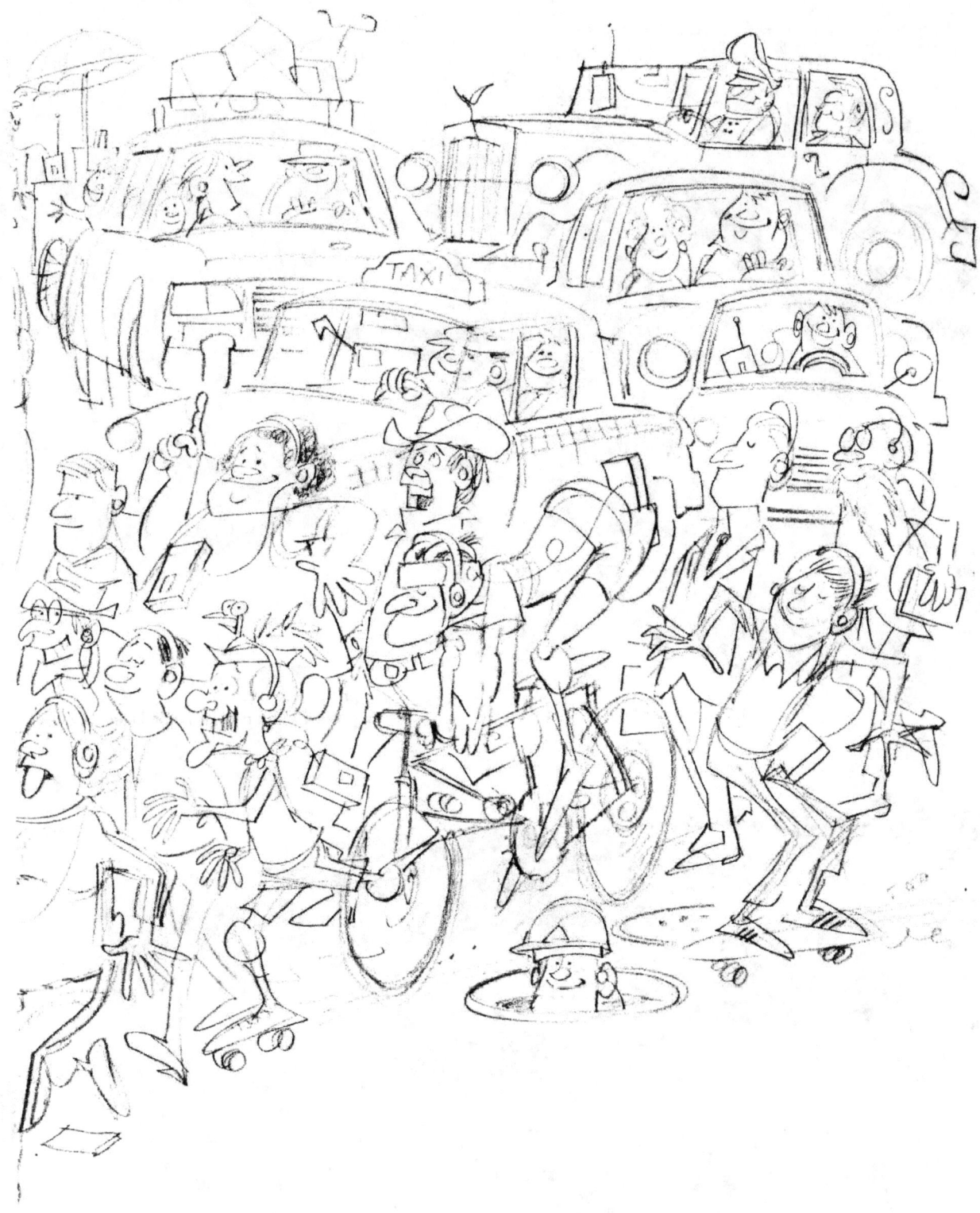

City Traffic
Pencil rough on illustration board

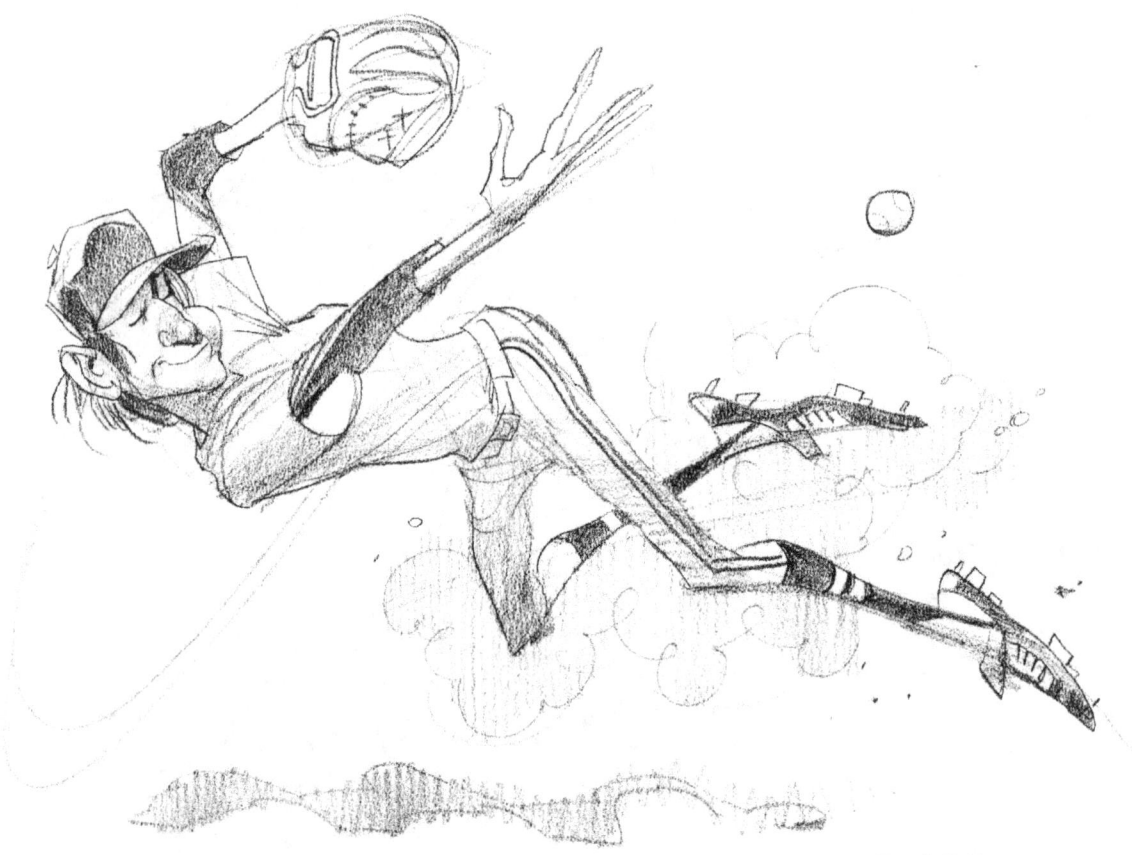

Baseball Player
Pencil rough on illustration board

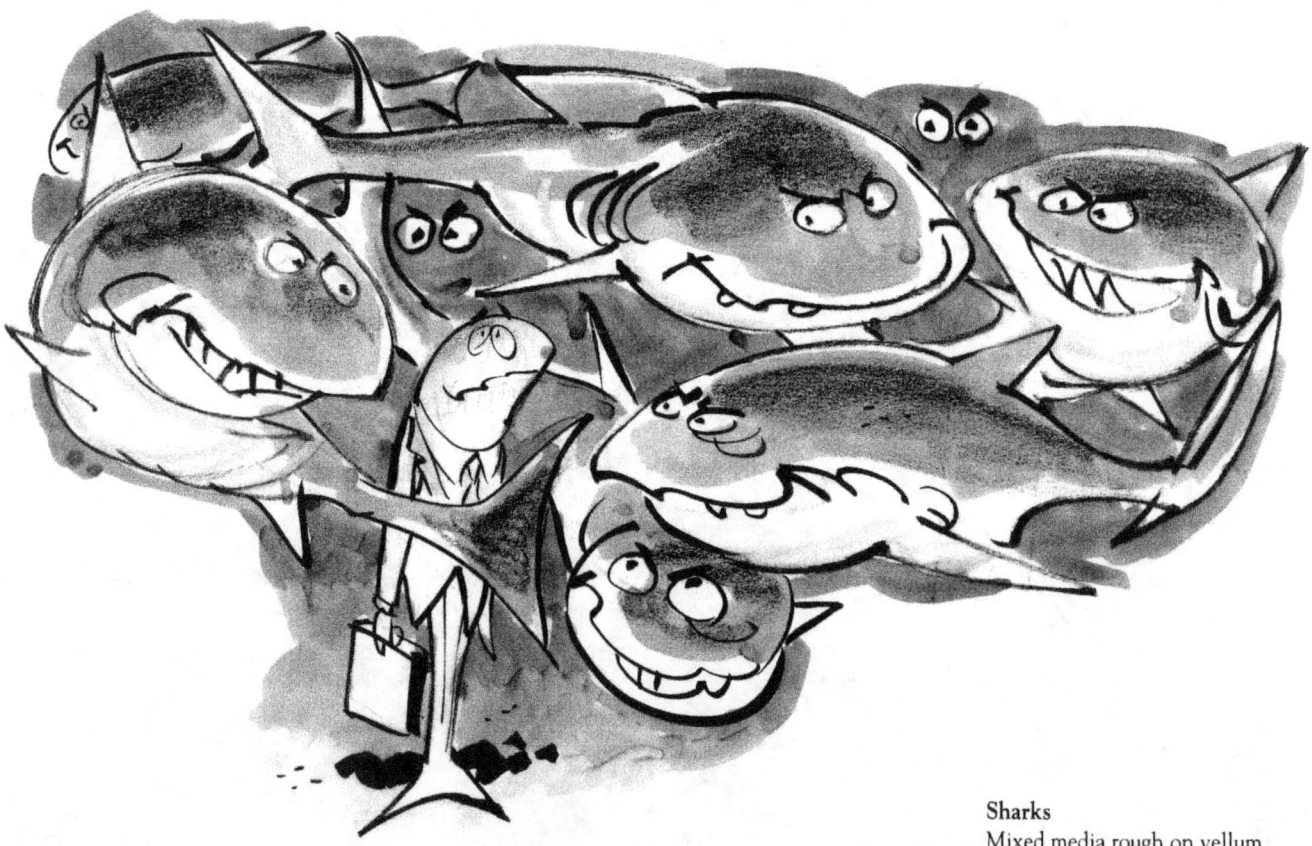

Sharks
Mixed media rough on vellum

Soda Jerk
Pencil rough on Strathmore

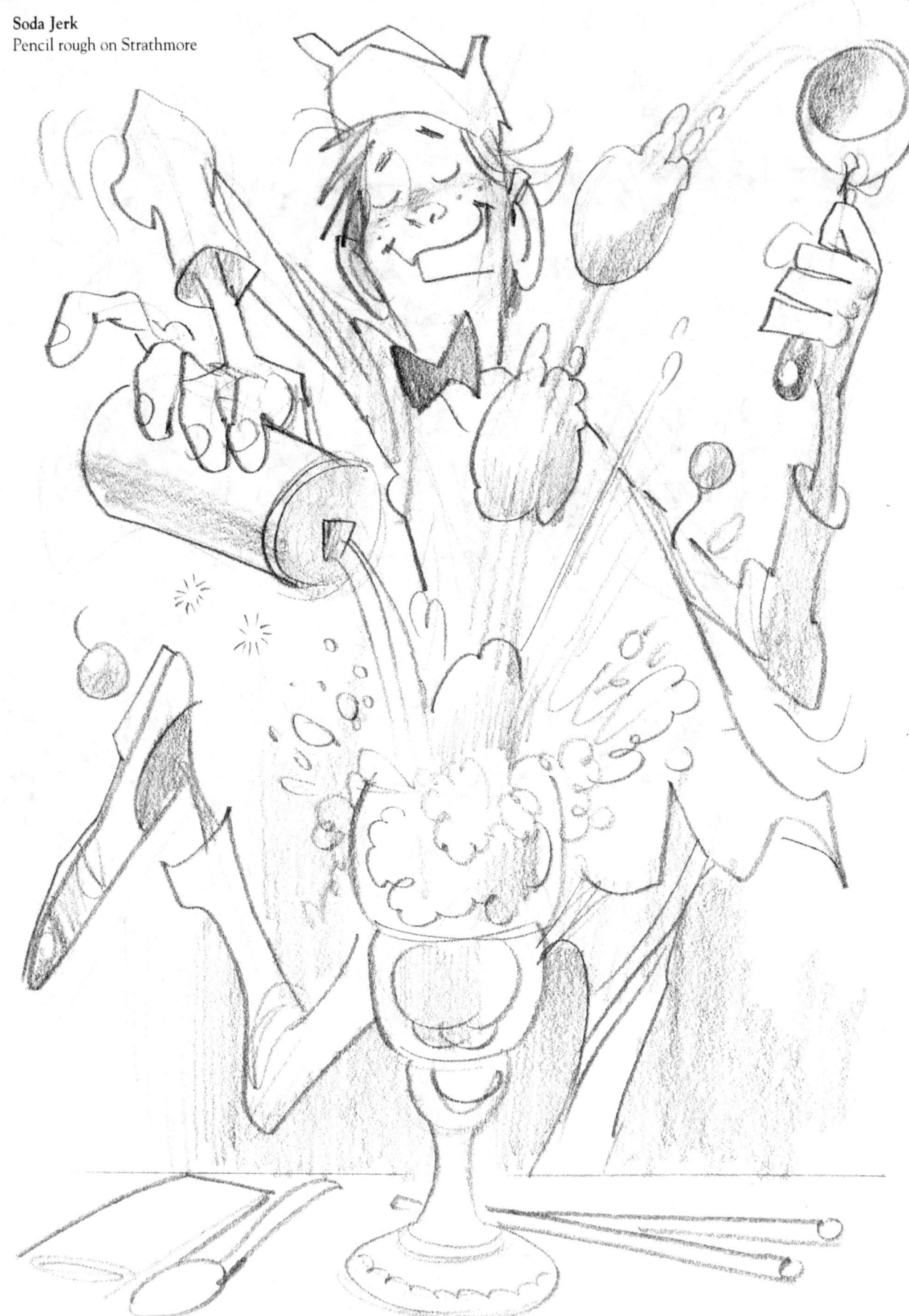

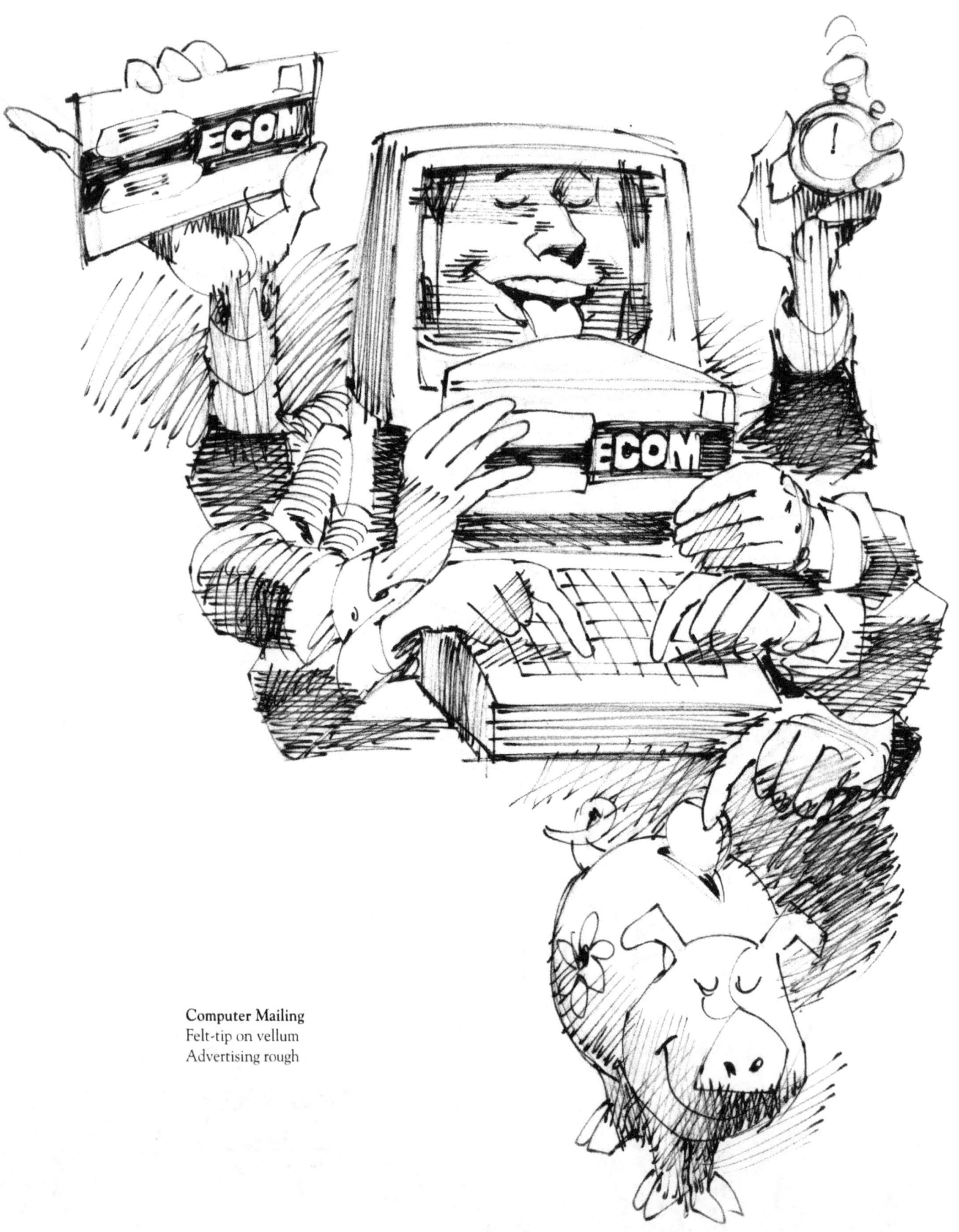

Computer Mailing
Felt-tip on vellum
Advertising rough

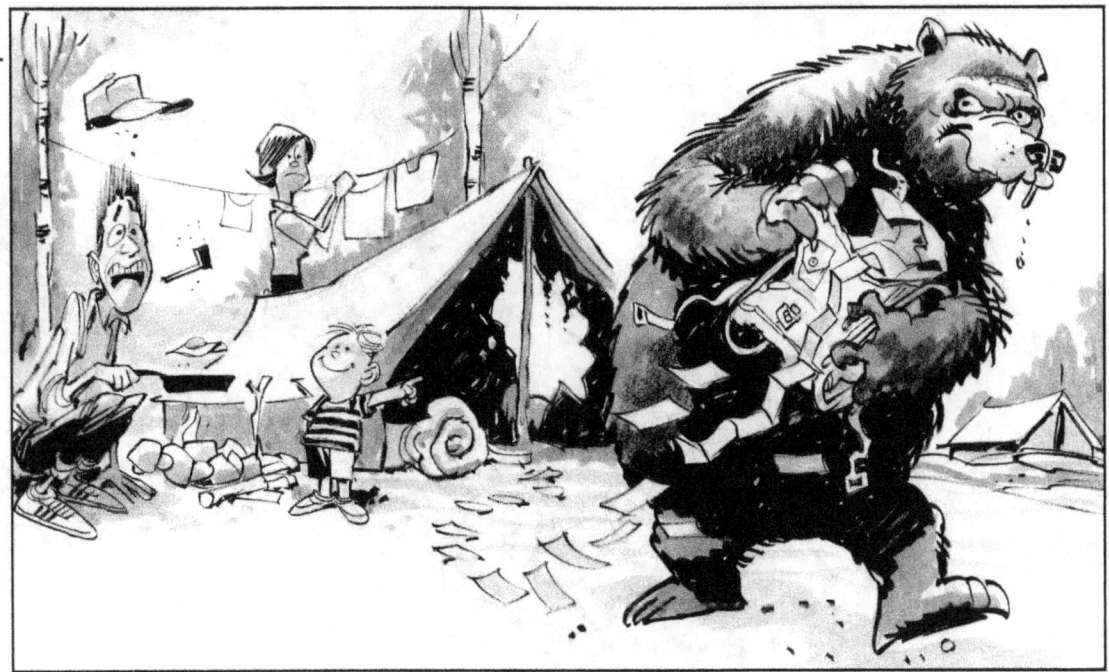

Camping Fun
Brush & ink and marker rough
on vellum

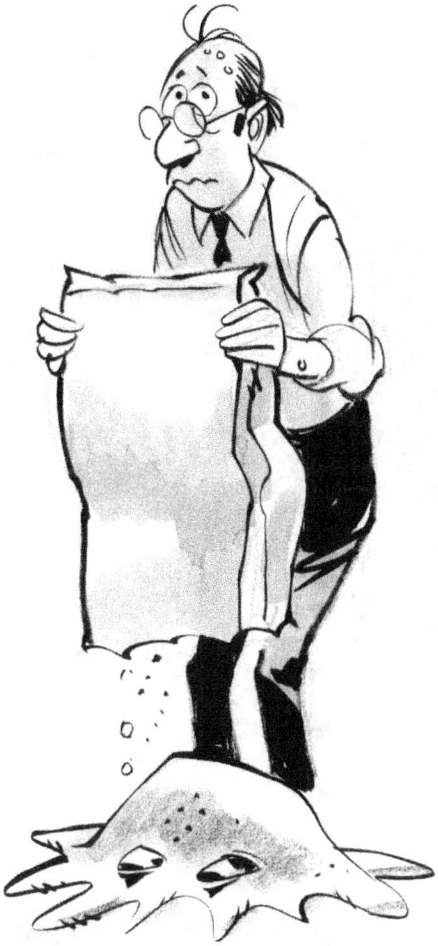

Fallout
Mixed media on vellum
Advertising rough

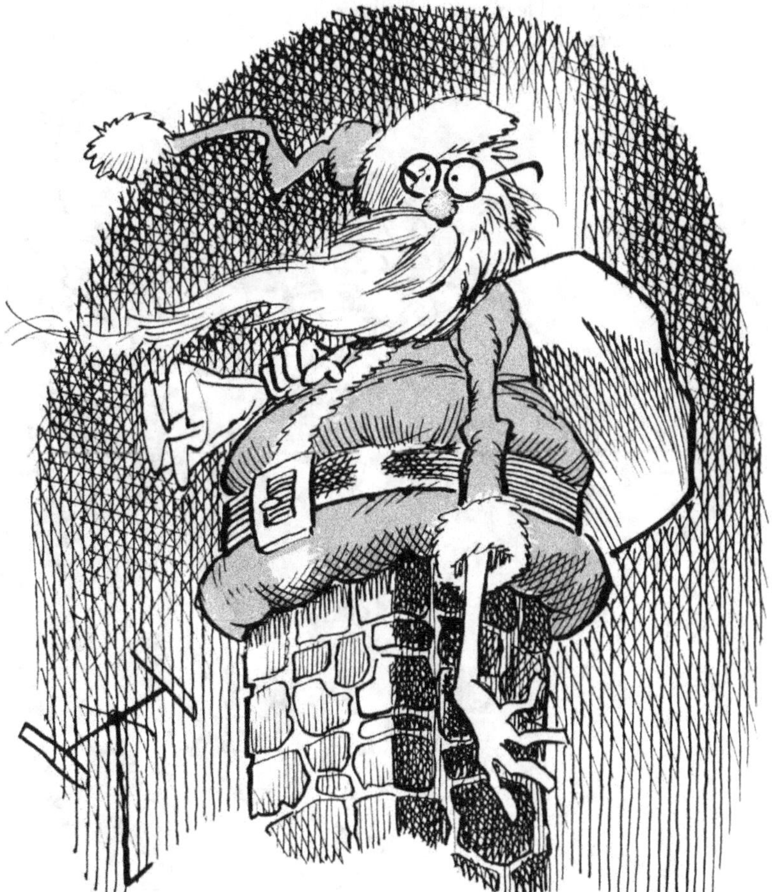

Stuck!
Pen & ink on Strathmore
Davis Family Christmas card

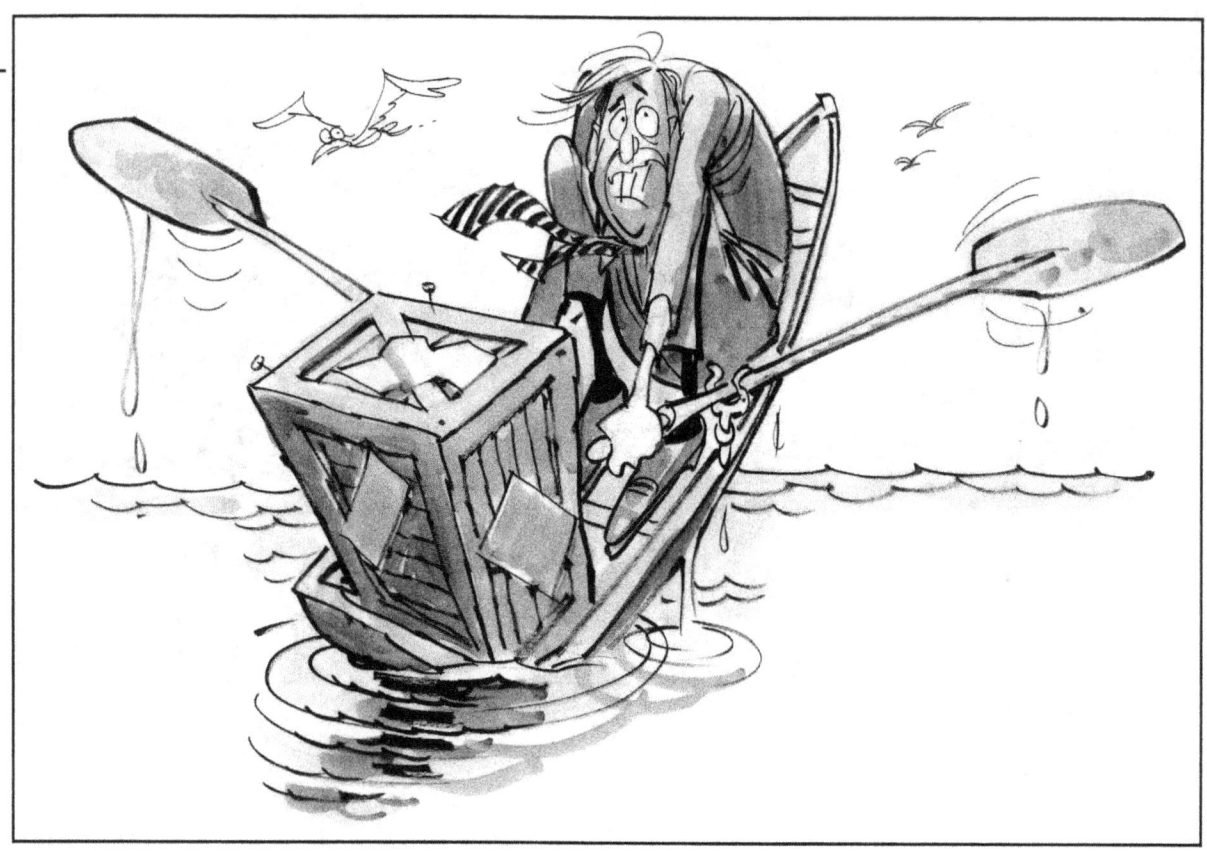

That sinking feeling...
Brush & ink and marker on vellum
Advertising rough

Superbowl Fight
Brush & ink and marker rough
on vellum

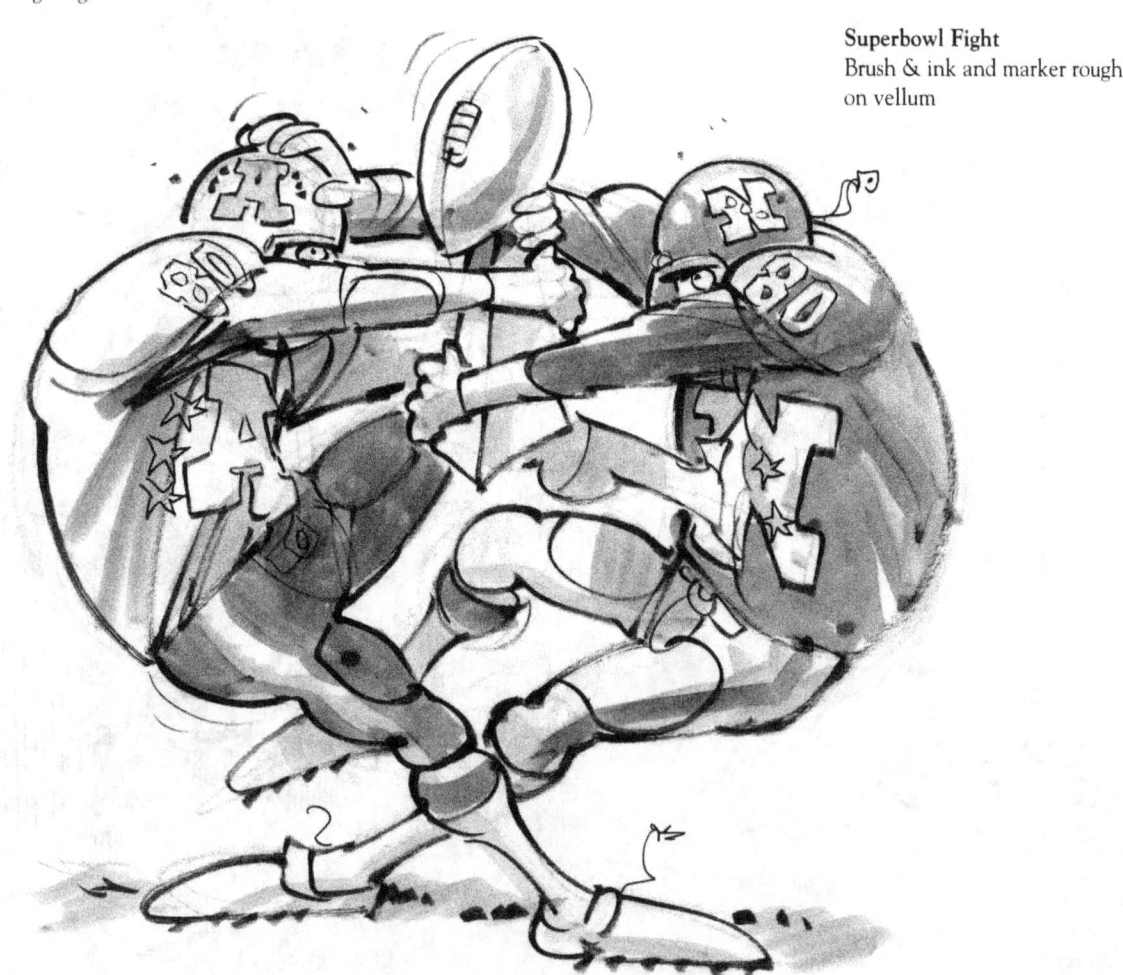

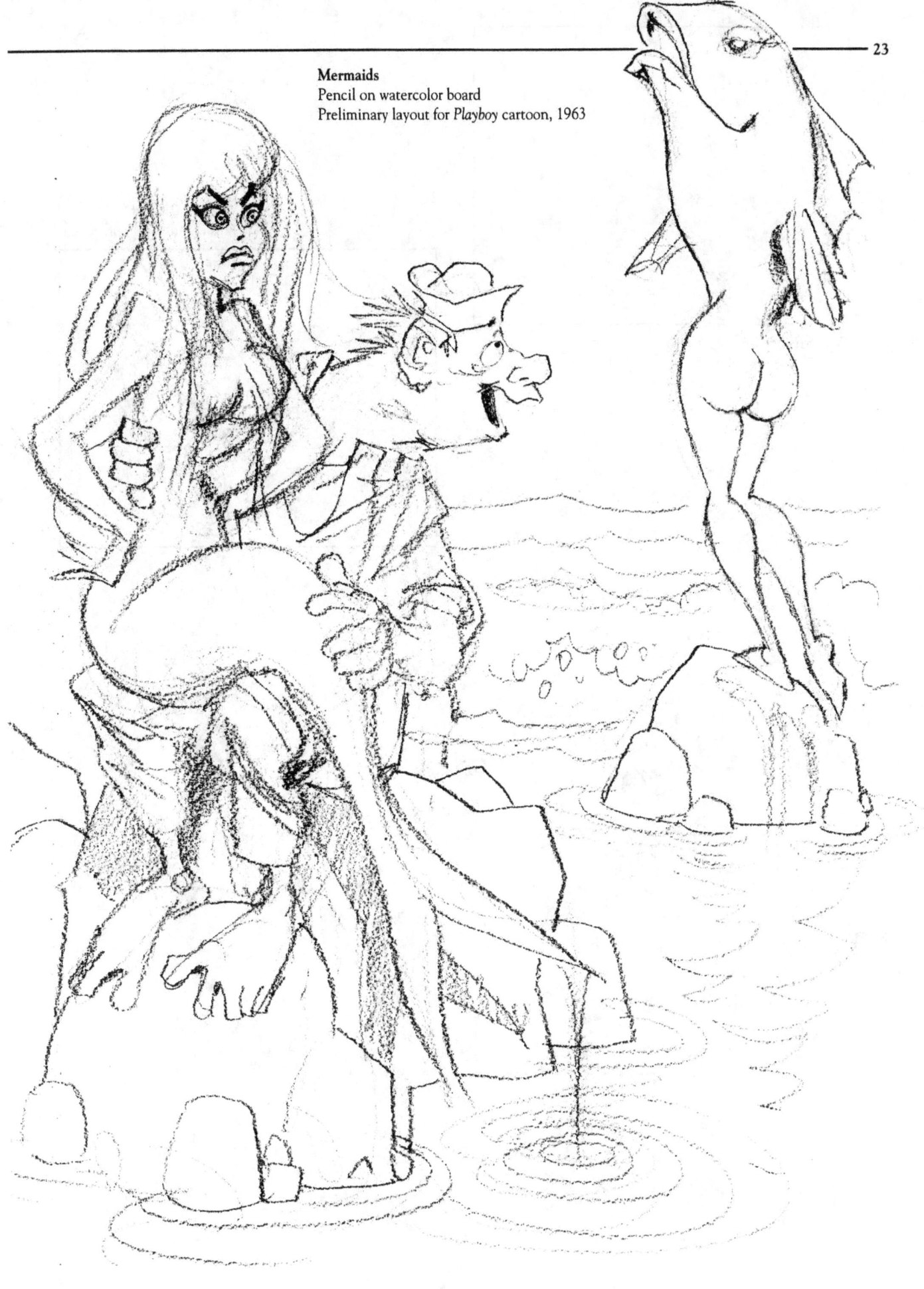

Mermaids
Pencil on watercolor board
Preliminary layout for *Playboy* cartoon, 1963

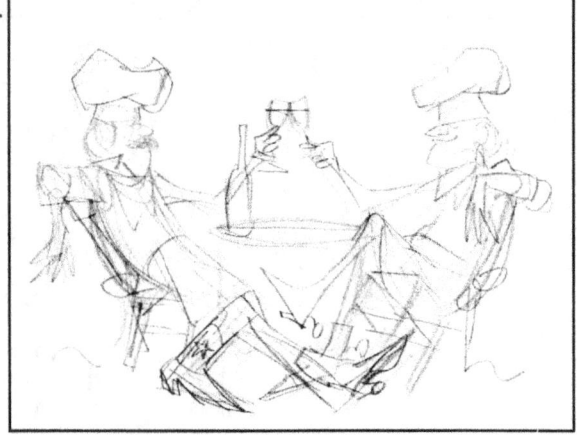

Western Chefs #1
Pencil layout on vellum

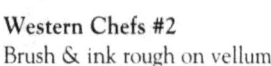

Western Chefs #2
Brush & ink rough on vellum

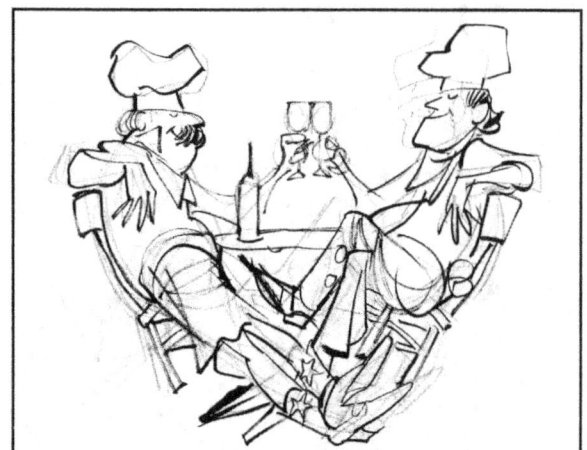

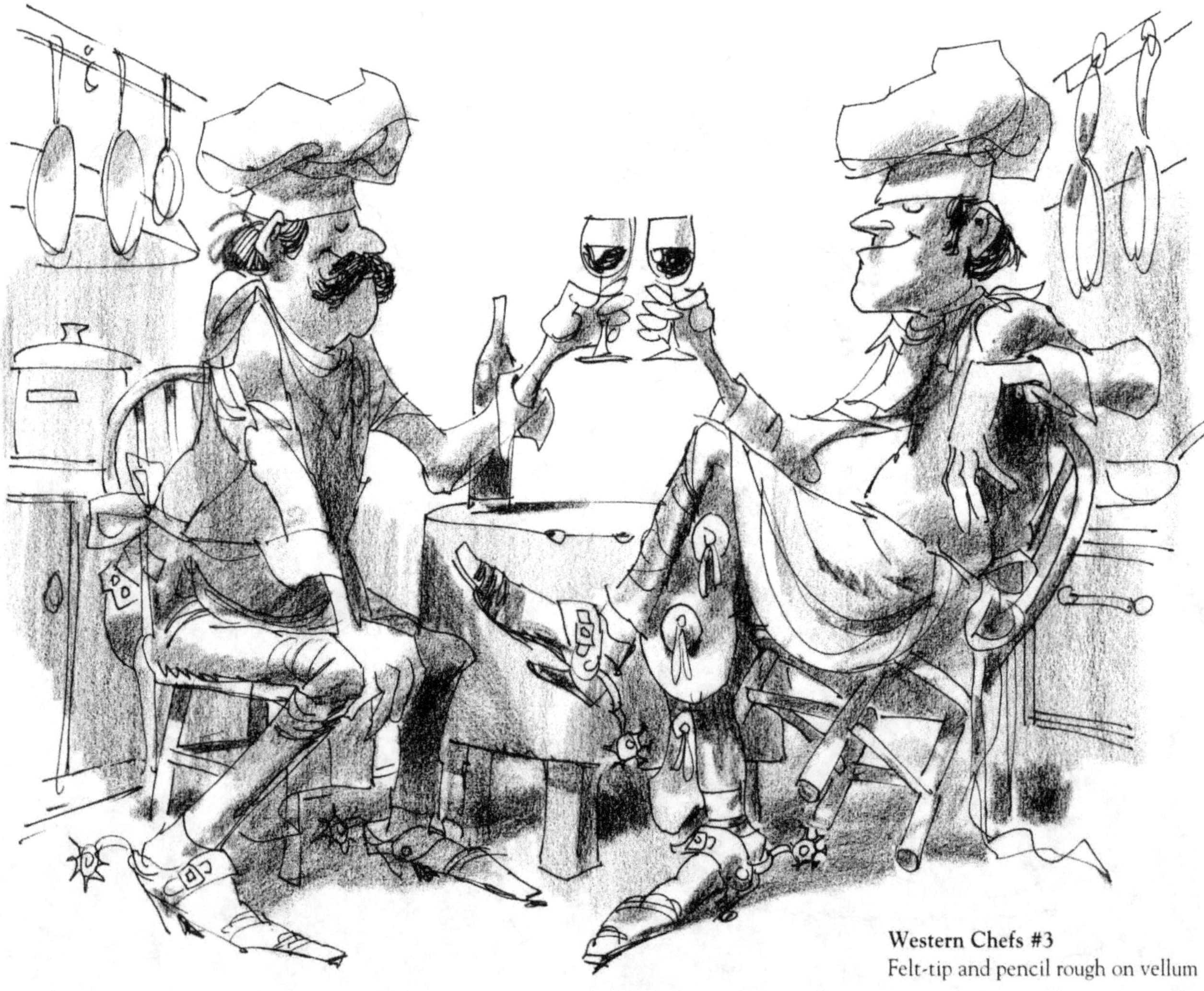

Western Chefs #3
Felt-tip and pencil rough on vellum

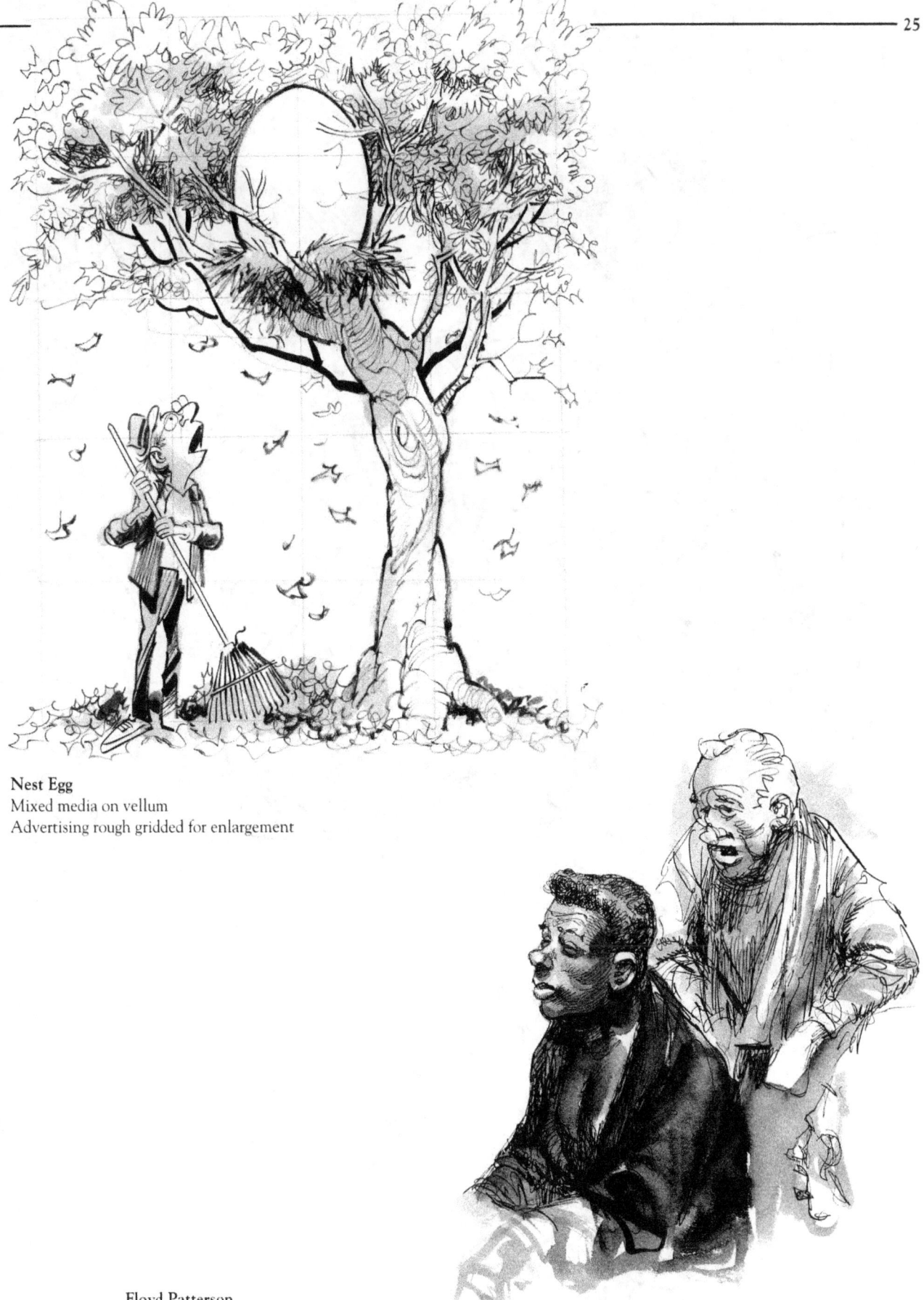

Nest Egg
Mixed media on vellum
Advertising rough gridded for enlargement

Floyd Patterson
Pen & ink and wash on illustration board
Alternate illustration for *HELP!* #11, 1961

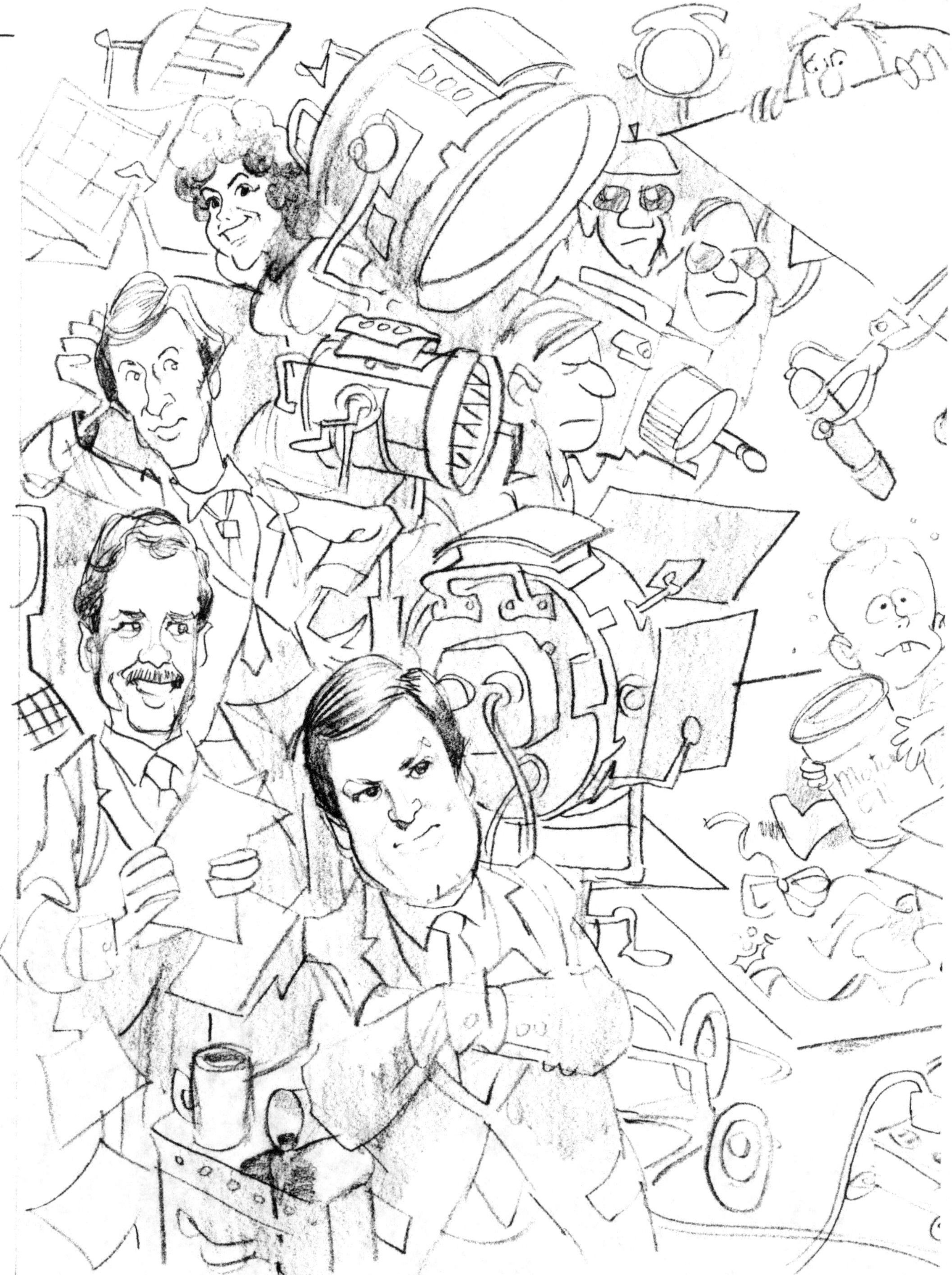

Shooting a TV Commercial
Pencil on Strathmore
Advertising layout

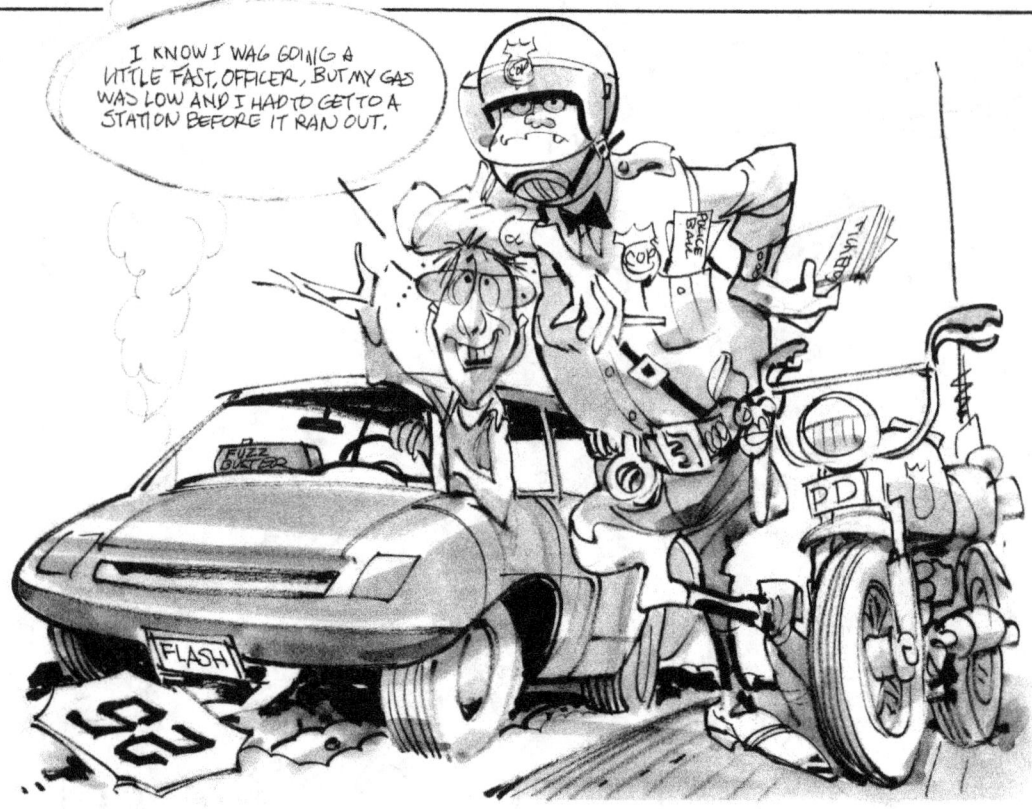

I know I was going a little fast...
Brush & ink and marker rough
on vellum

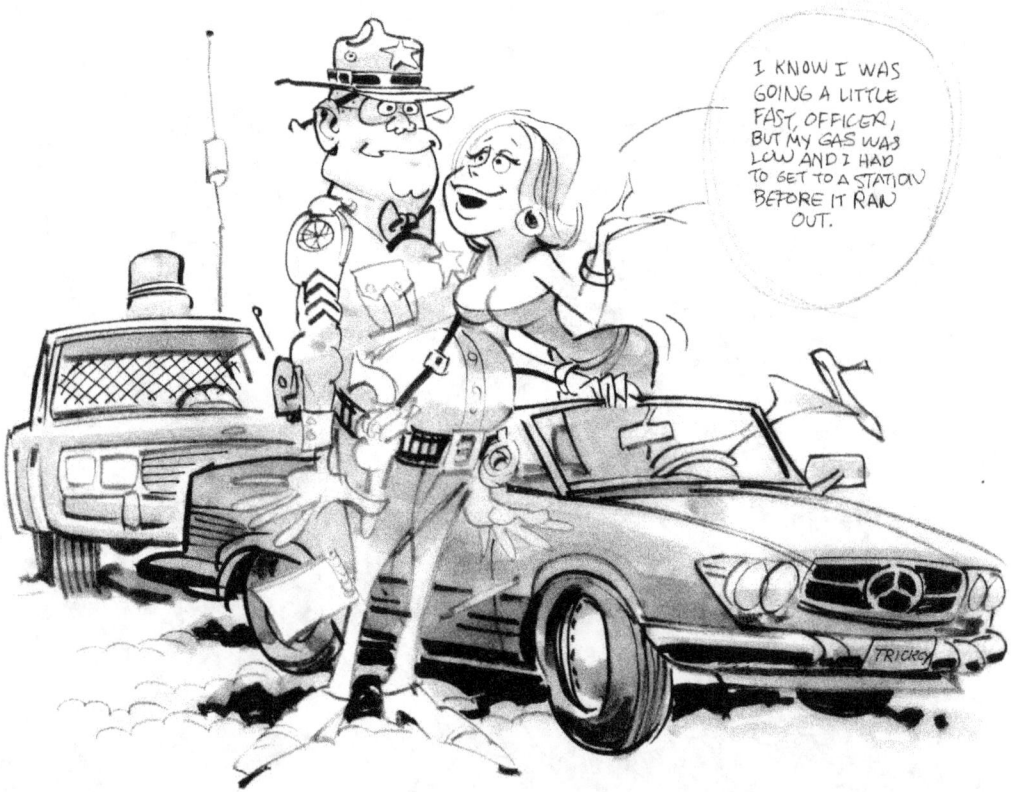

I know I was going a little fast...
Brush & ink and marker rough
on vellum

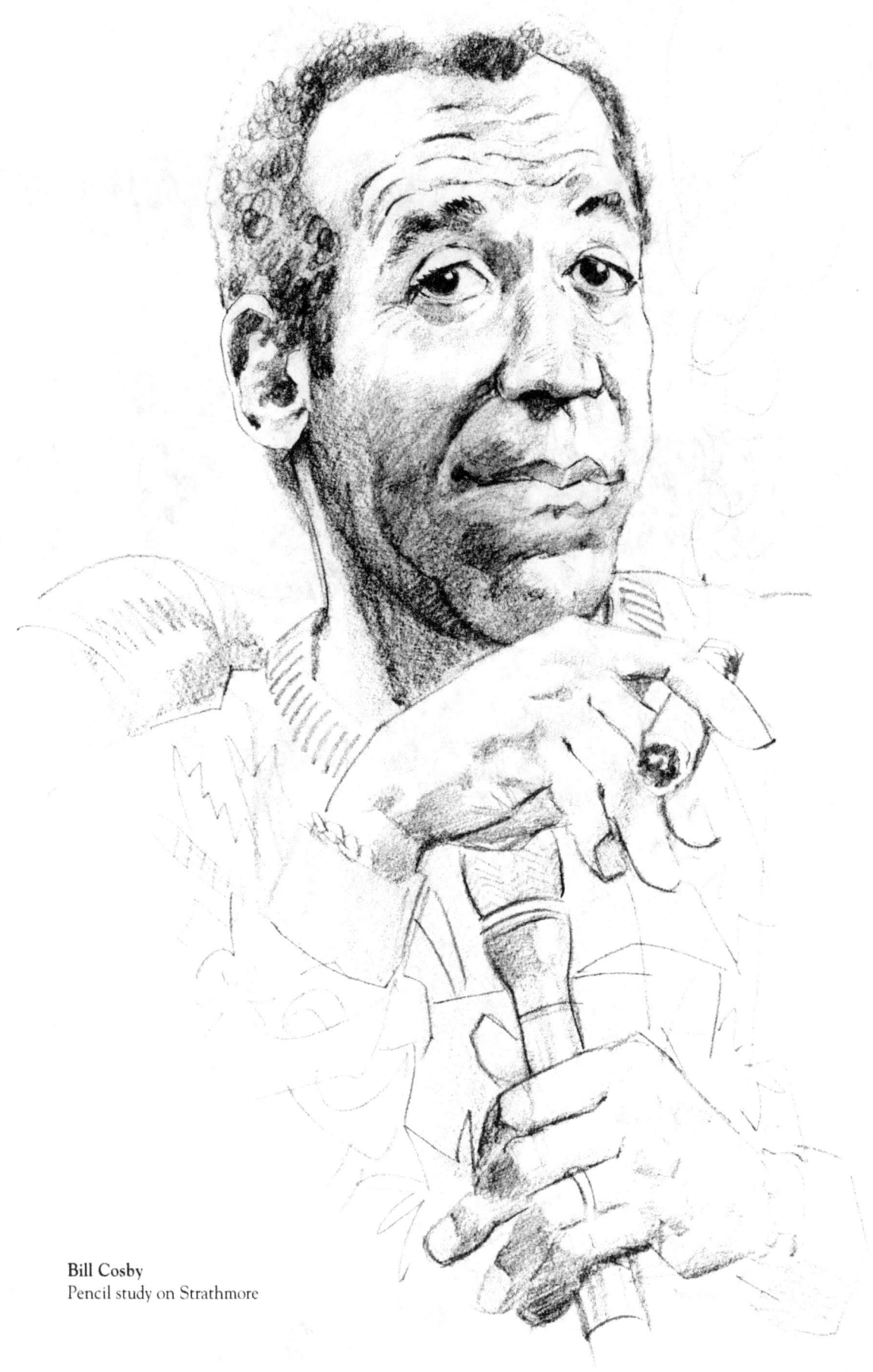

Bill Cosby
Pencil study on Strathmore

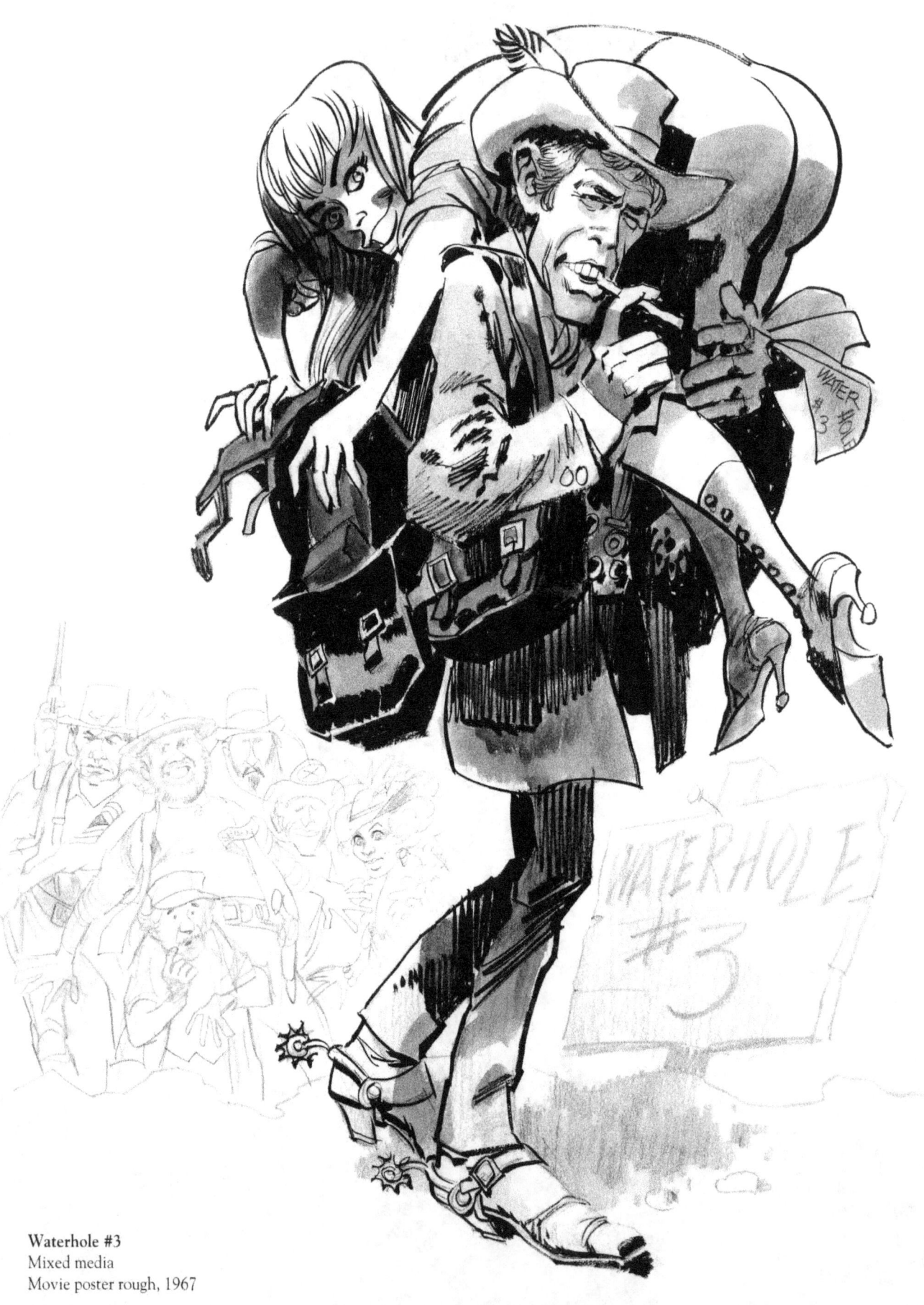

Waterhole #3
Mixed media
Movie poster rough, 1967

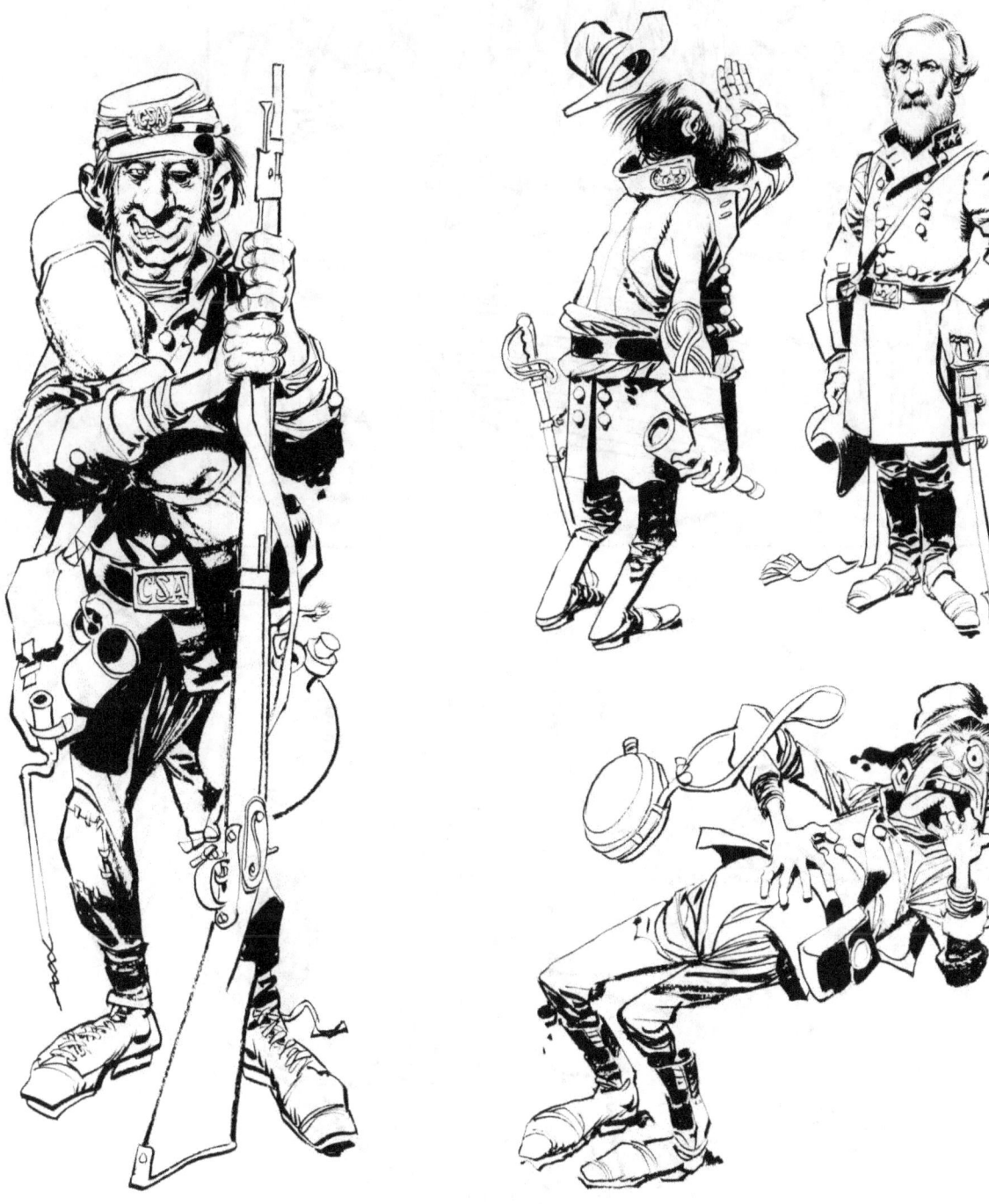

Confederate Soldiers
Brush & ink on colored paper

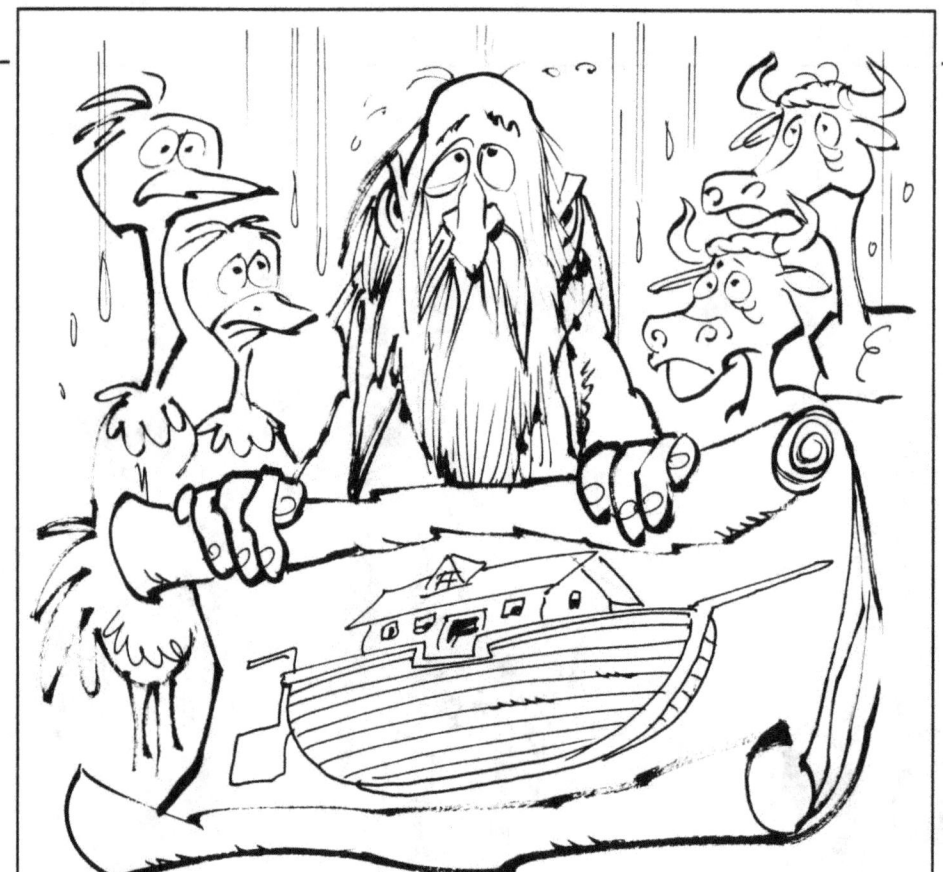

Noah's Ark
Brush & ink and pen & ink
rough on vellum

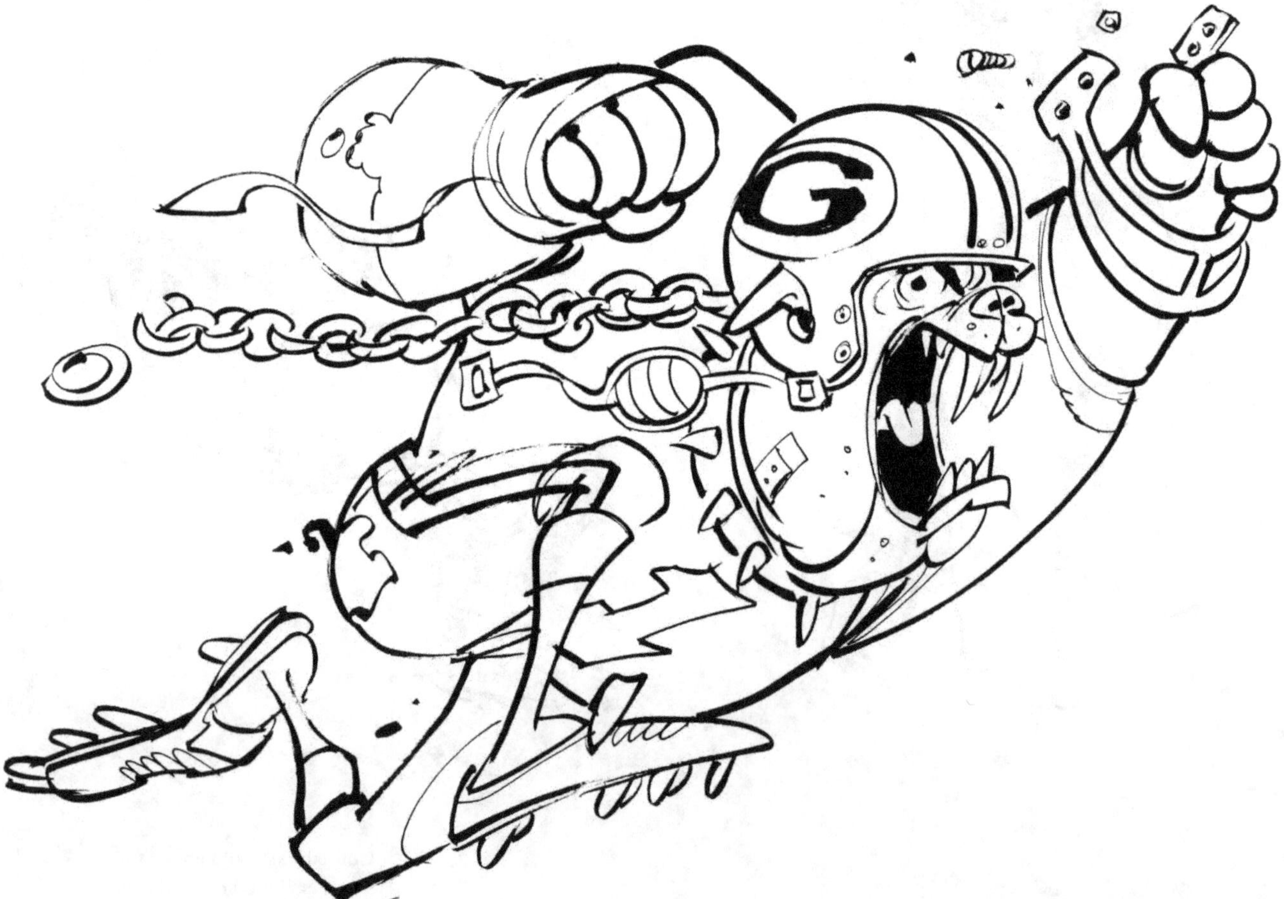

Sic 'em Dawgs!
Brush & ink on vellum
For Georgia University Bulldogs

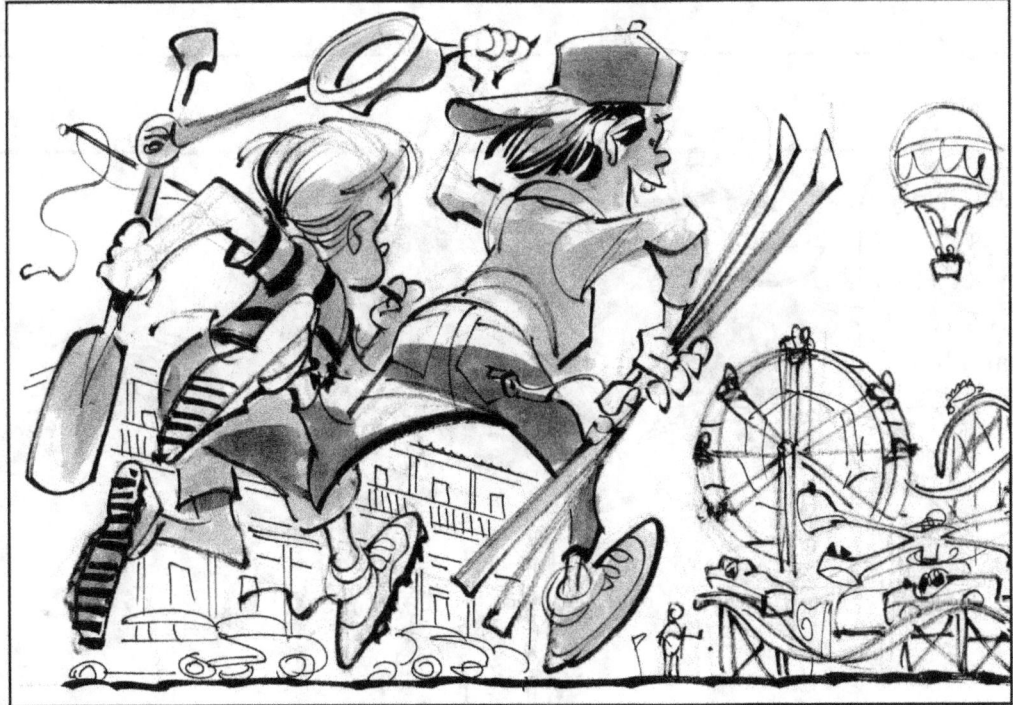

Going to the Fair
Brush & ink and pen & ink
rough on vellum

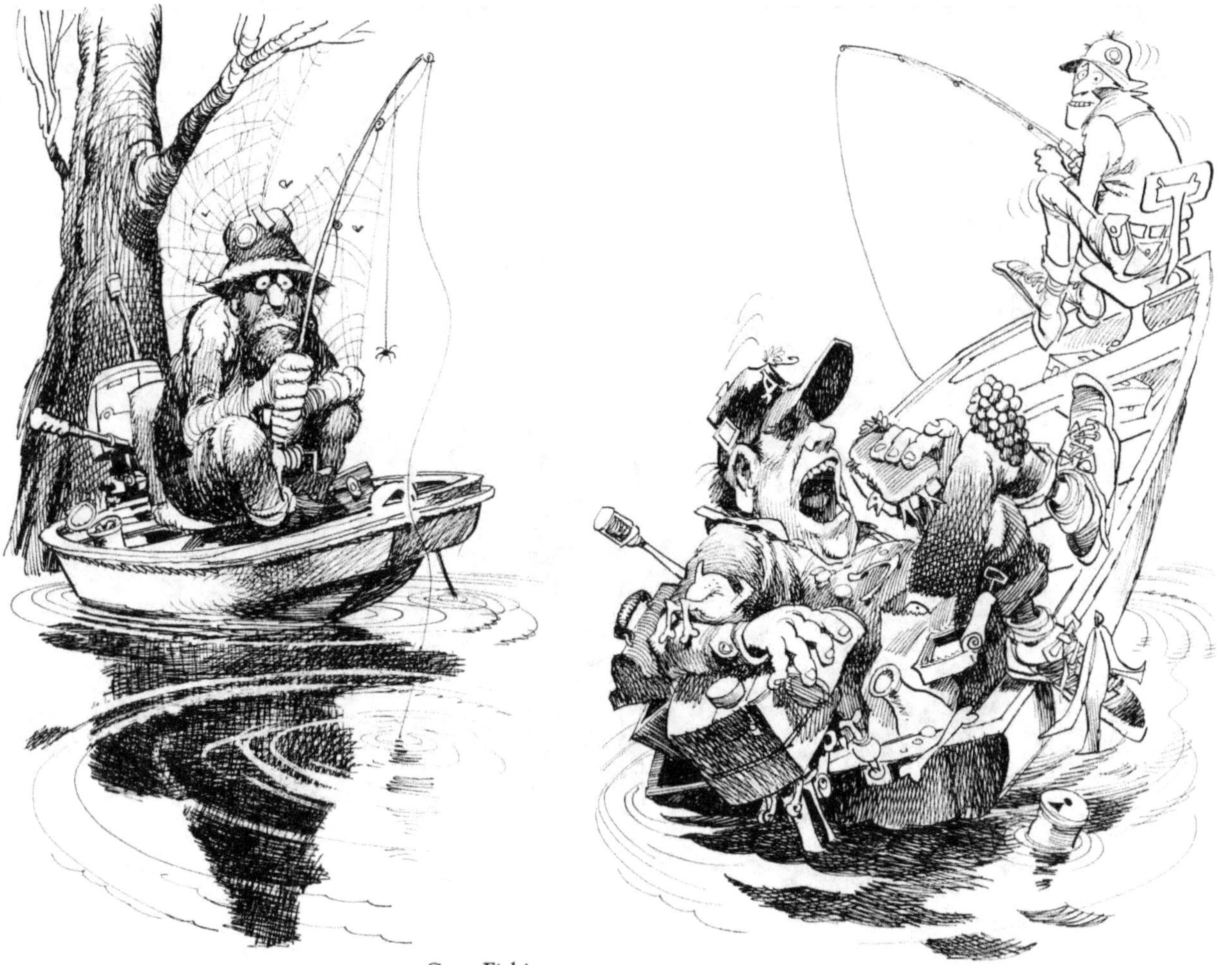

Gone Fishing
Pen & ink on illustration board
Magazine illustrations, *Sports Afield*, 1973

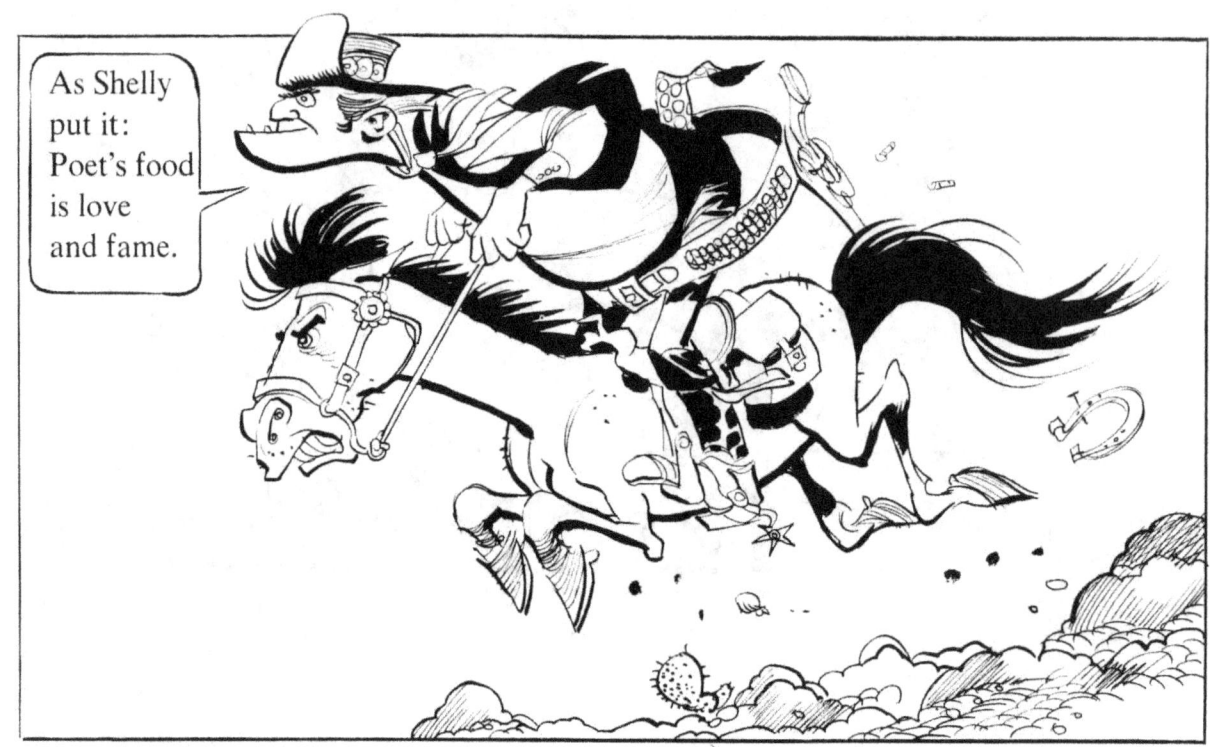

As Shelly put it...
Mixed media on Strathmore
Unfinished comic strip panel

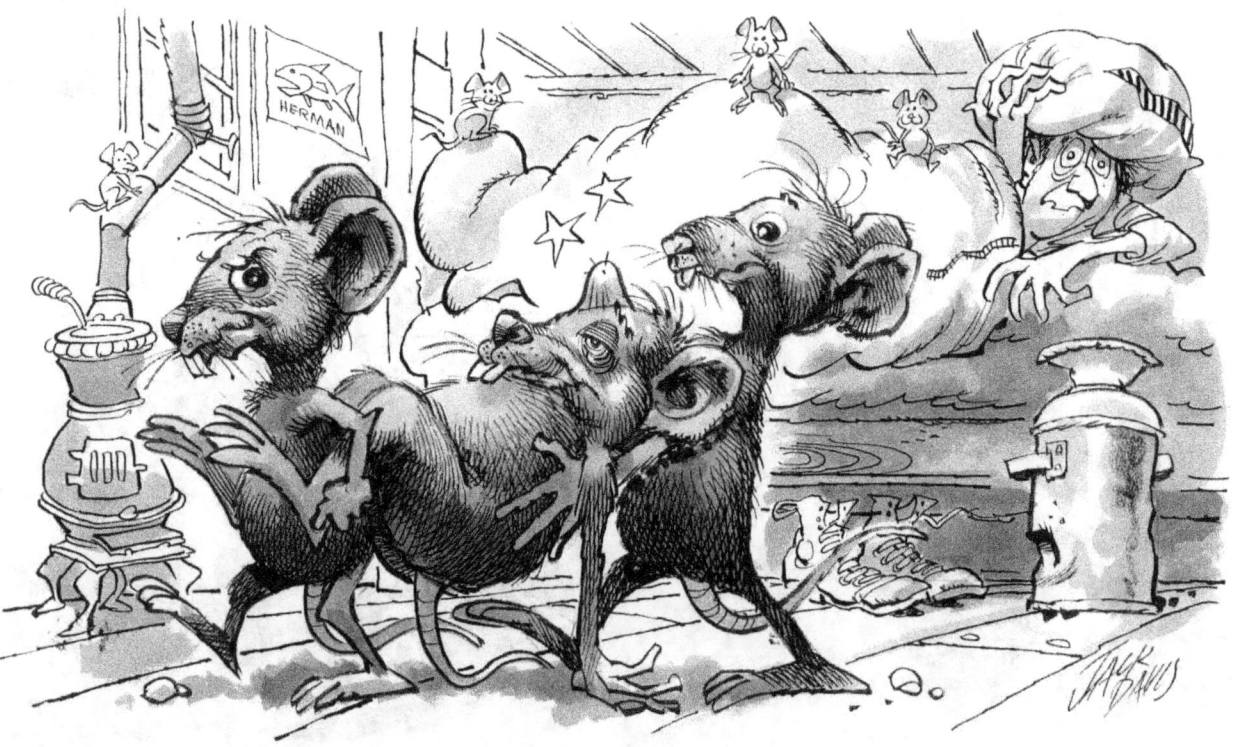

Three Mice
Brush & ink and pen & ink with wash
Magazine illustration, *Sports Afield*, 1975

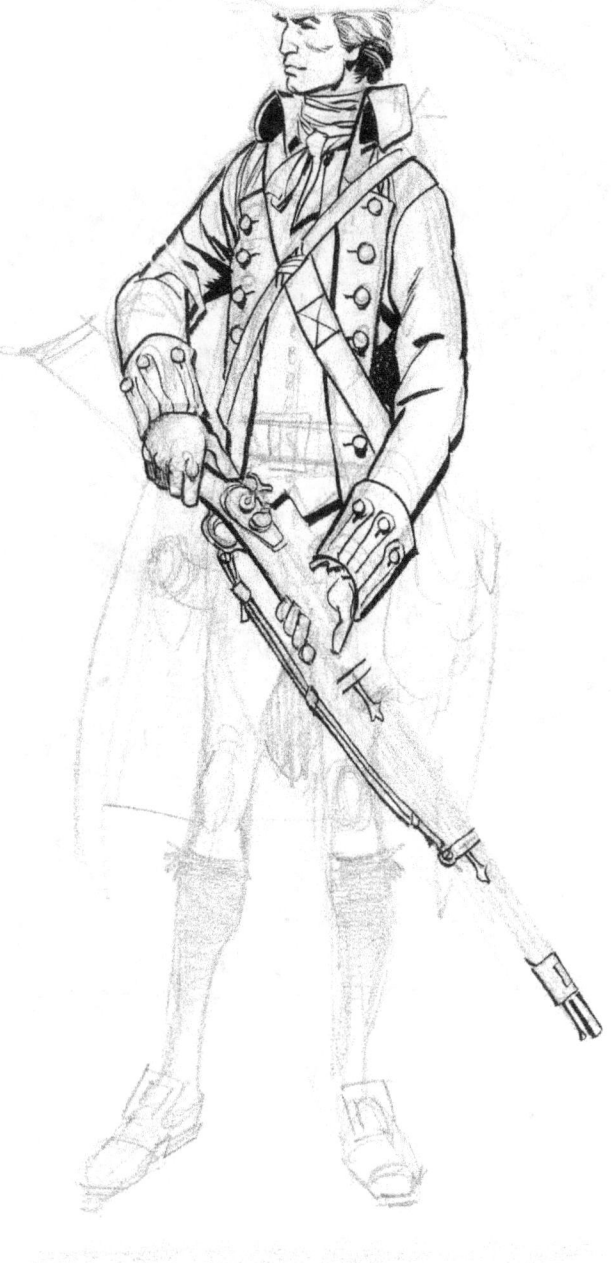

Revolutionary War Soldier
Pencil and brush & ink on Strathmore
Unfinished illustration

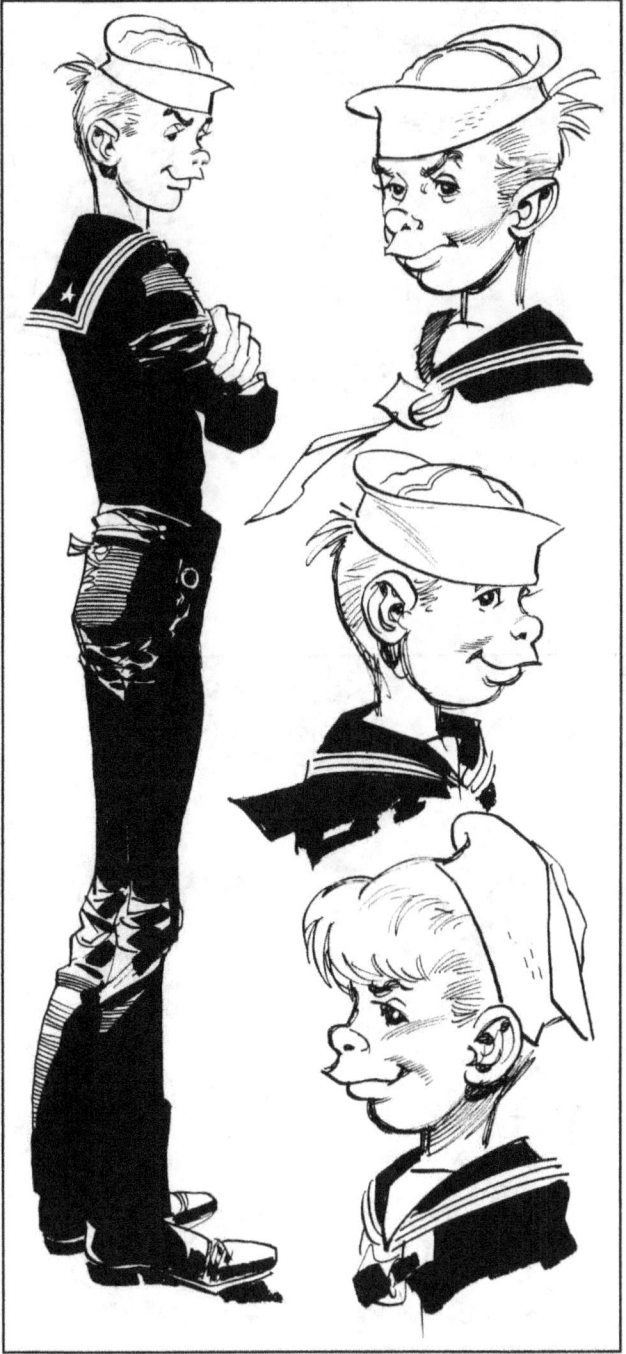

In the Navy
Pen & ink on Strathmore
Study for possible comic strip character

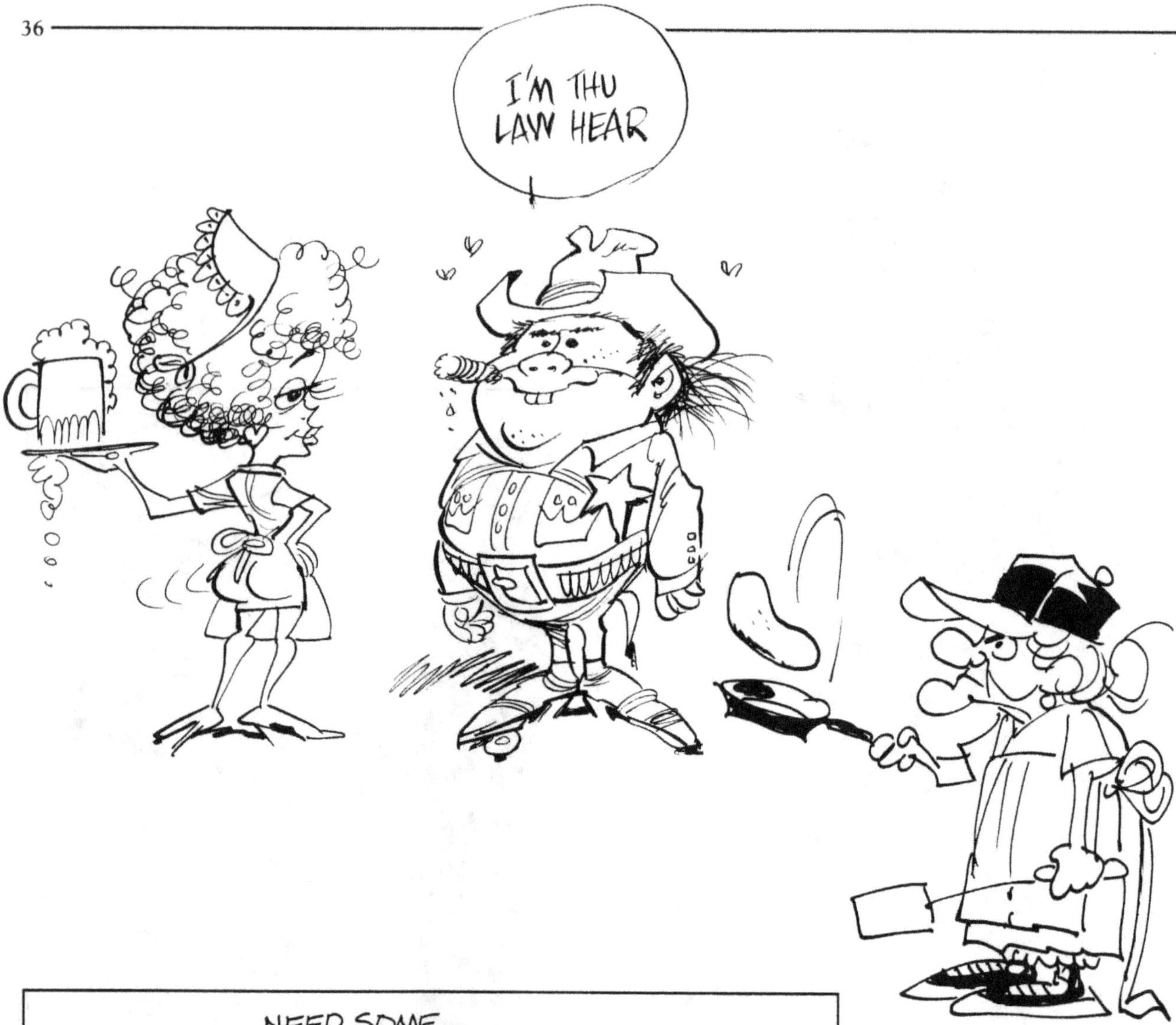

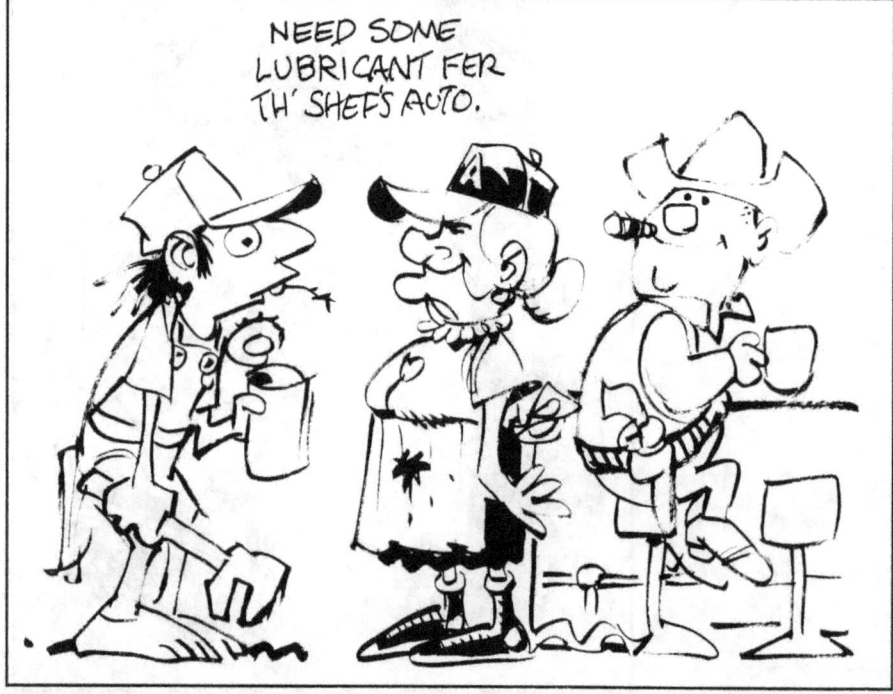

I'm thu Law
Mixed media sketches for possible
comic strip characters

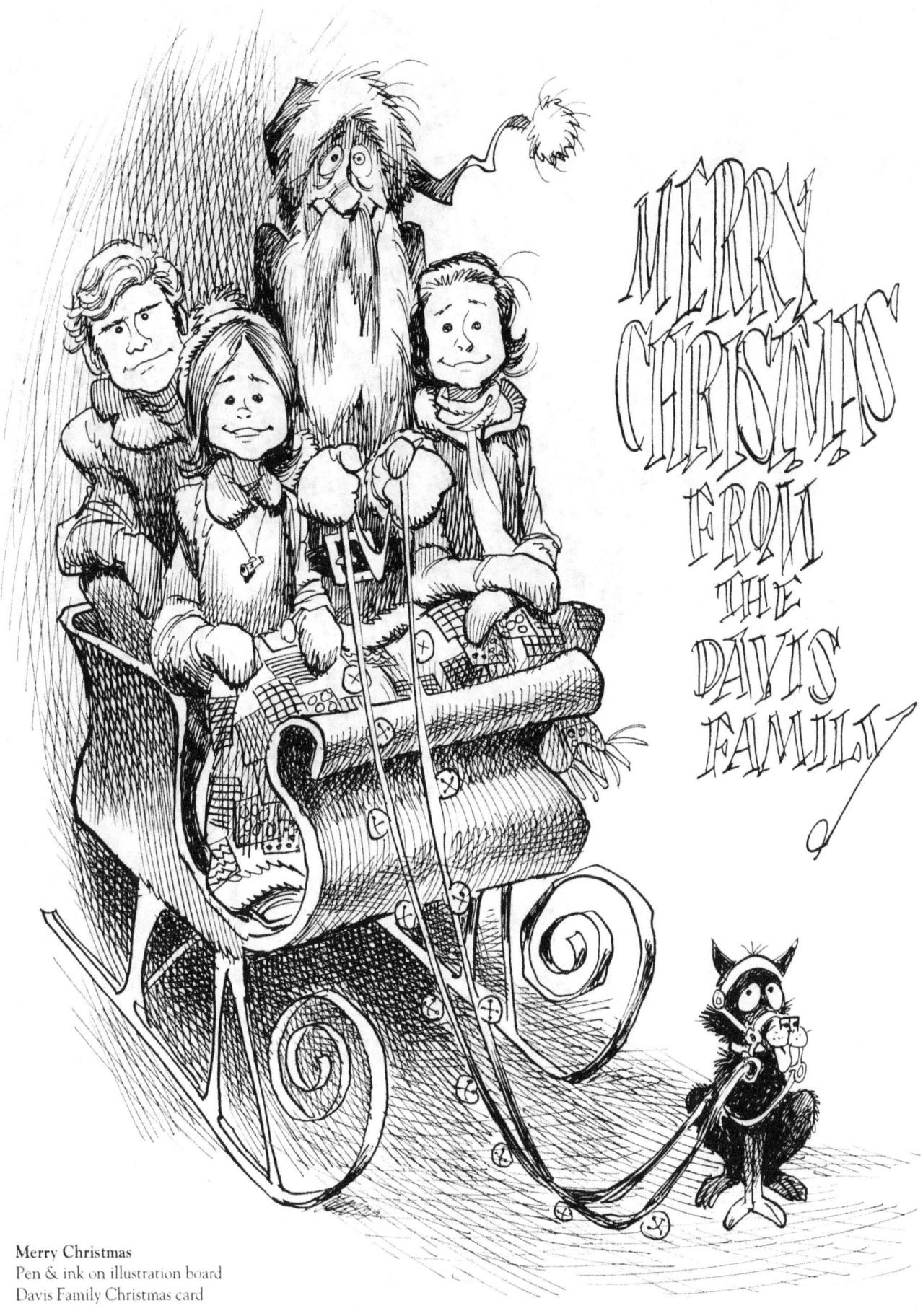

Merry Christmas
Pen & ink on illustration board
Davis Family Christmas card

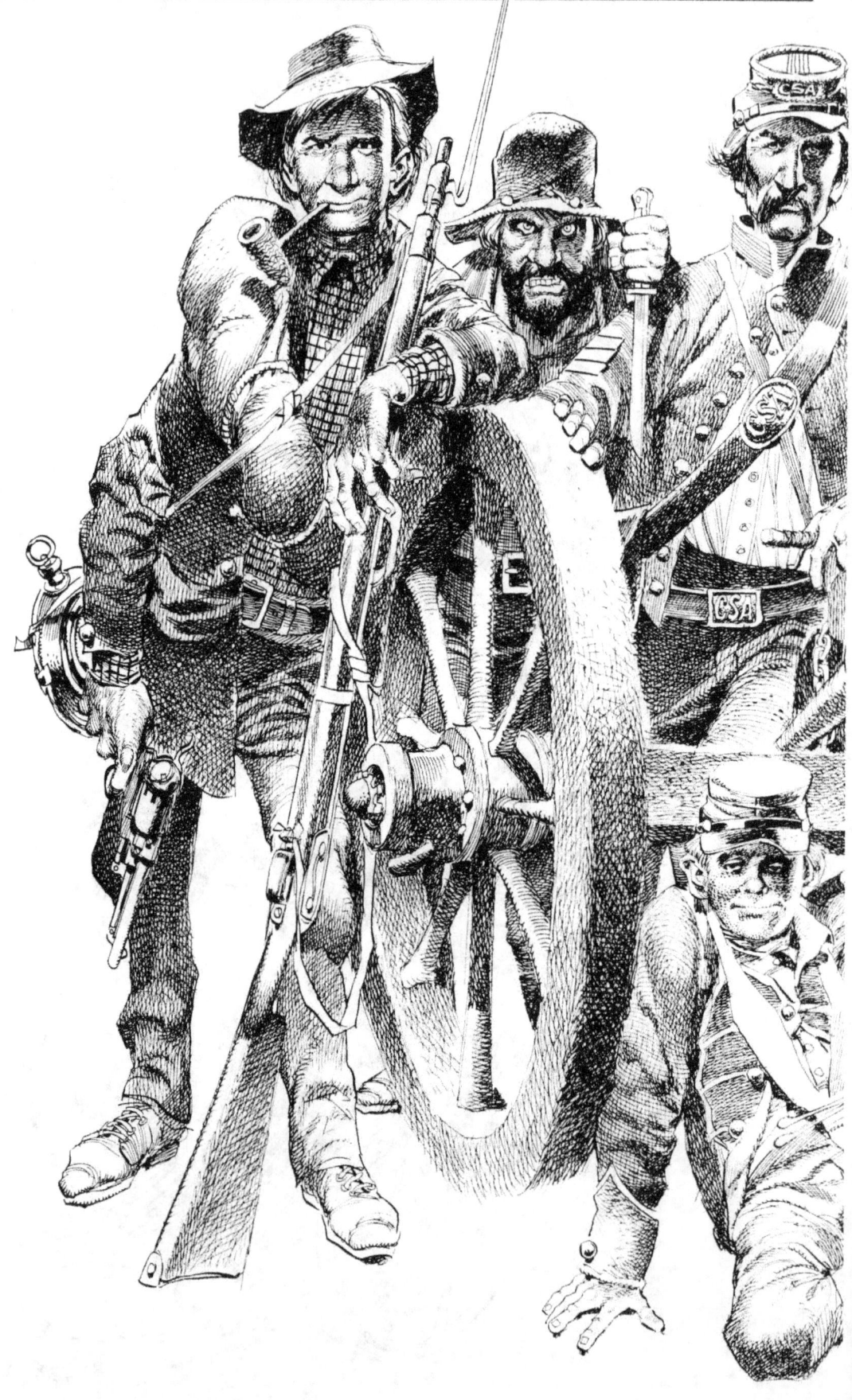

Some Confederate Militia Boys
Pen & ink, 1976

SOME GEORGI

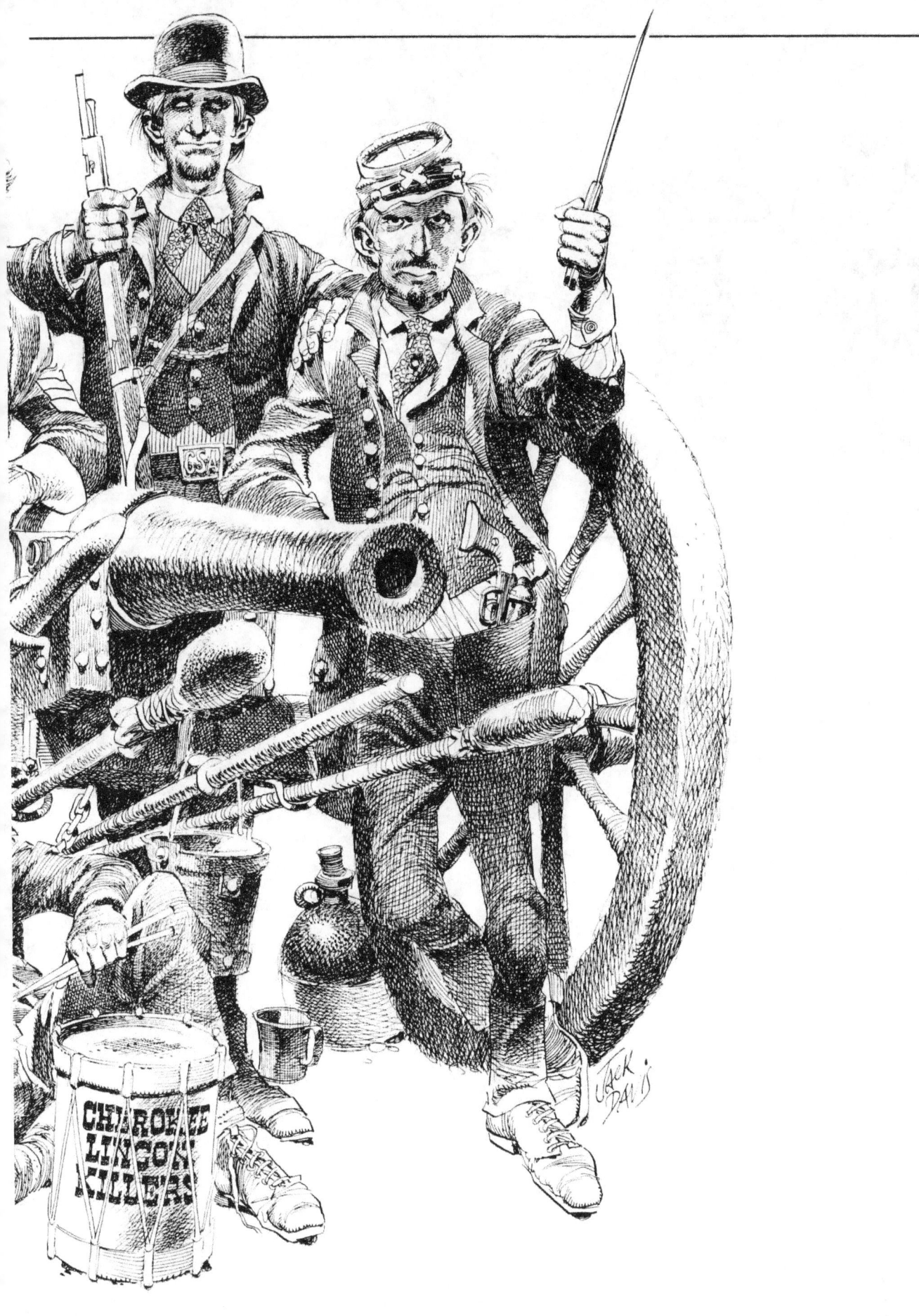

MILITIA BOYS

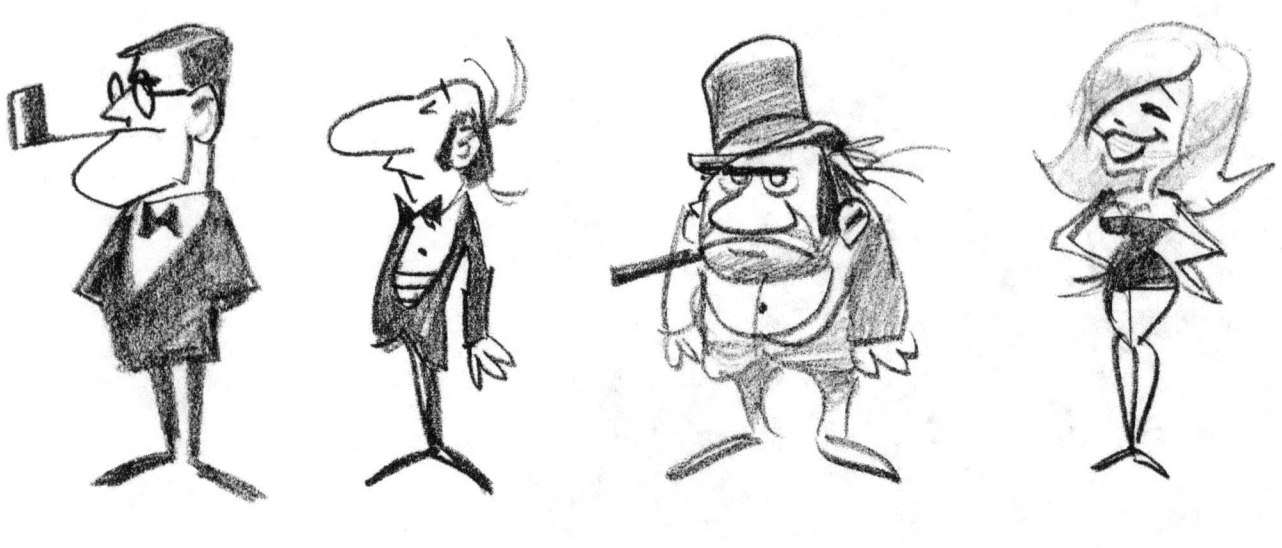

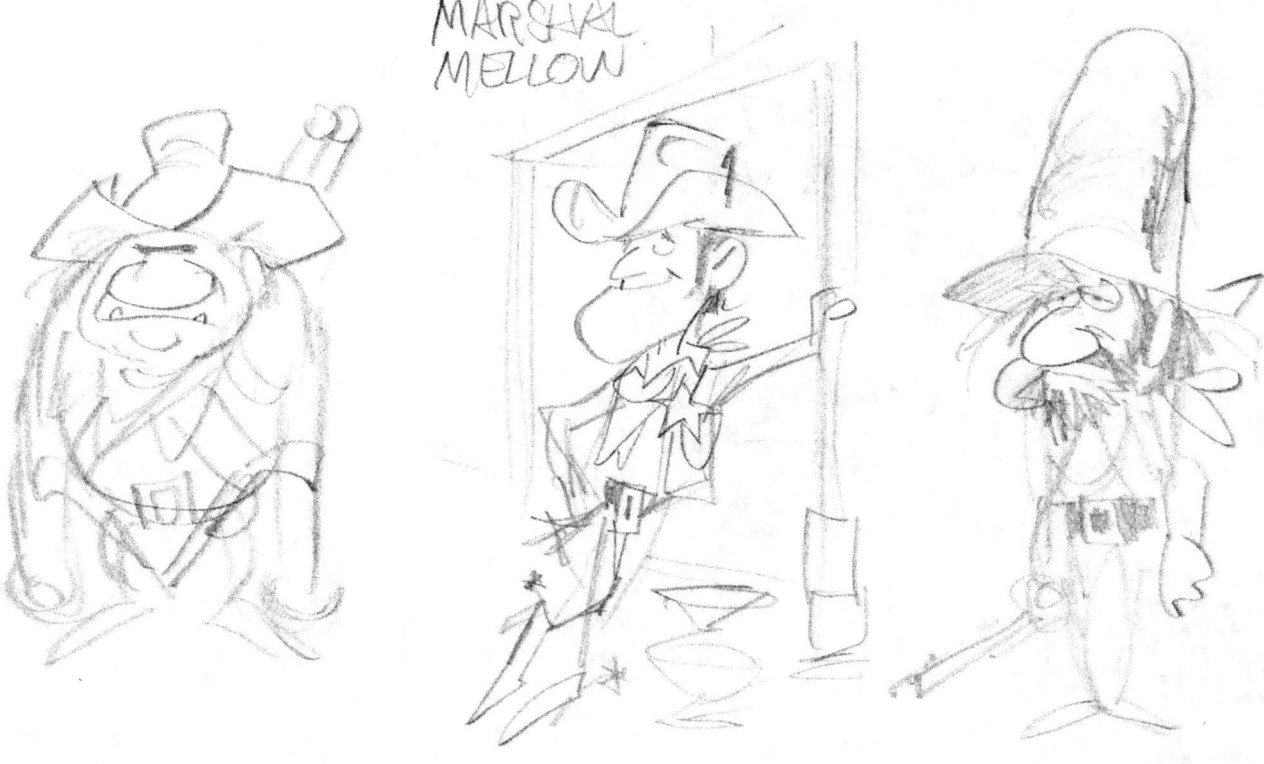

MARSHAL
MELLON

Sketchpad
Mixed media on paper
Sketches of possible comic strip characters

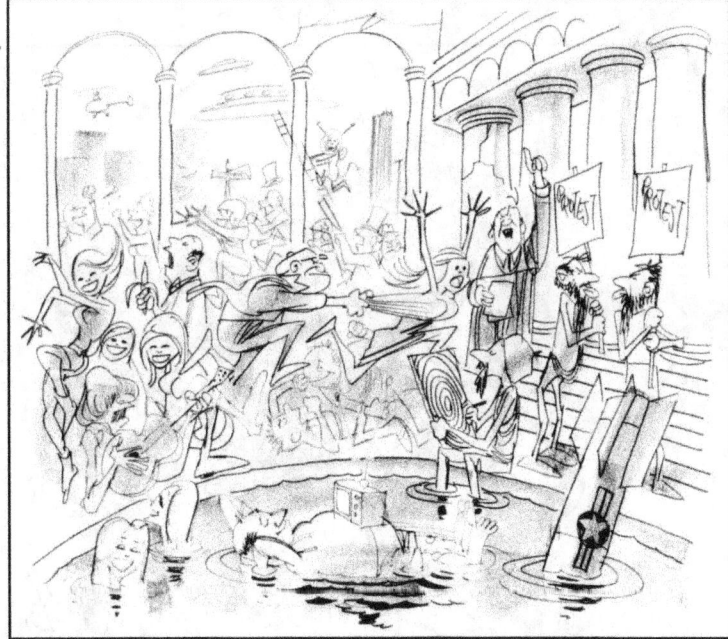

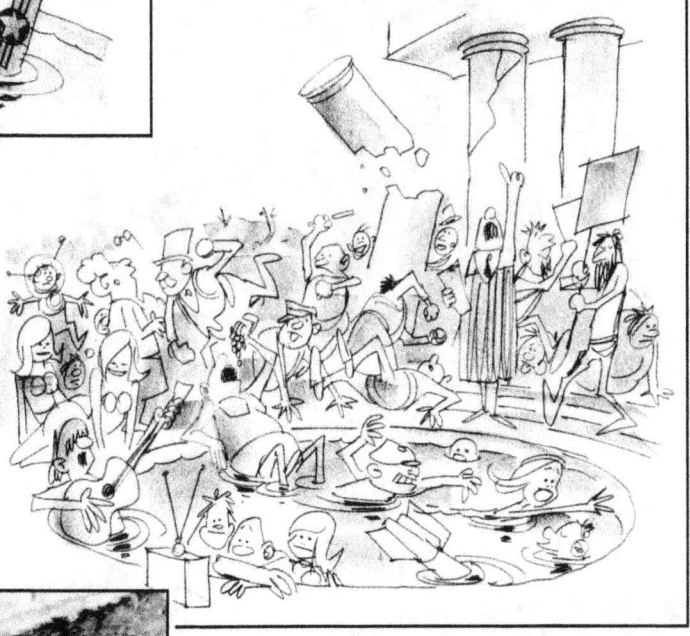

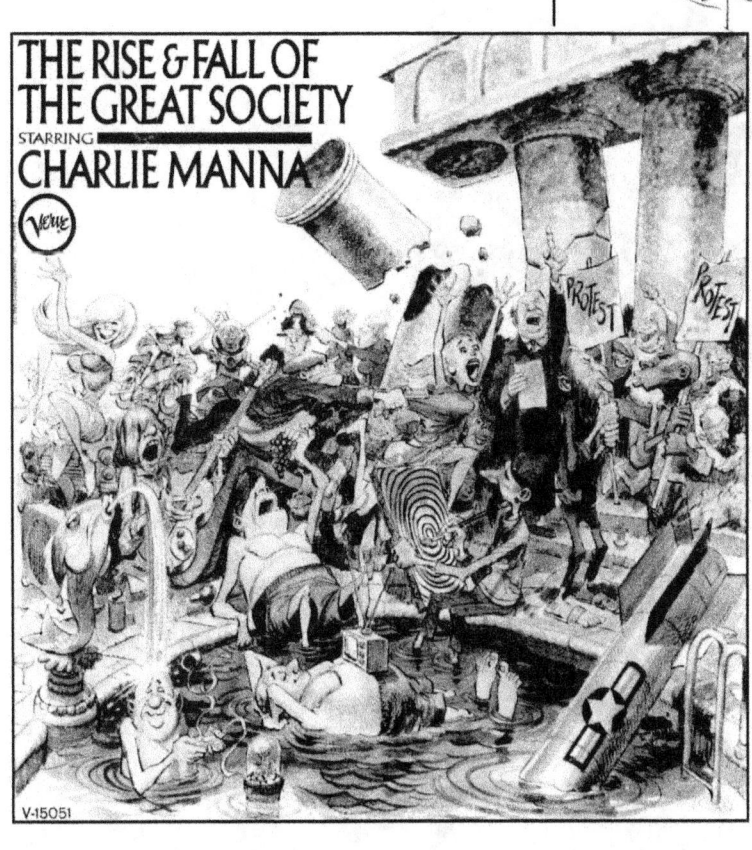

Rise and Fall #1 and #2
Marker and pencil on vellum
(Ideas from both roughs were used on
the completed album cover.)

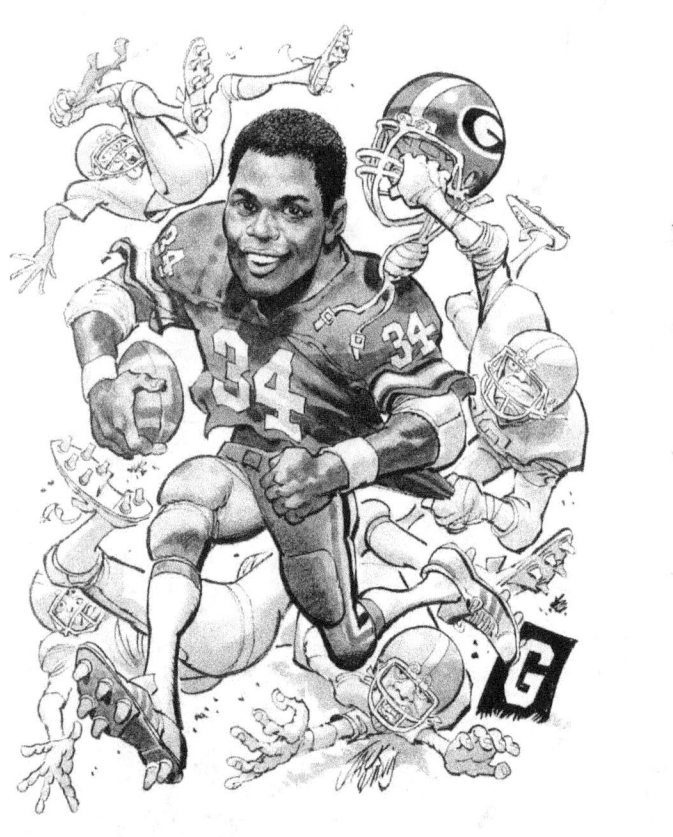
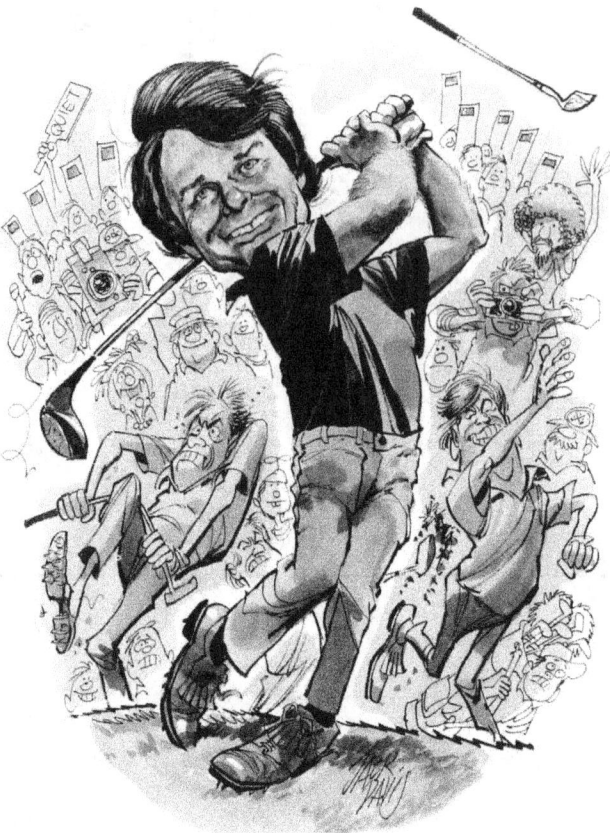

Pressure Proof Athletes
Two of a series of caricatures of famous athletes
commissioned by George Dickel, 1982.

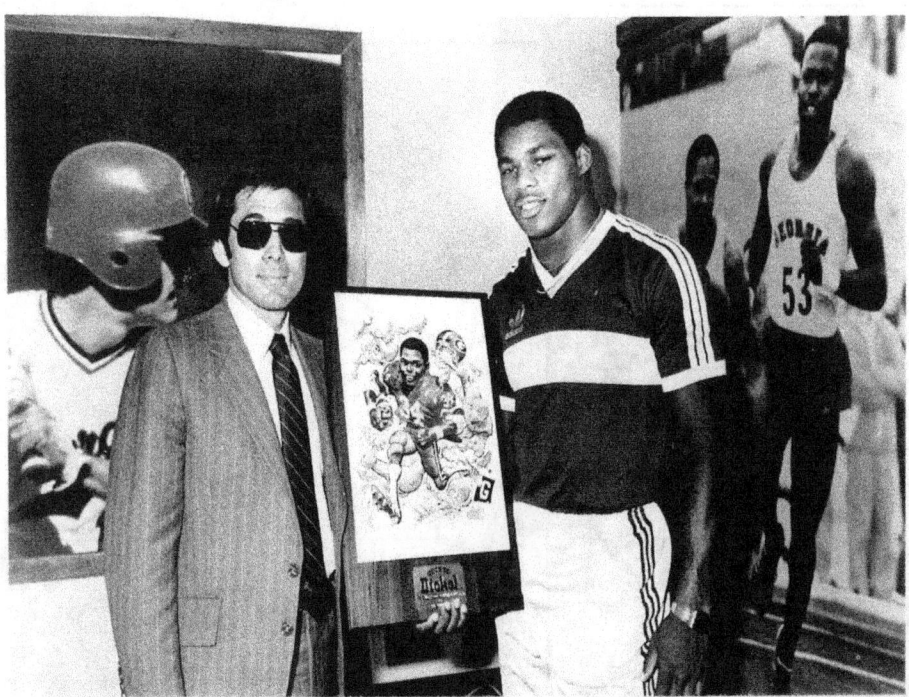

George Dickel representative
presenting Davis drawing to
Herschel Walker.

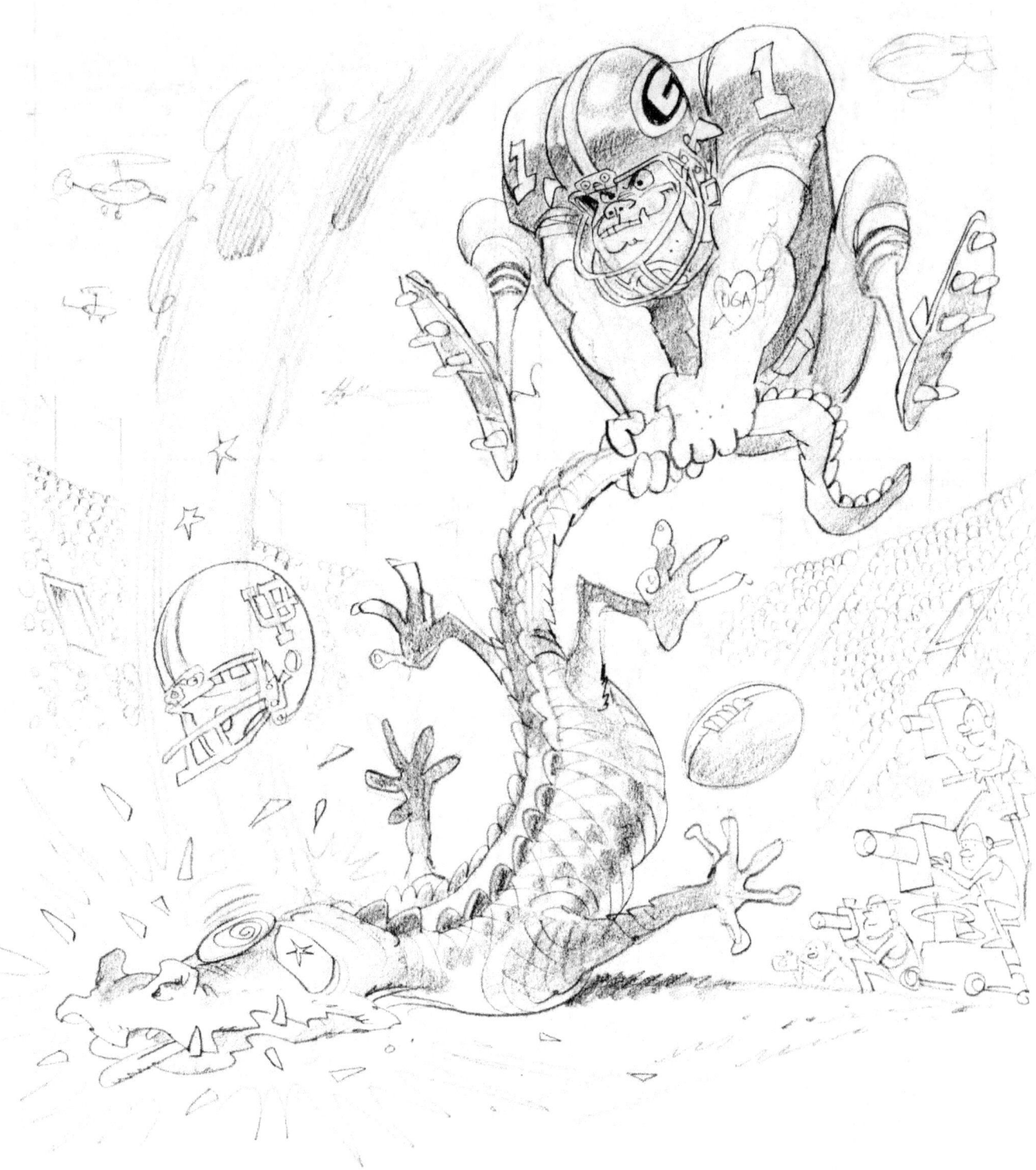

Dawgs vs. Gators
Pencil on illustration board
Georgia University football program cover

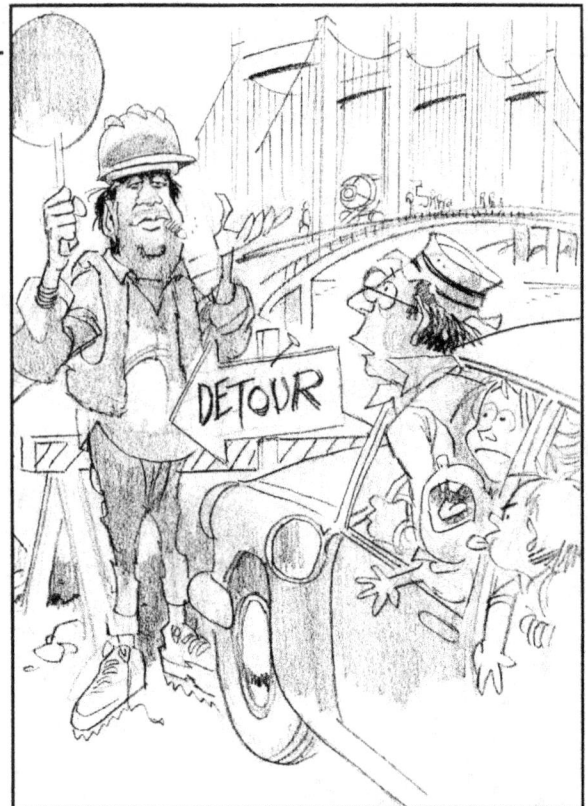

Detour #1
Pencil on Strathmore
Advertising rough

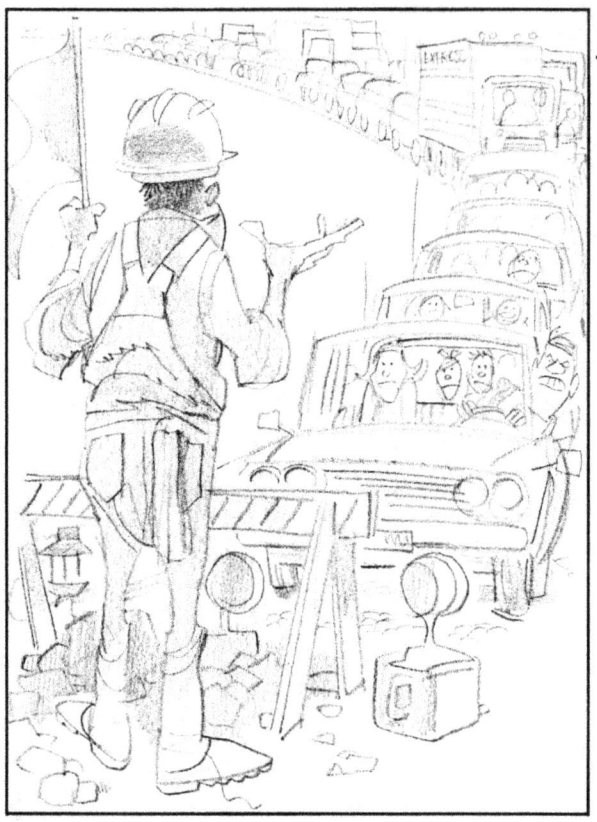

Detour #2
Pencil on Strathmore
Advertising rough

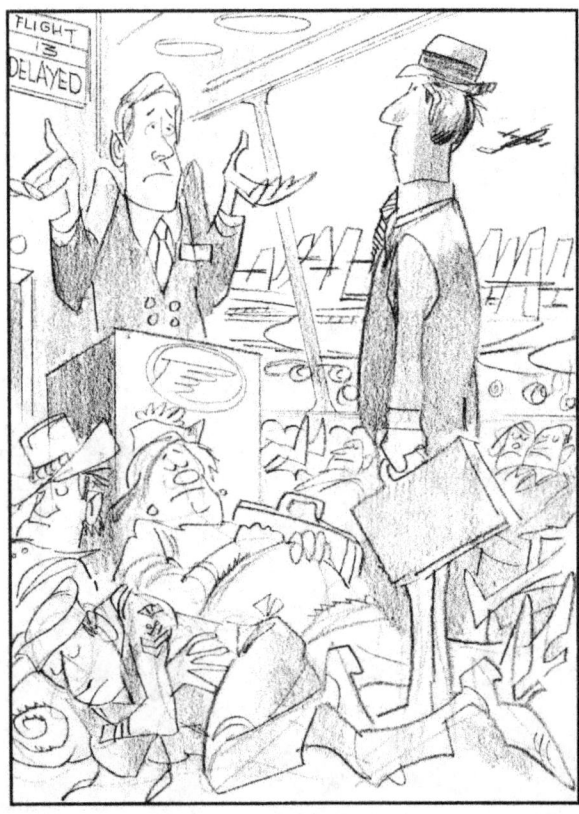

Flight 13
Pencil on Strathmore
Advertising rough

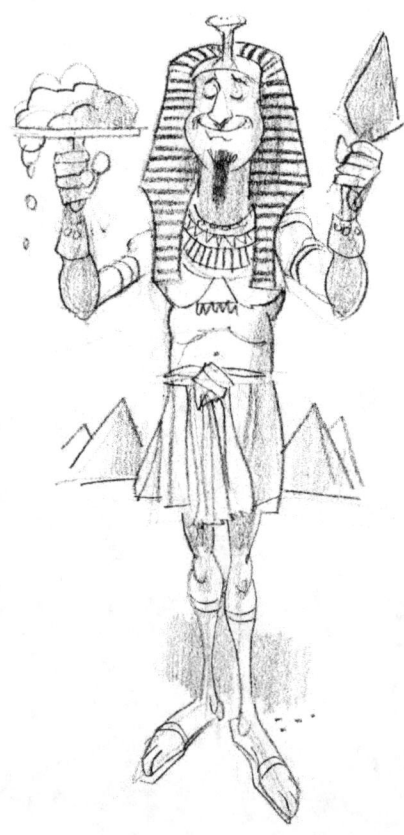

Pharoah
Pencil on Strathmore
Advertising rough

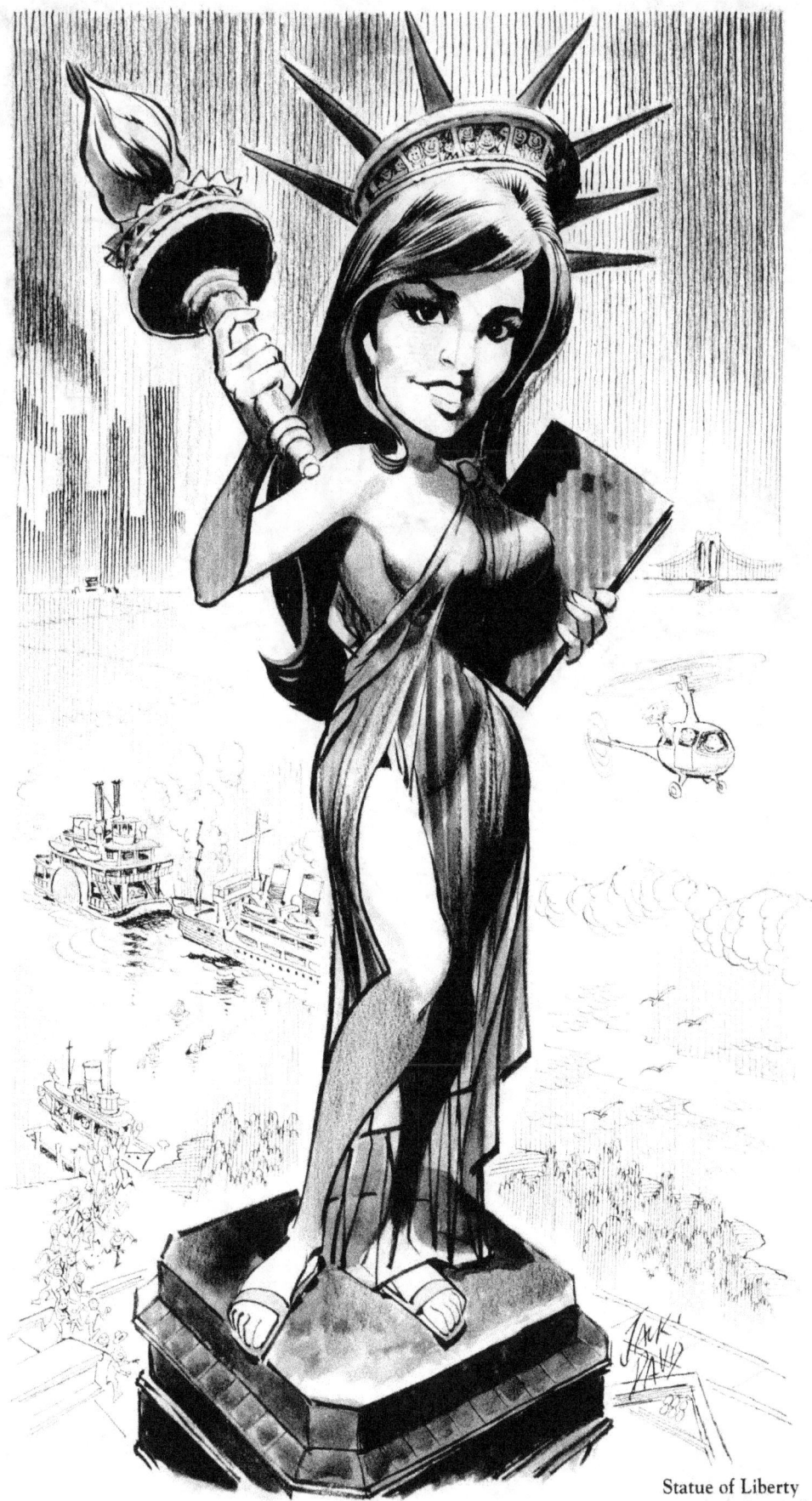

Statue of Liberty
Mixed media on illustration board
Magazine illustration

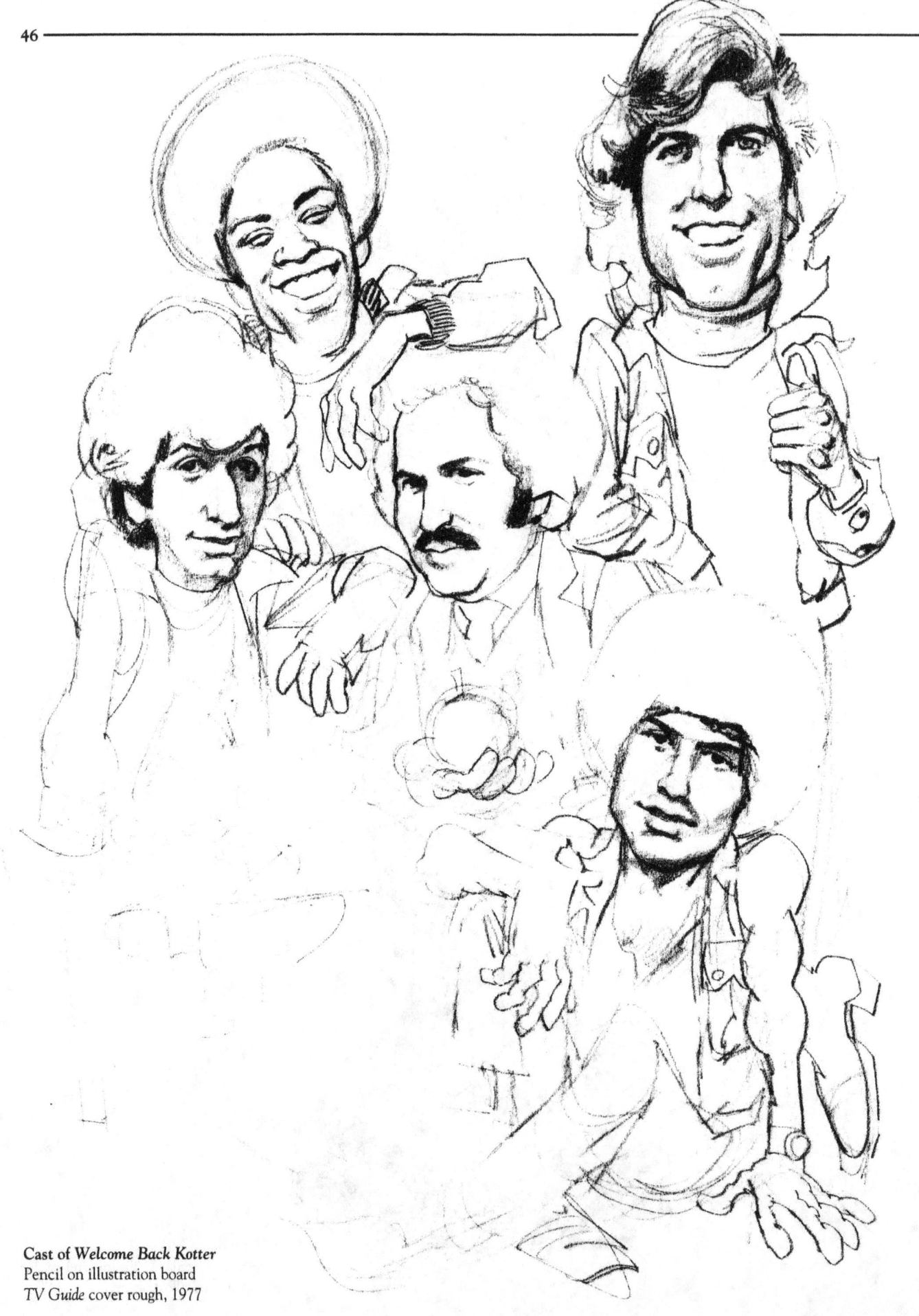

Cast of Welcome Back Kotter
Pencil on illustration board
TV Guide cover rough, 1977

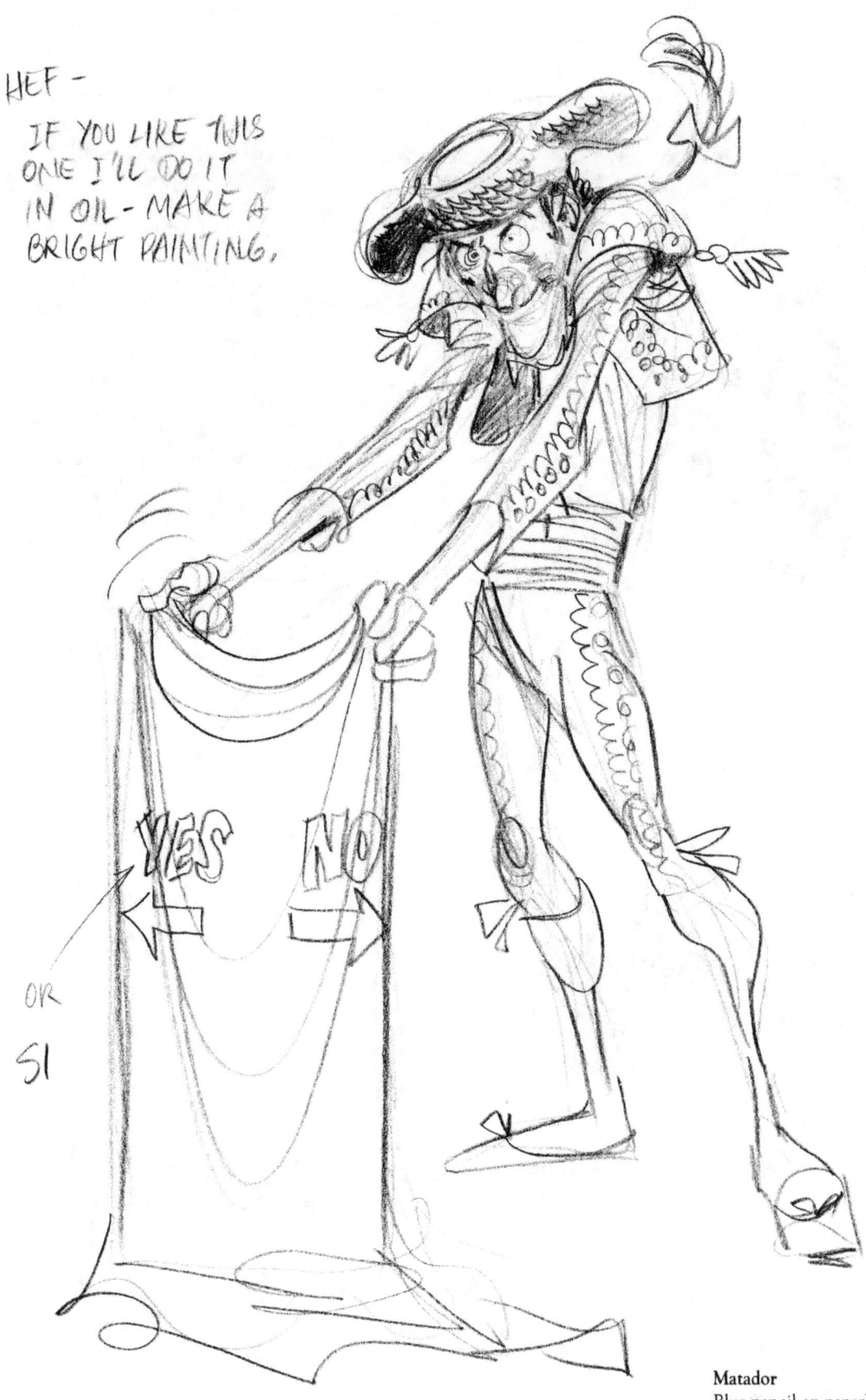

HEF —

IF YOU LIKE THIS
ONE I'LL DO IT
IN OIL — MAKE A
BRIGHT PAINTING.

YES

NO

OR

SI

Matador
Blue pencil on paperl
Idea sketch for *Playboy* cartoon

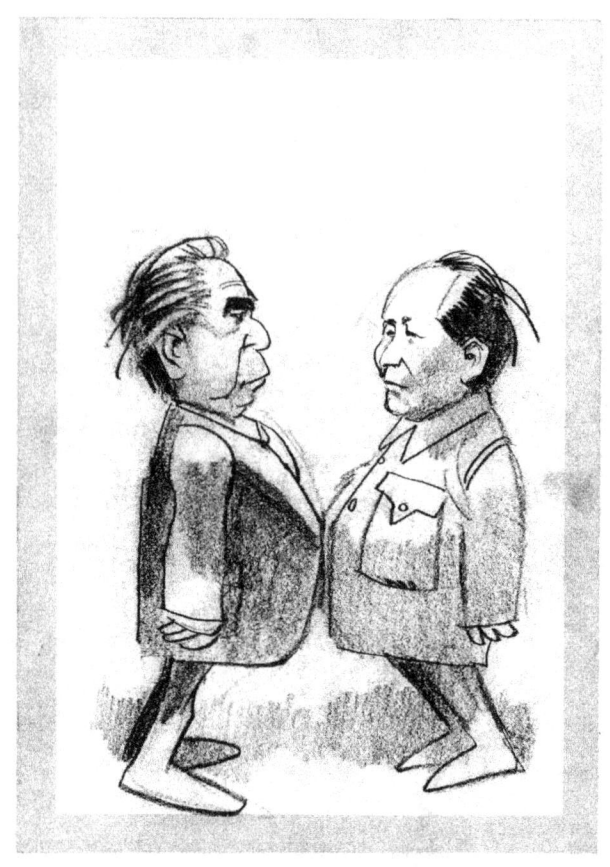
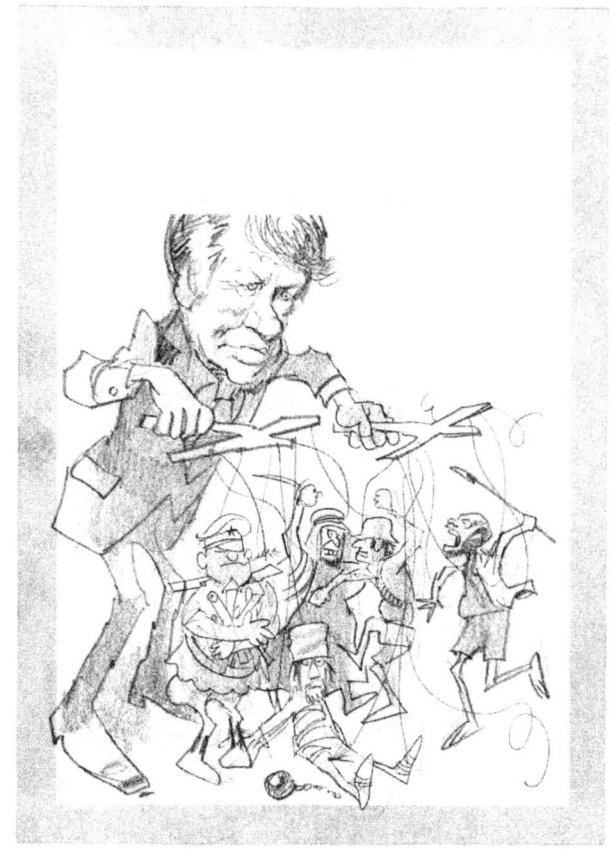
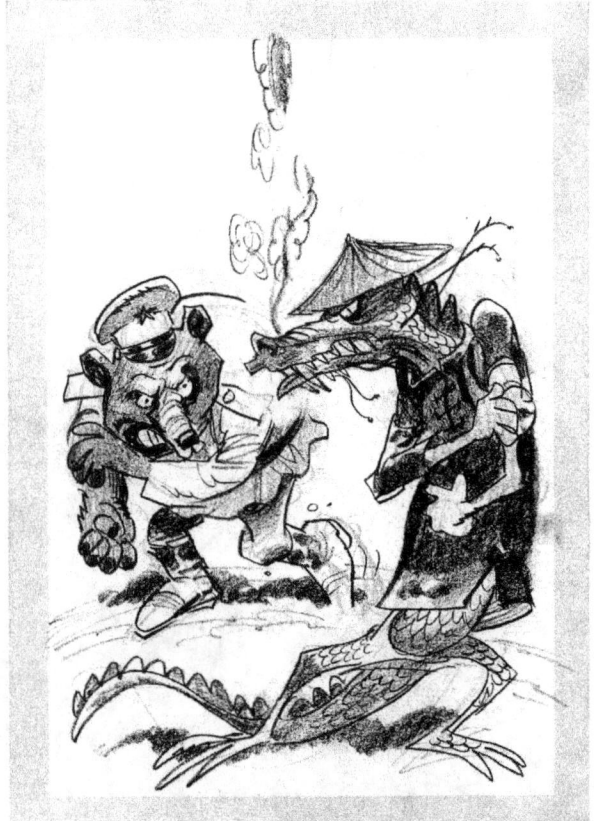
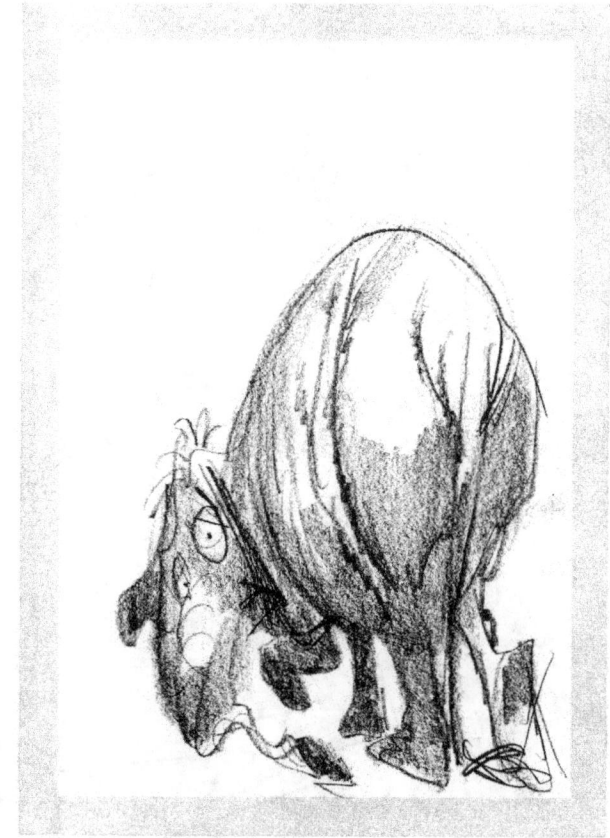

TIME *Magazine* Cover Ideas
Pencil on prepared sketch pad

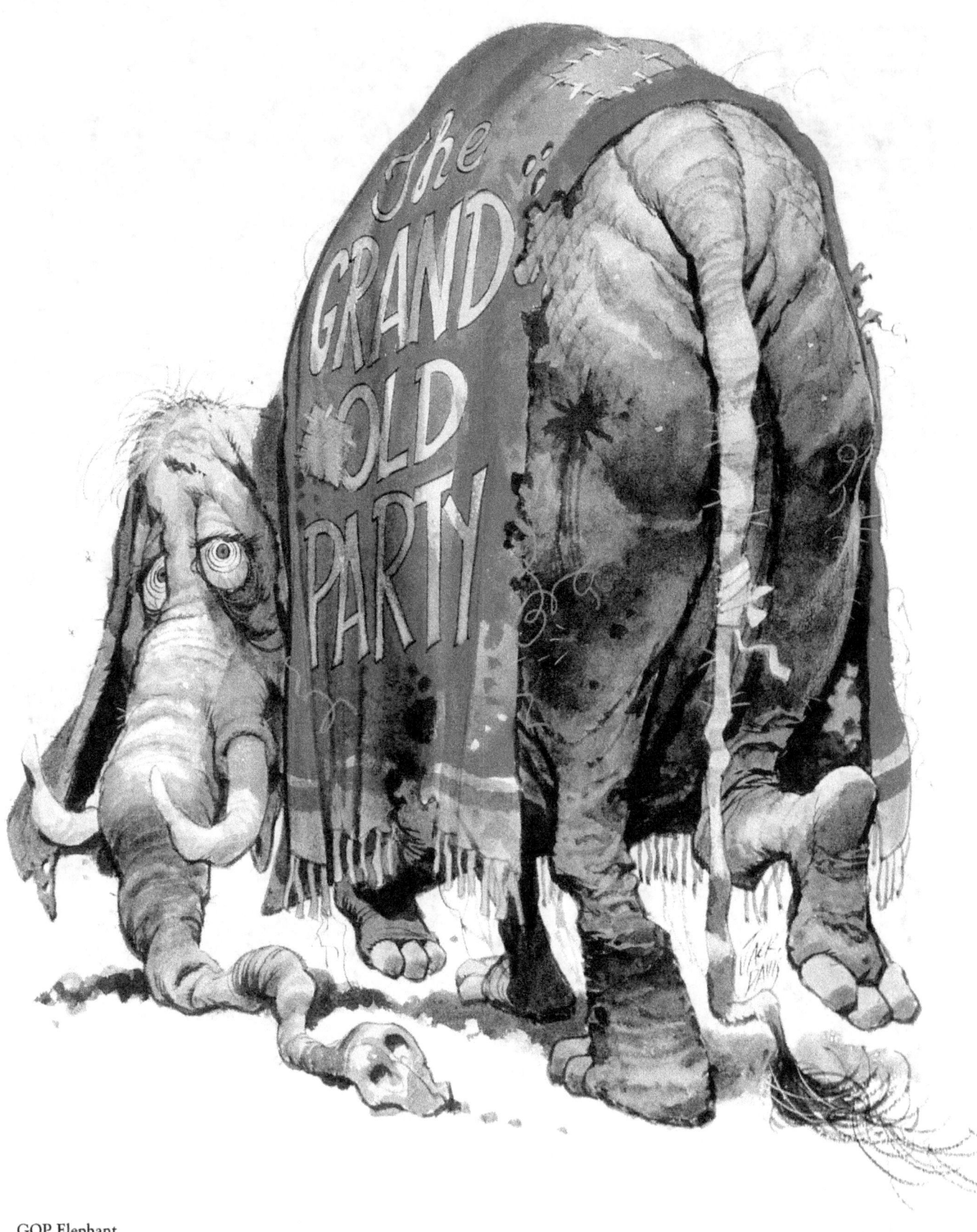

GOP Elephant
Brush & ink and watercolor on illustration board
Unused *TIME Magazine* cover

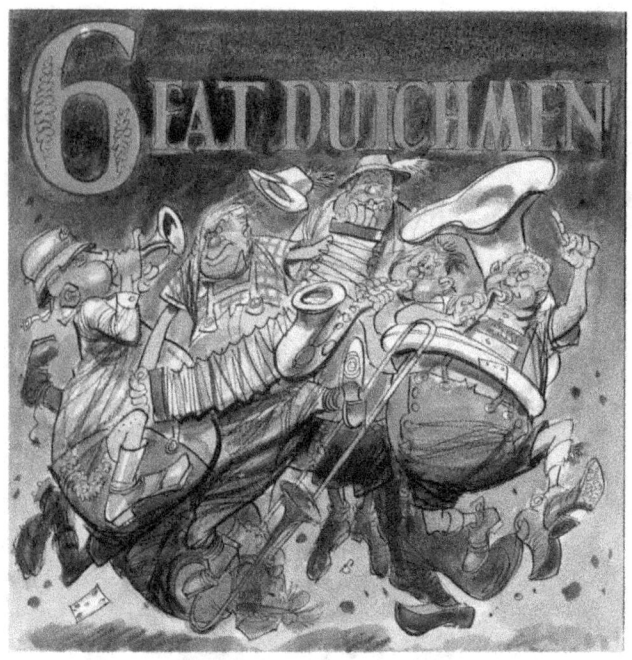

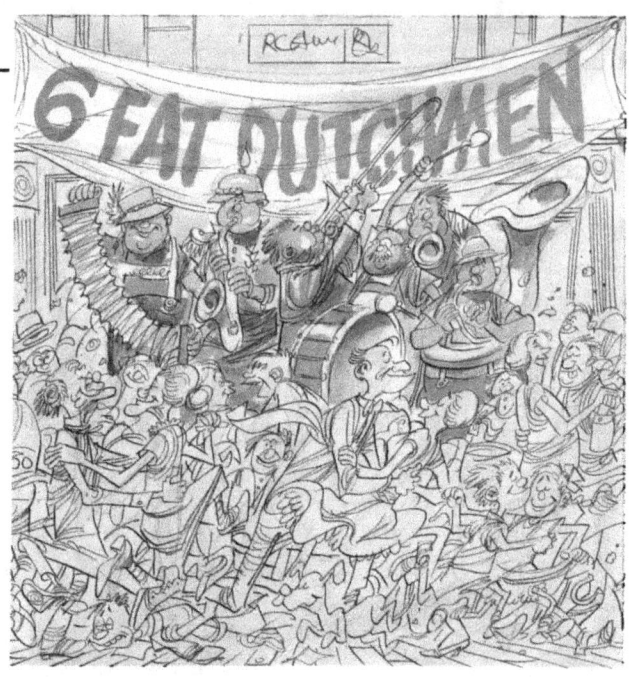

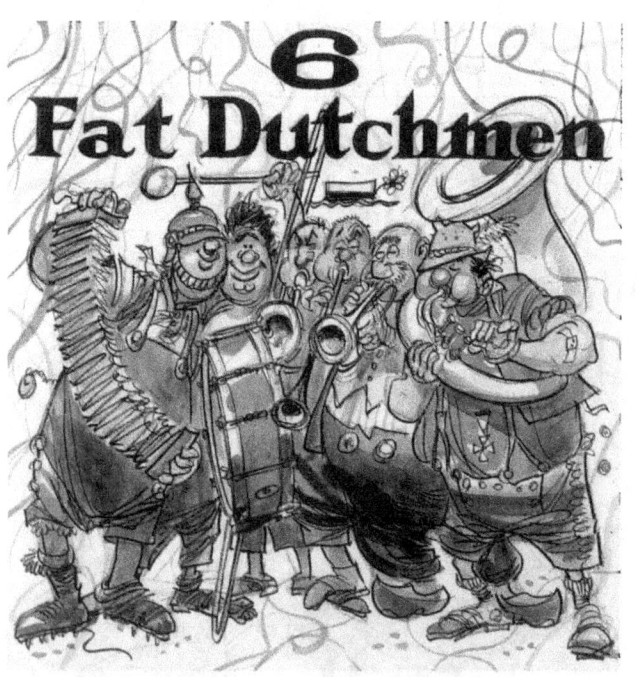

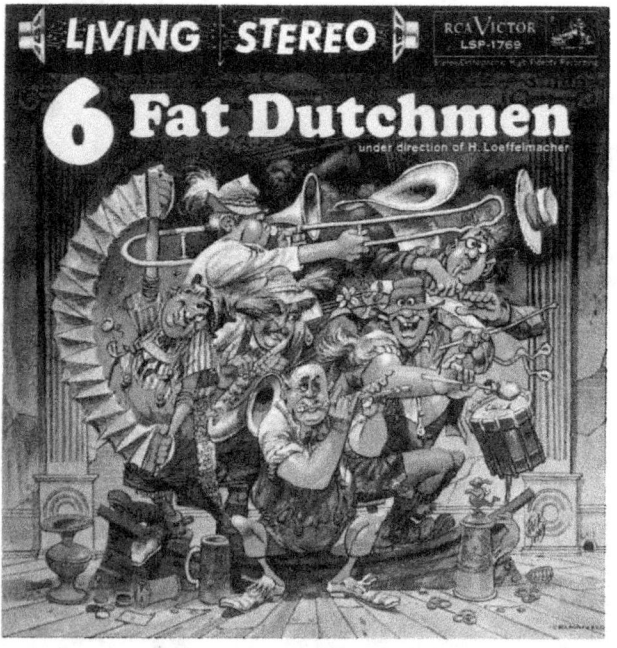

6 Fat Dutchmen
Pen & ink and watercolor on illustration board
Three roughs and finished album jacket, 1958

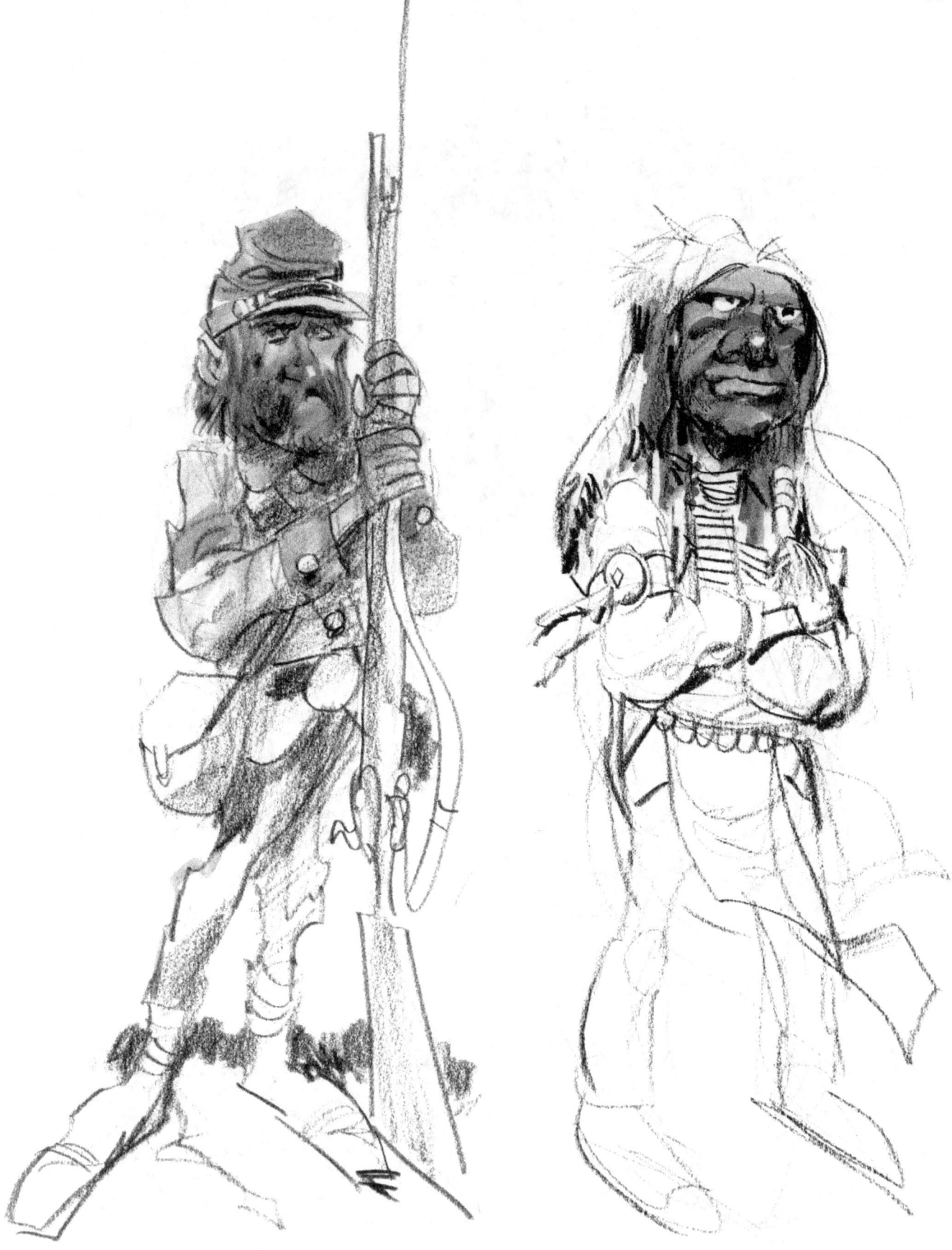

Civil War Soldier
Pencil and watercolor sketch on Strathmore

Indian
Pencil and watercolor sketch on Strathmore

I Can't Jog
Brush & ink and watercolor on illustration board

Trapped
Mixed media on watercolor board
Alternate illustration for *Cavalier* magazine, 1963

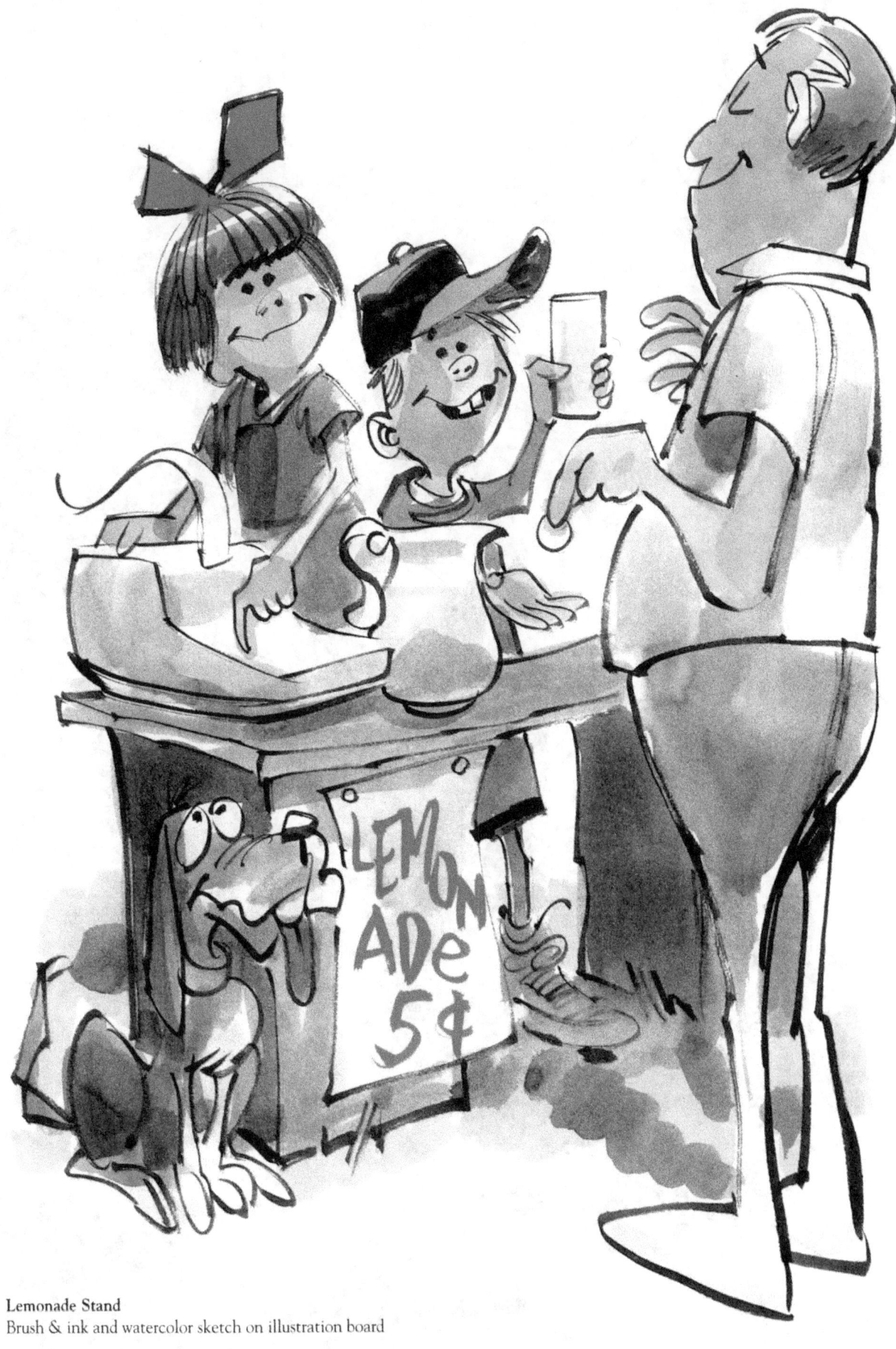

Lemonade Stand
Brush & ink and watercolor sketch on illustration board

High-Tech Fishing
Mixed media on illustration board
Magazine illustration

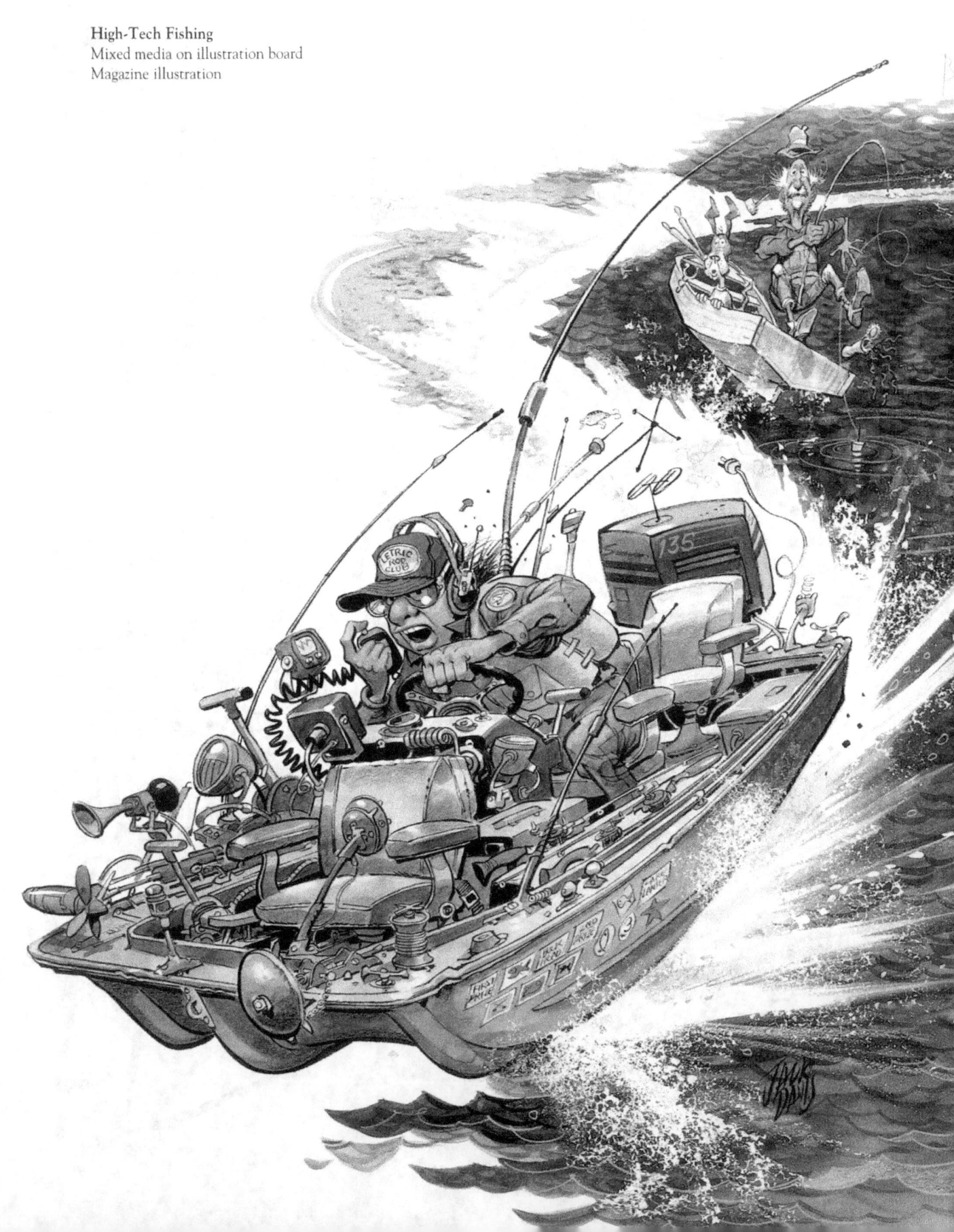

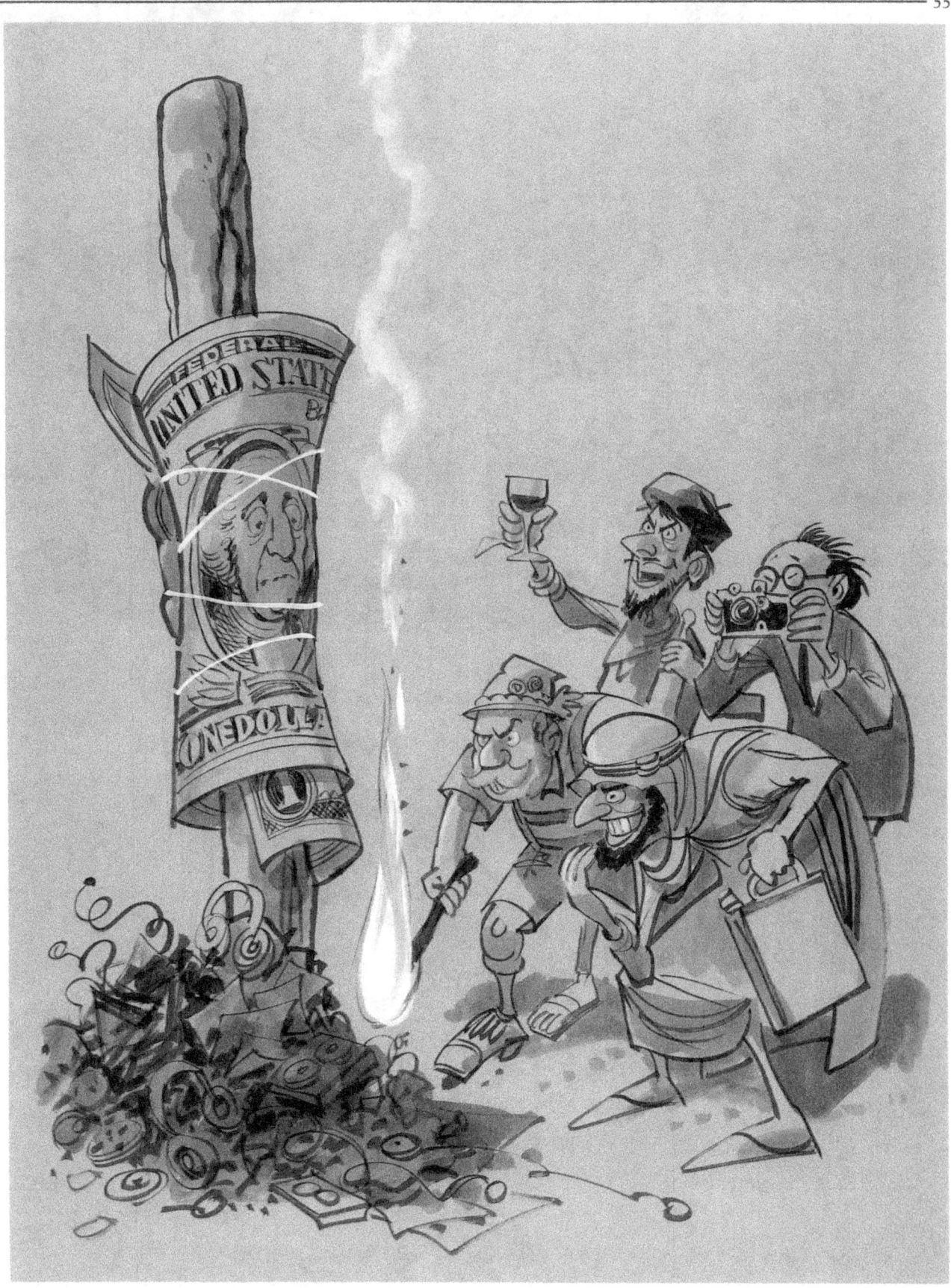

The Dollar in Trouble
Brush & ink and watercolor on colored board
Unused magazine cover

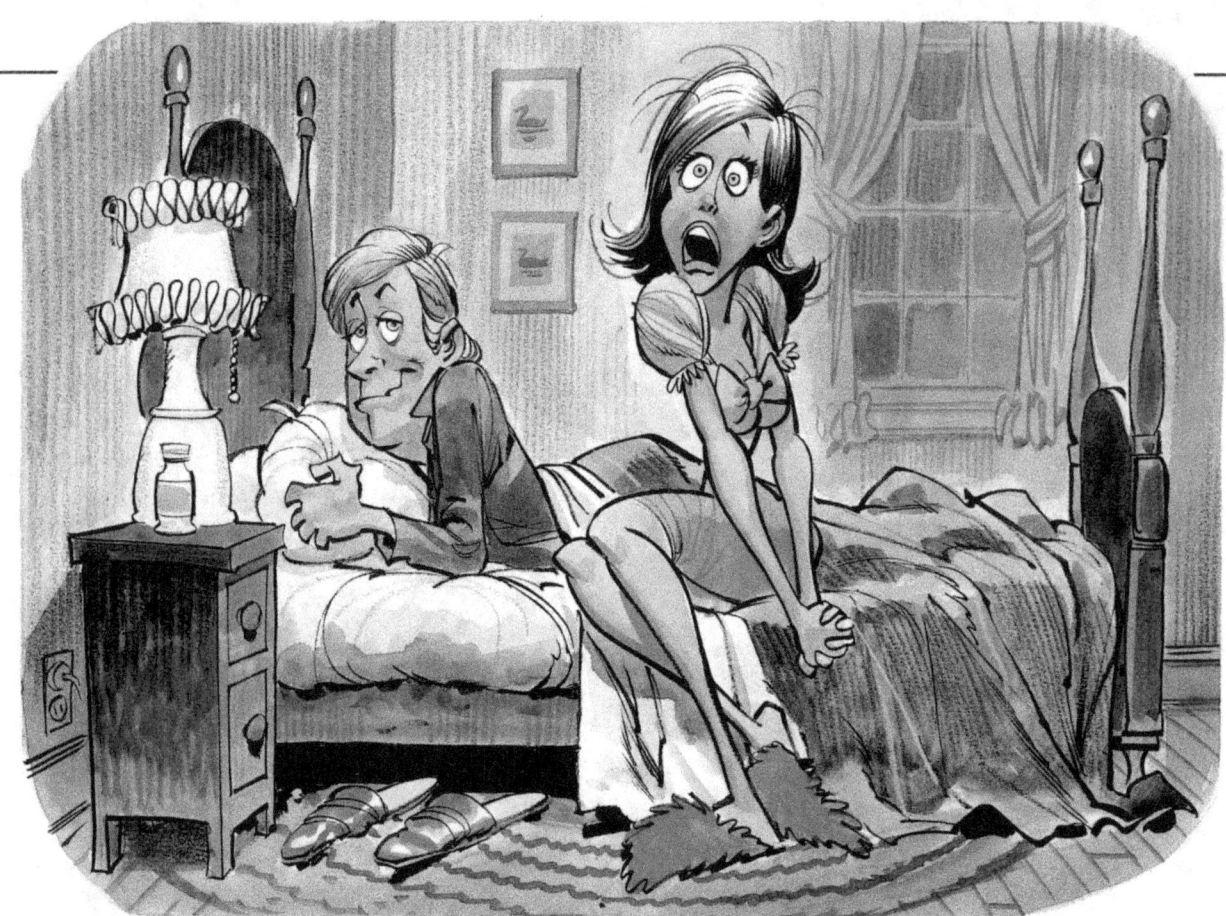

Can't Sleep?
Mixed media on illustration board
Preliminary idea for animated commercial

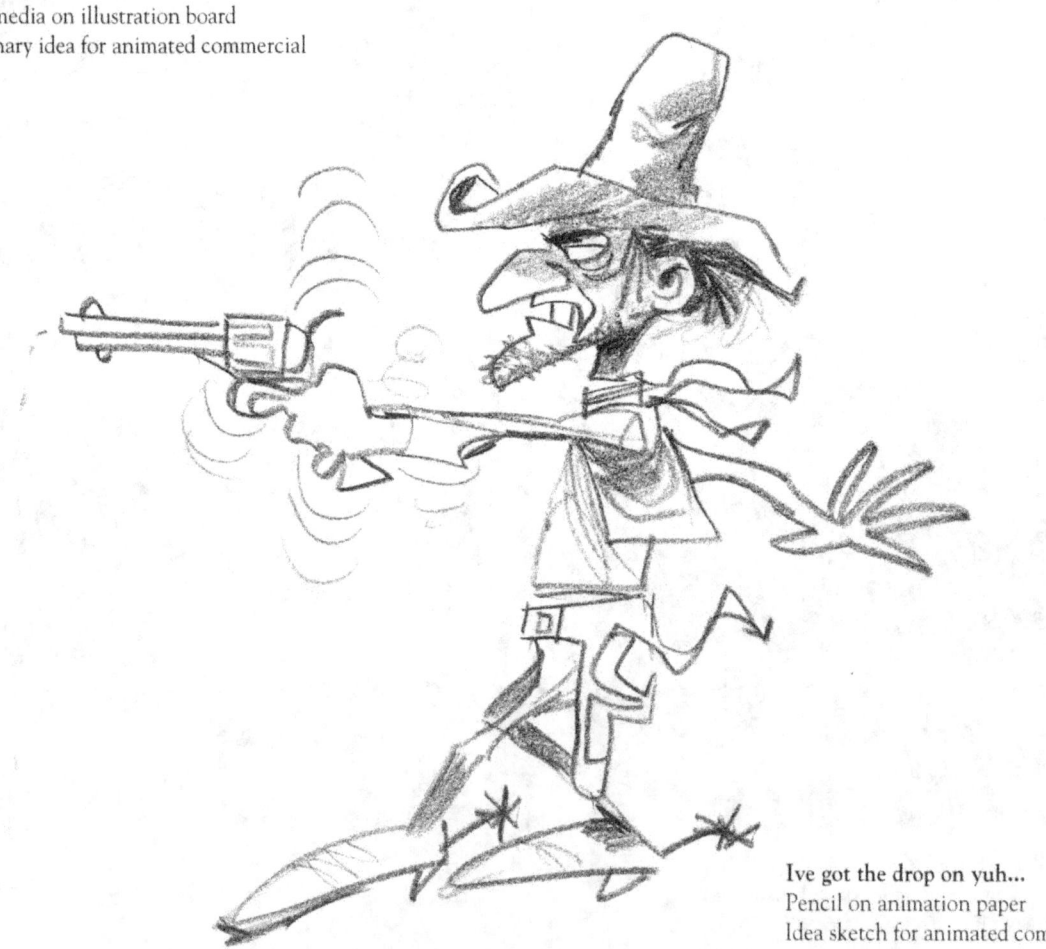

Ive got the drop on yuh...
Pencil on animation paper
Idea sketch for animated commercial

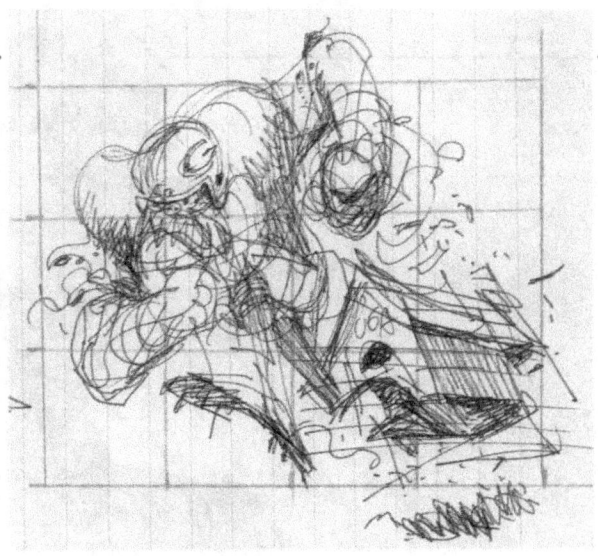

Georgia Dawghouse
Felt-tip on legal pad, gridded for enlargement
Preliminary sketch for poster, actual size

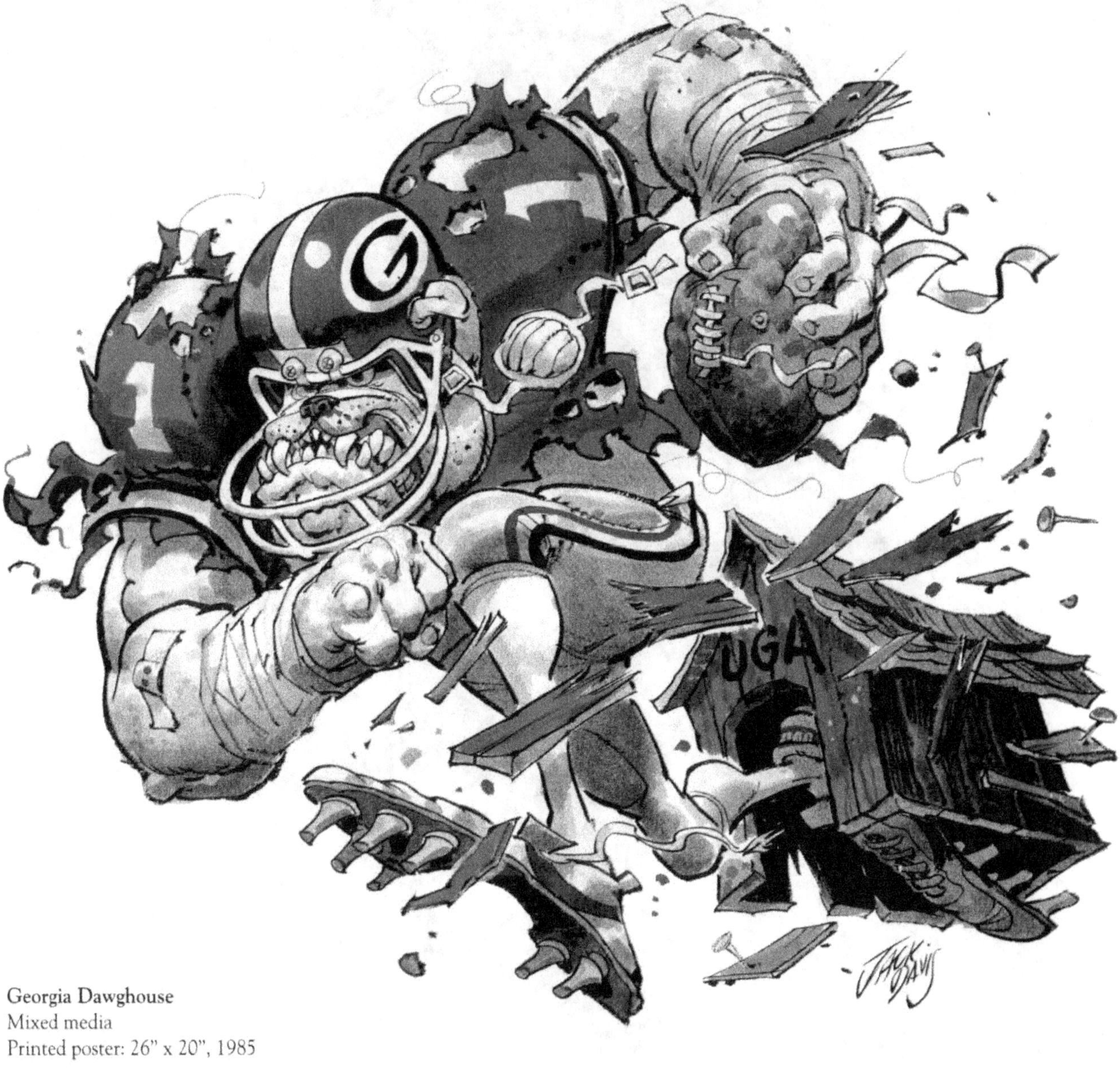

Georgia Dawghouse
Mixed media
Printed poster: 26" x 20", 1985

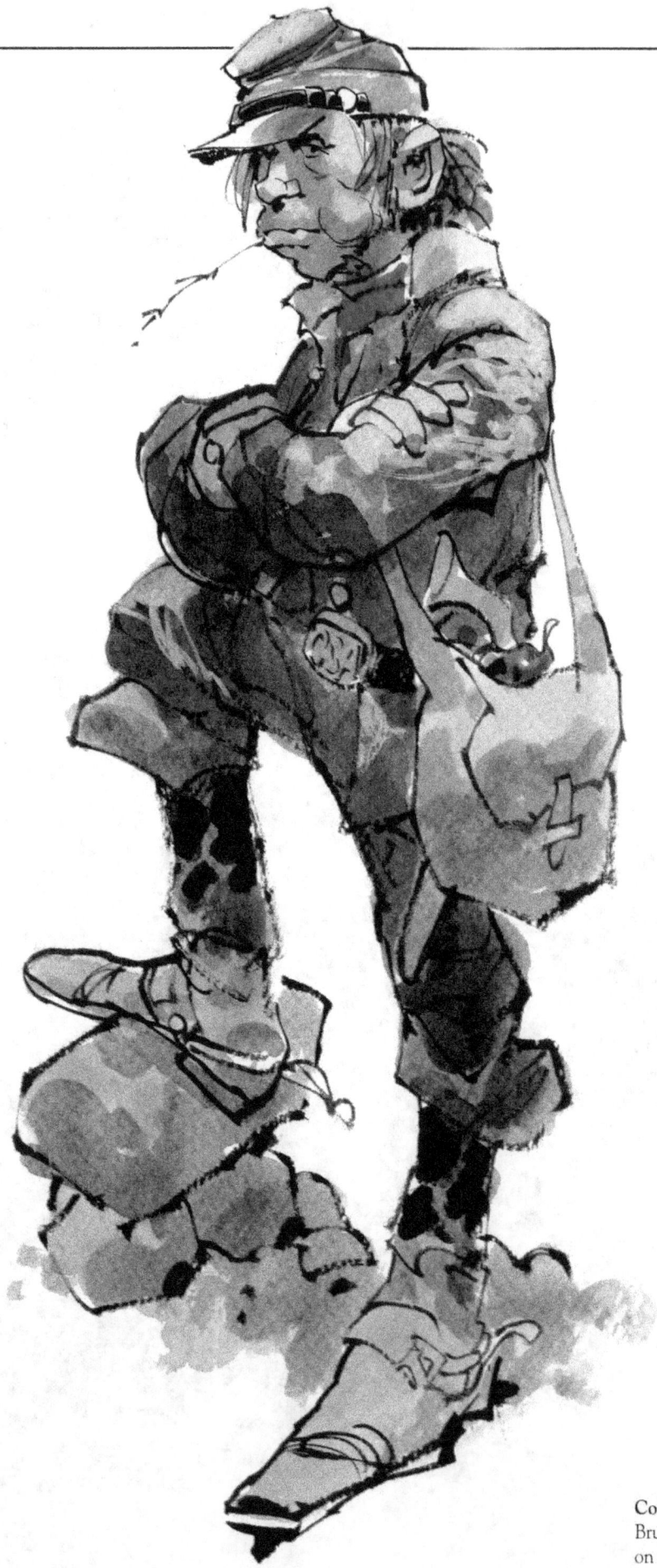

Confederate Soldier
Brush & ink and watercolor
on watercolor paper

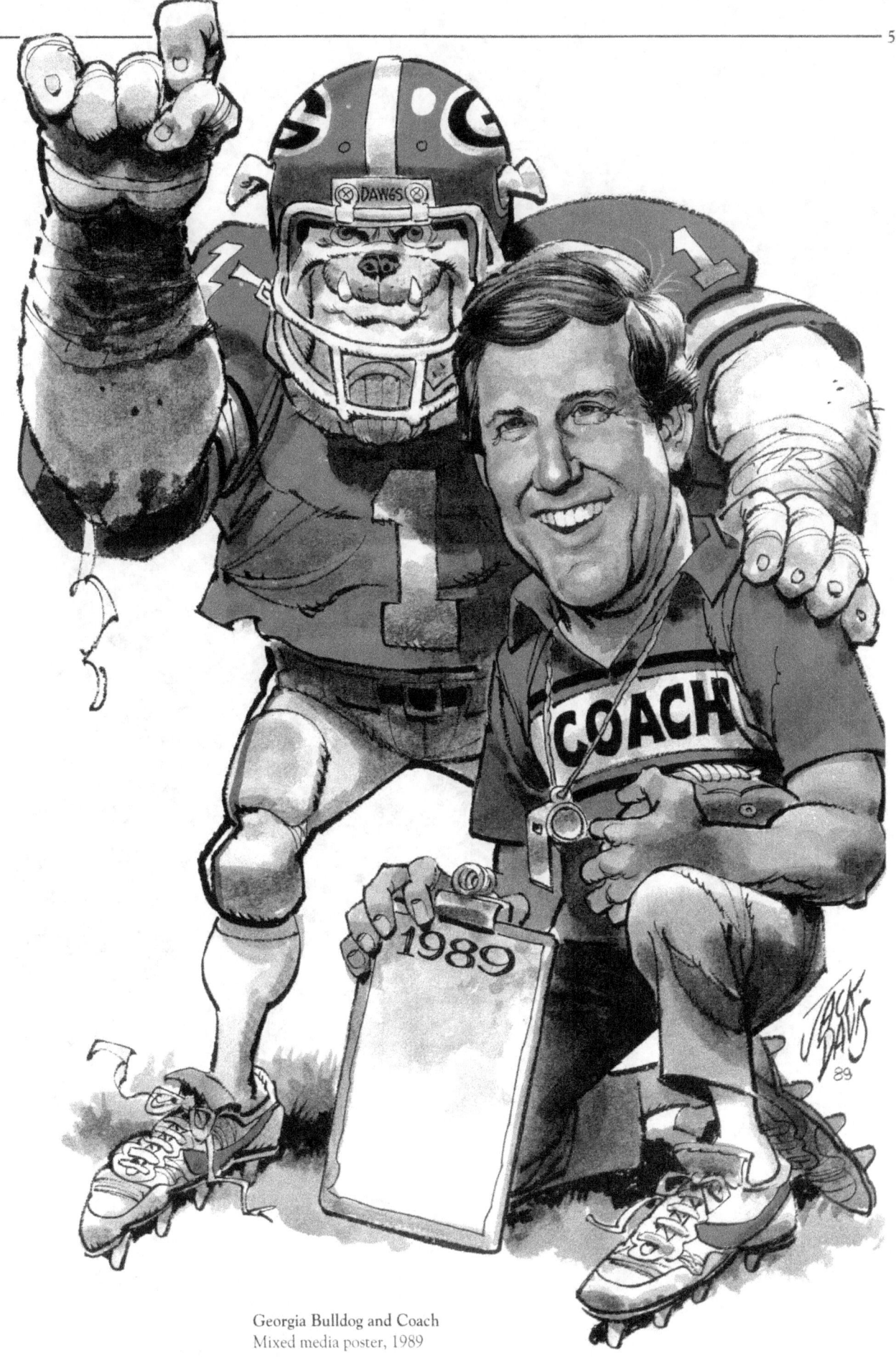

Georgia Bulldog and Coach
Mixed media poster, 1989

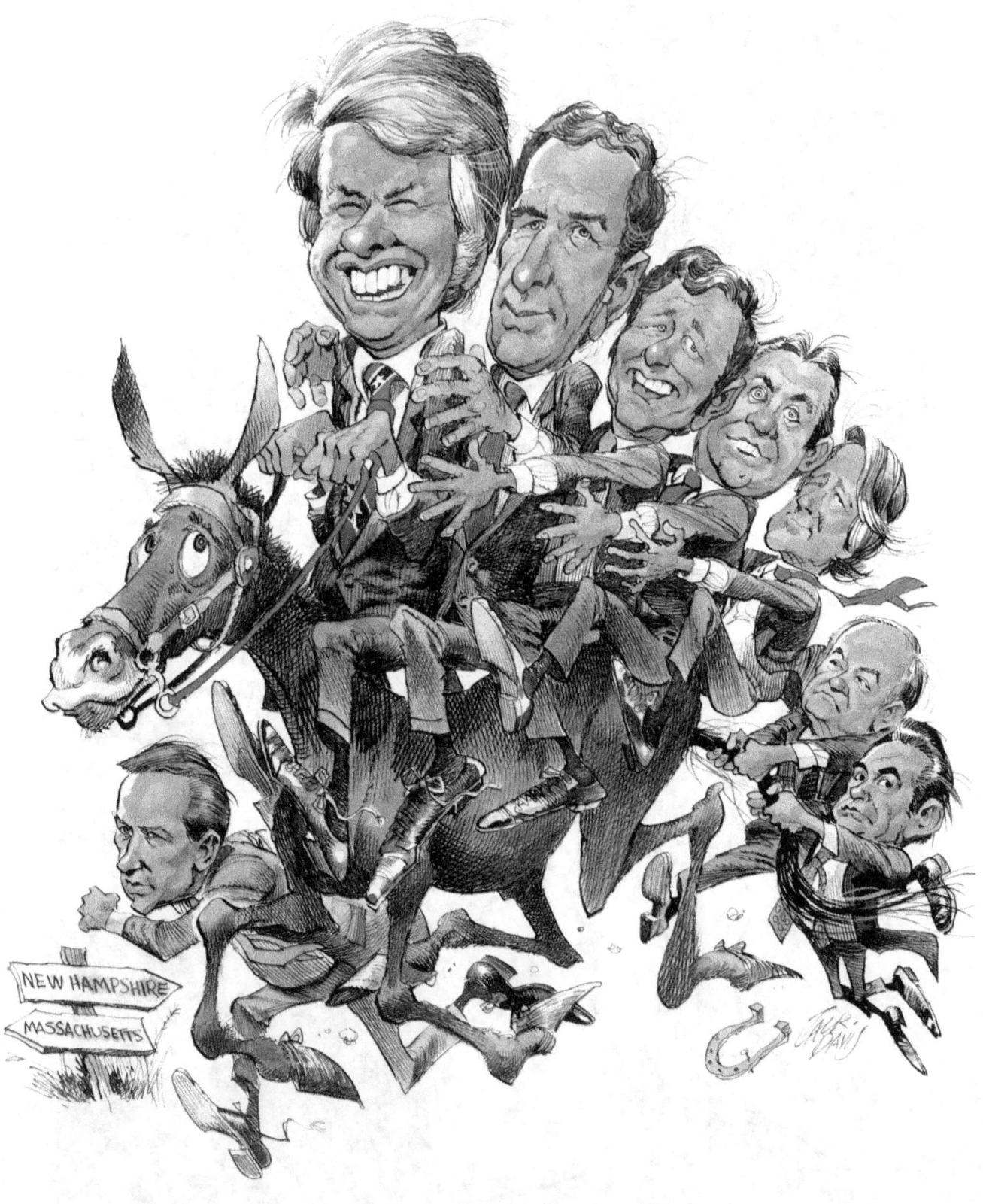

Massachusetts Presidential Primary
Pen & ink and watercolor on illustration board
Magazine illustration, 1976

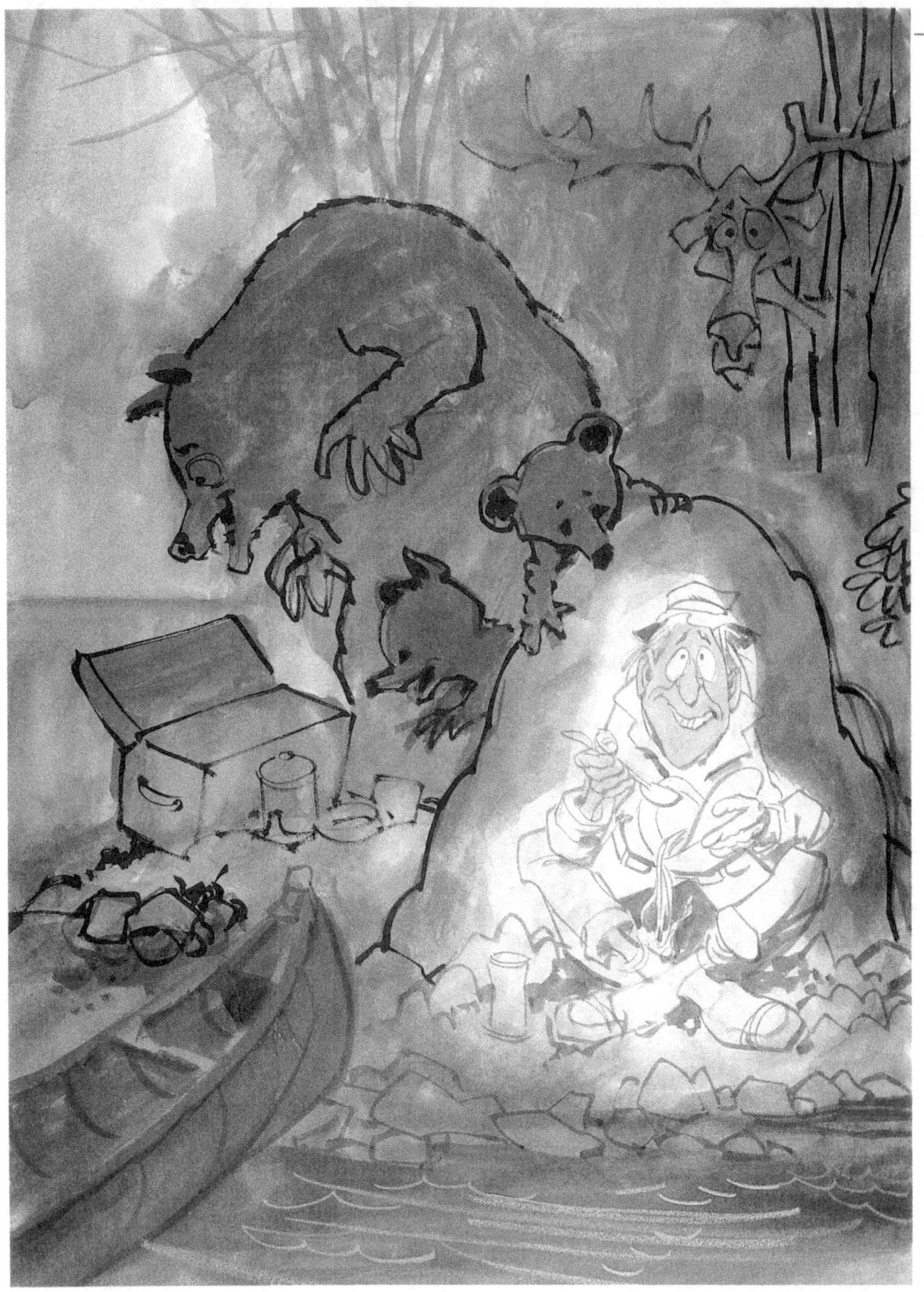

Three Bears
Mixed media rough on illustration board

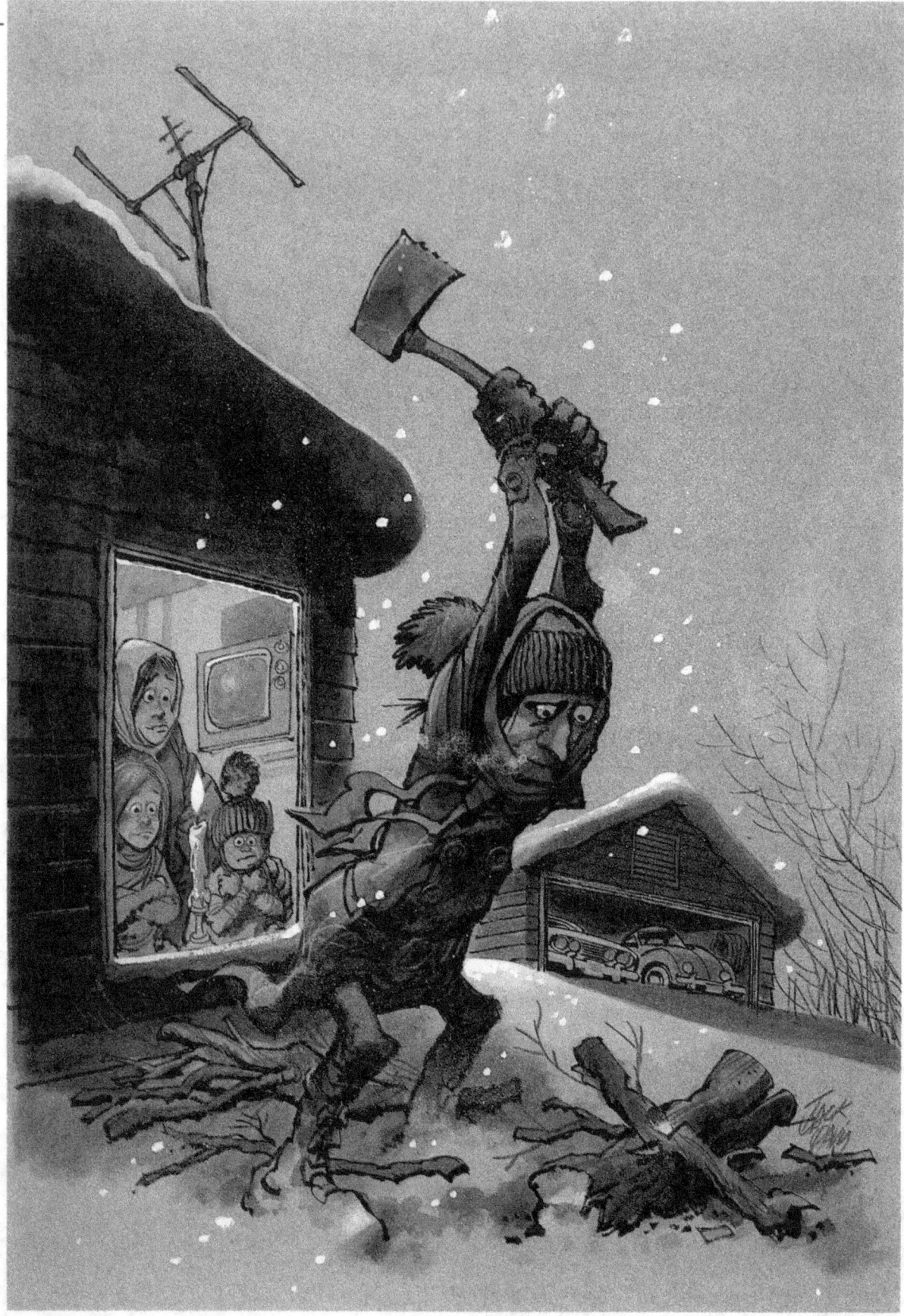

Energy Crisis
Mixed media on colored paper
Magazine cover

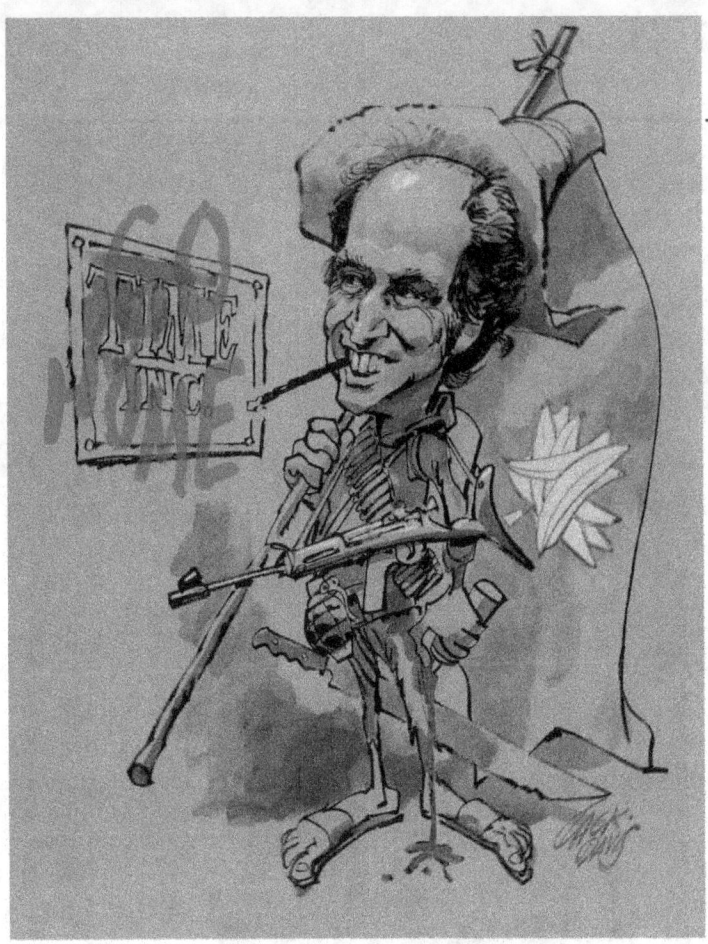

Pierre Trudeau
Mixed media on colored paper

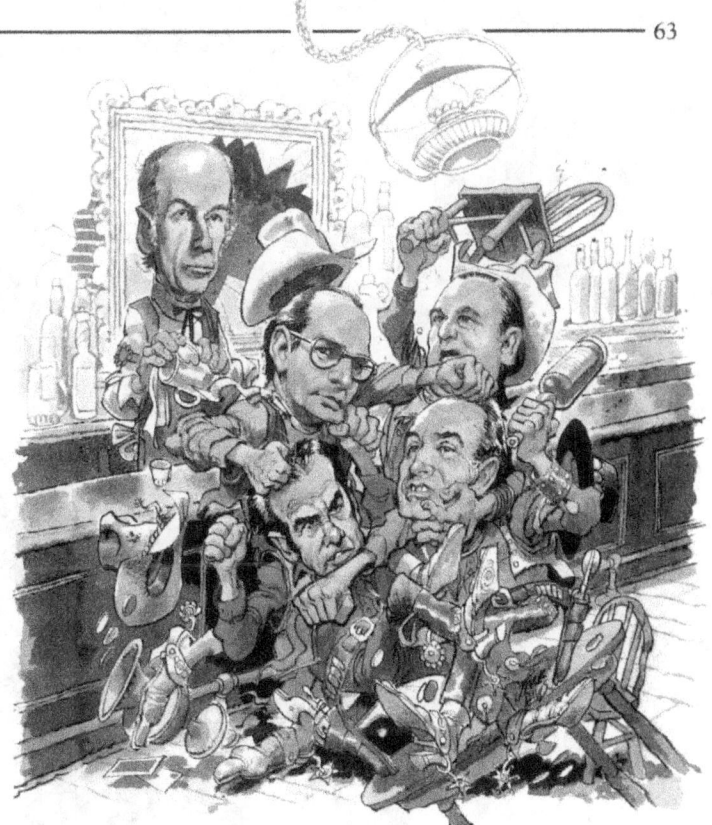

Nixon vs. the Watergate Investigators
Mixed media on watercolor board
Magazine illustration

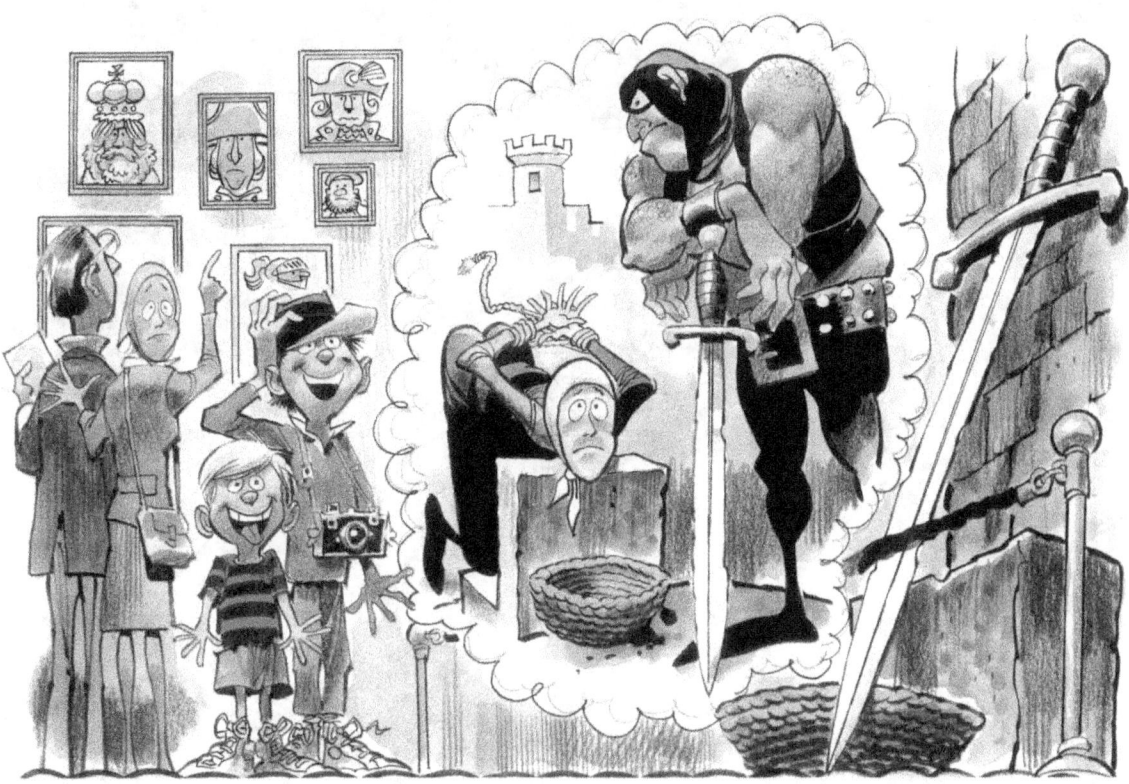

At the Museum
Mixed media on Strathmore
Magazine illustration

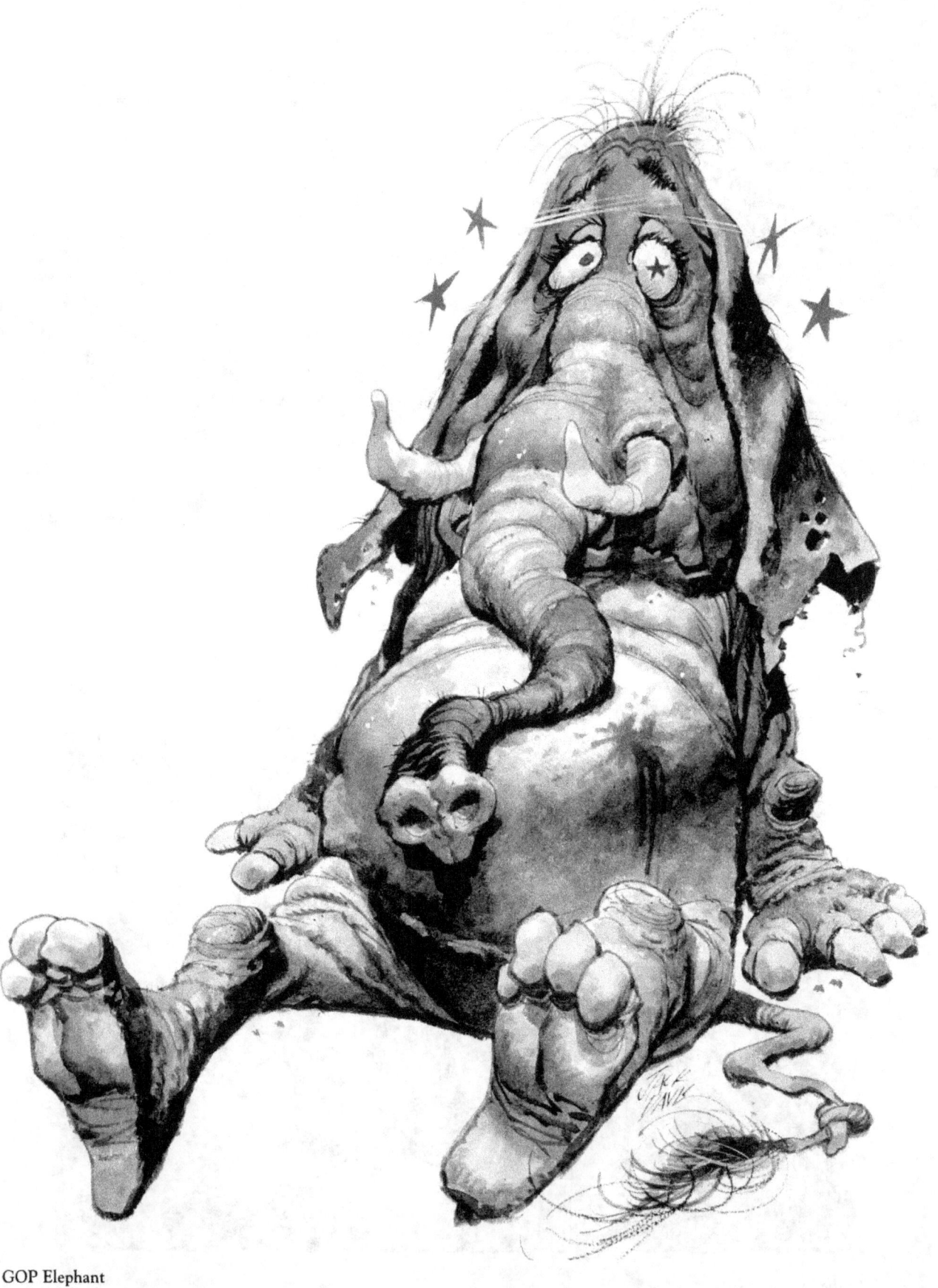

GOP Elephant
Mixed media on illustration board
Unused *TIME Magazine* cover

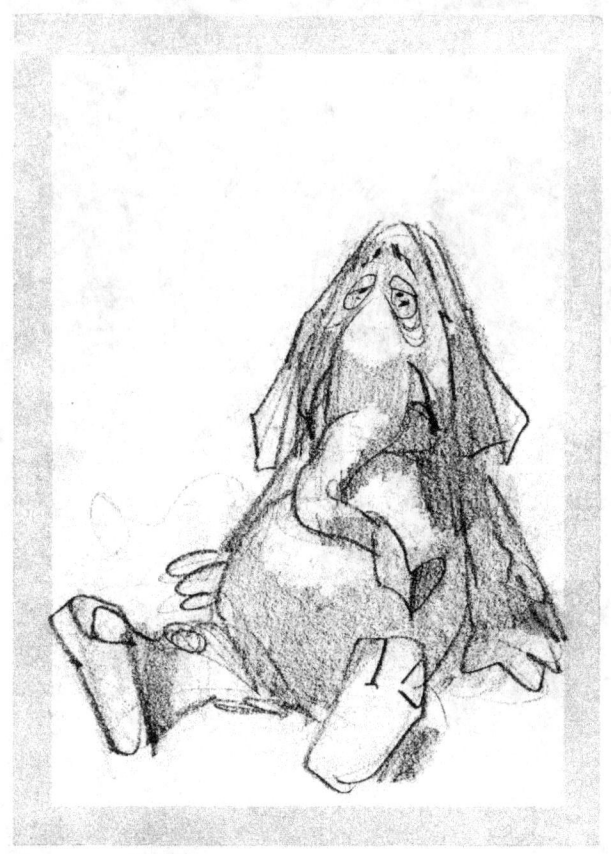

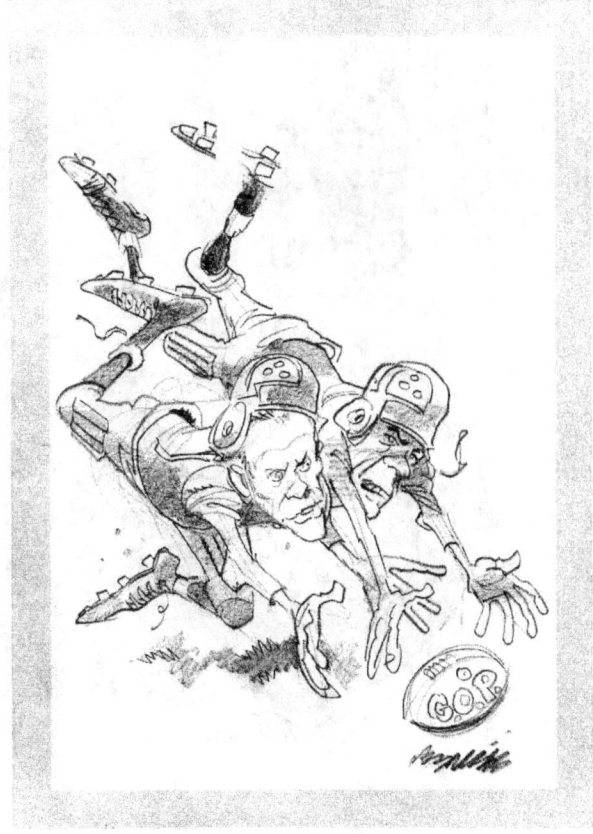

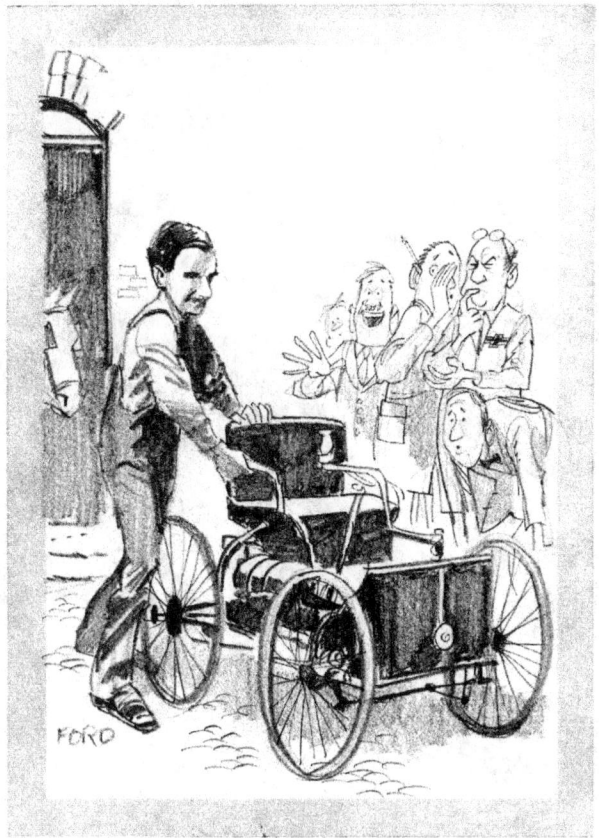

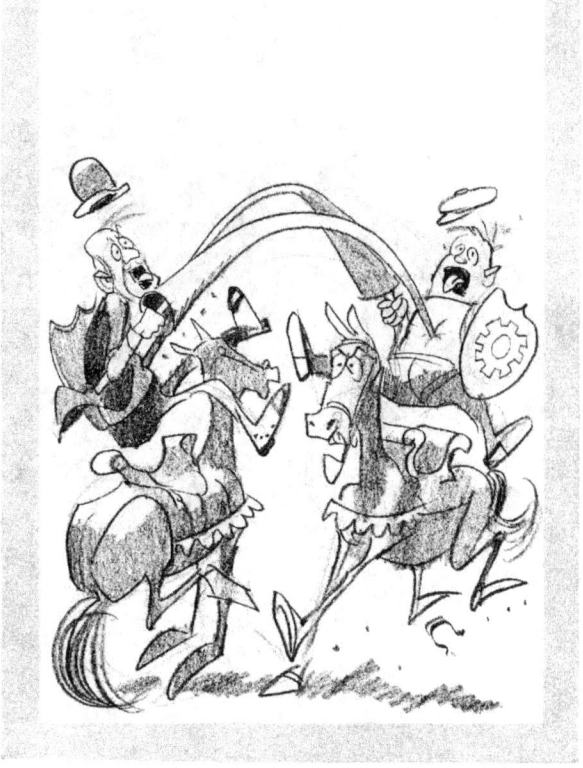

TIME *Magazine* Cover Ideas
Pencil on prepared sketch pad

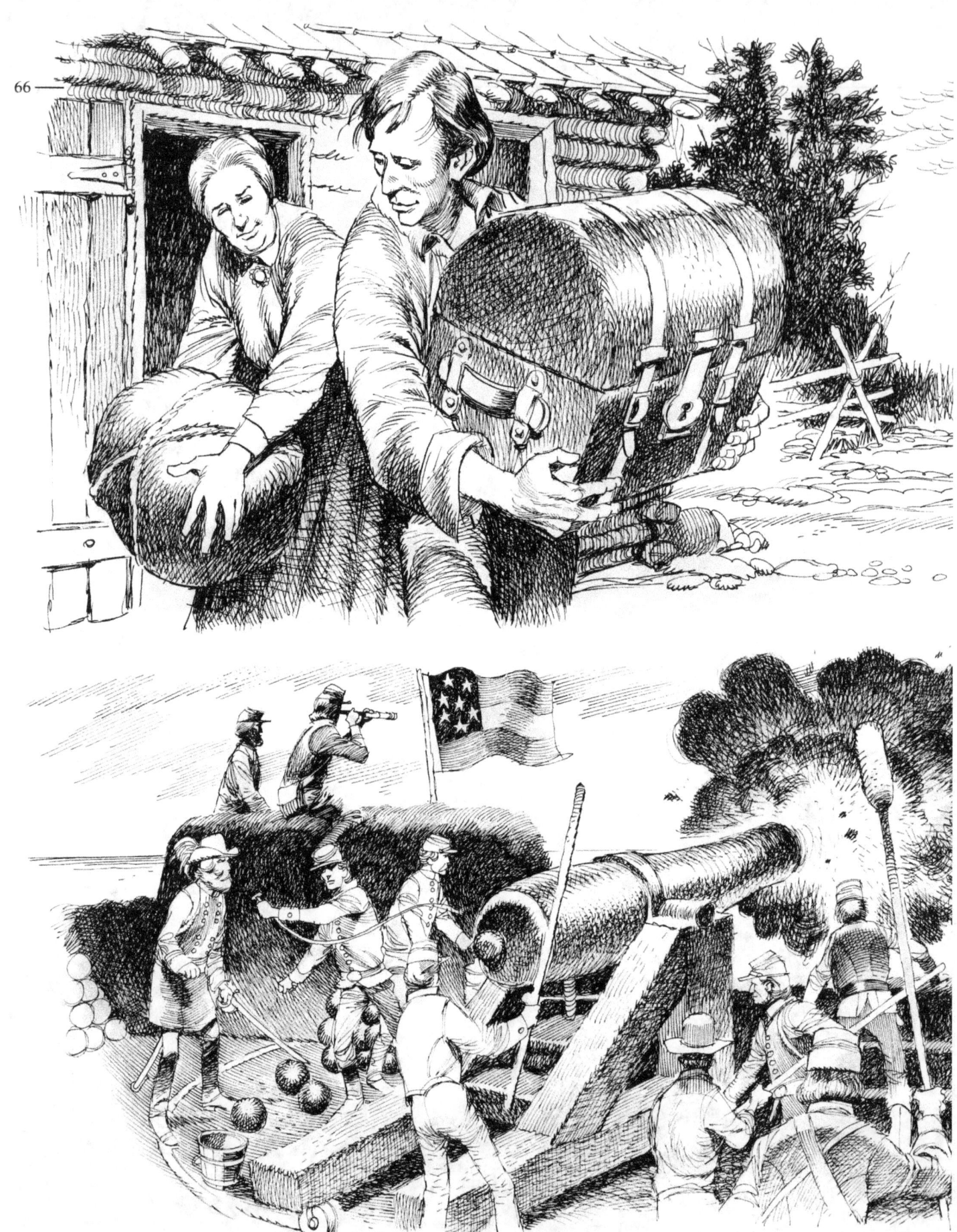

Fort Sumter
Pen & ink on illustration board
Meet Abraham Lincoln children's book, 1965

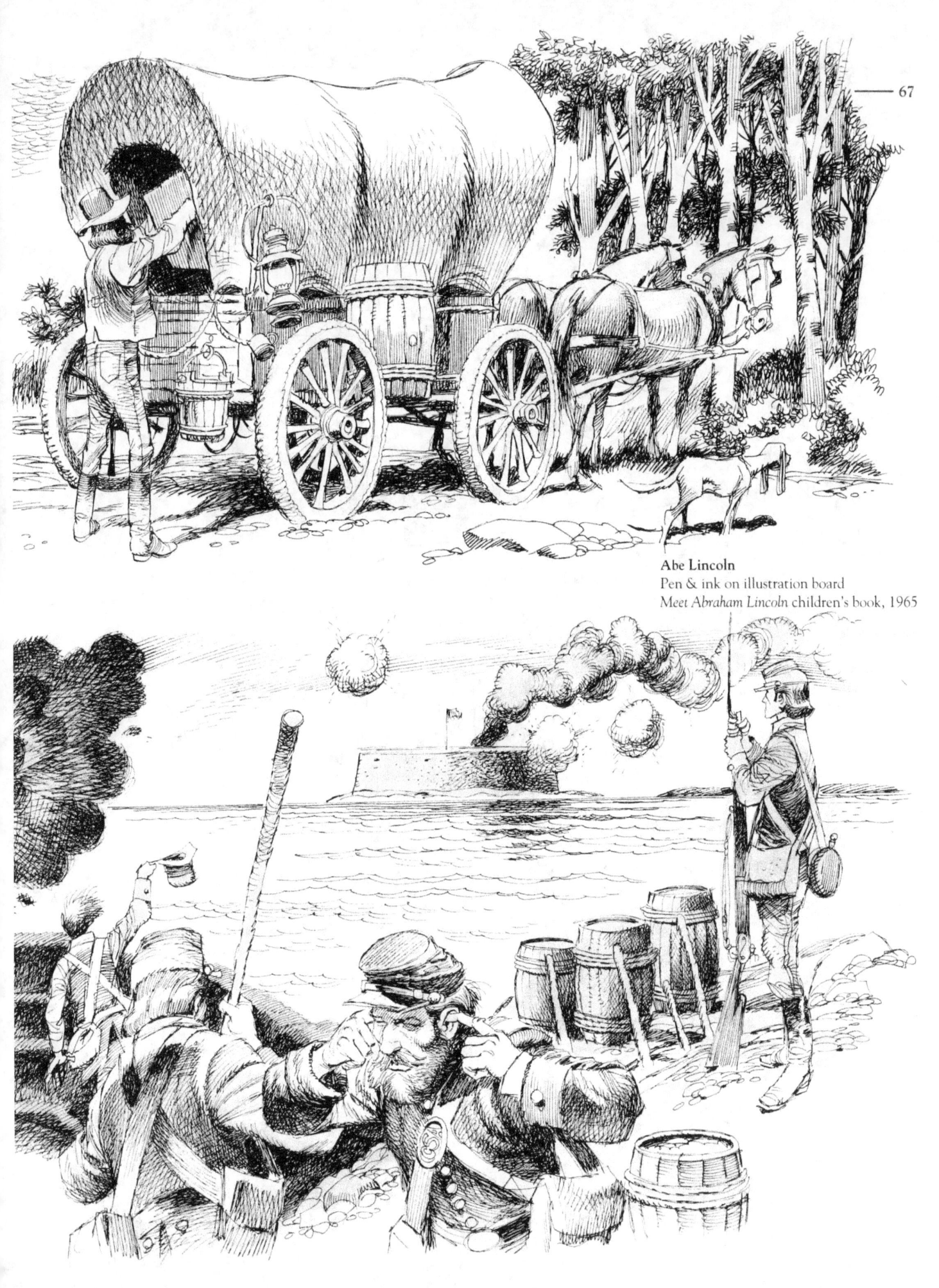

Abe Lincoln
Pen & ink on illustration board
Meet Abraham Lincoln children's book, 1965

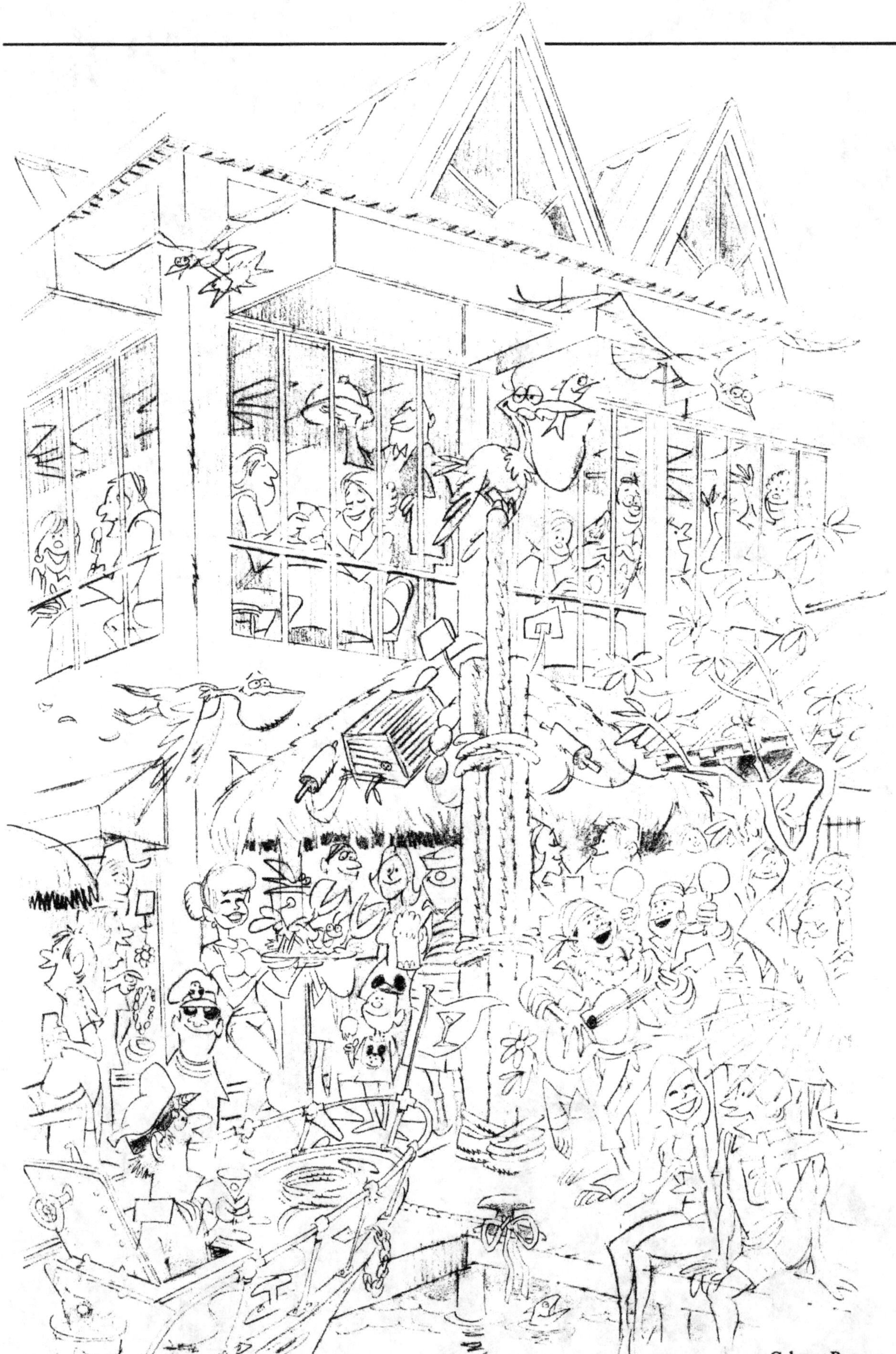

Calypso Party
Pencil on Strathmore
Advertising rough

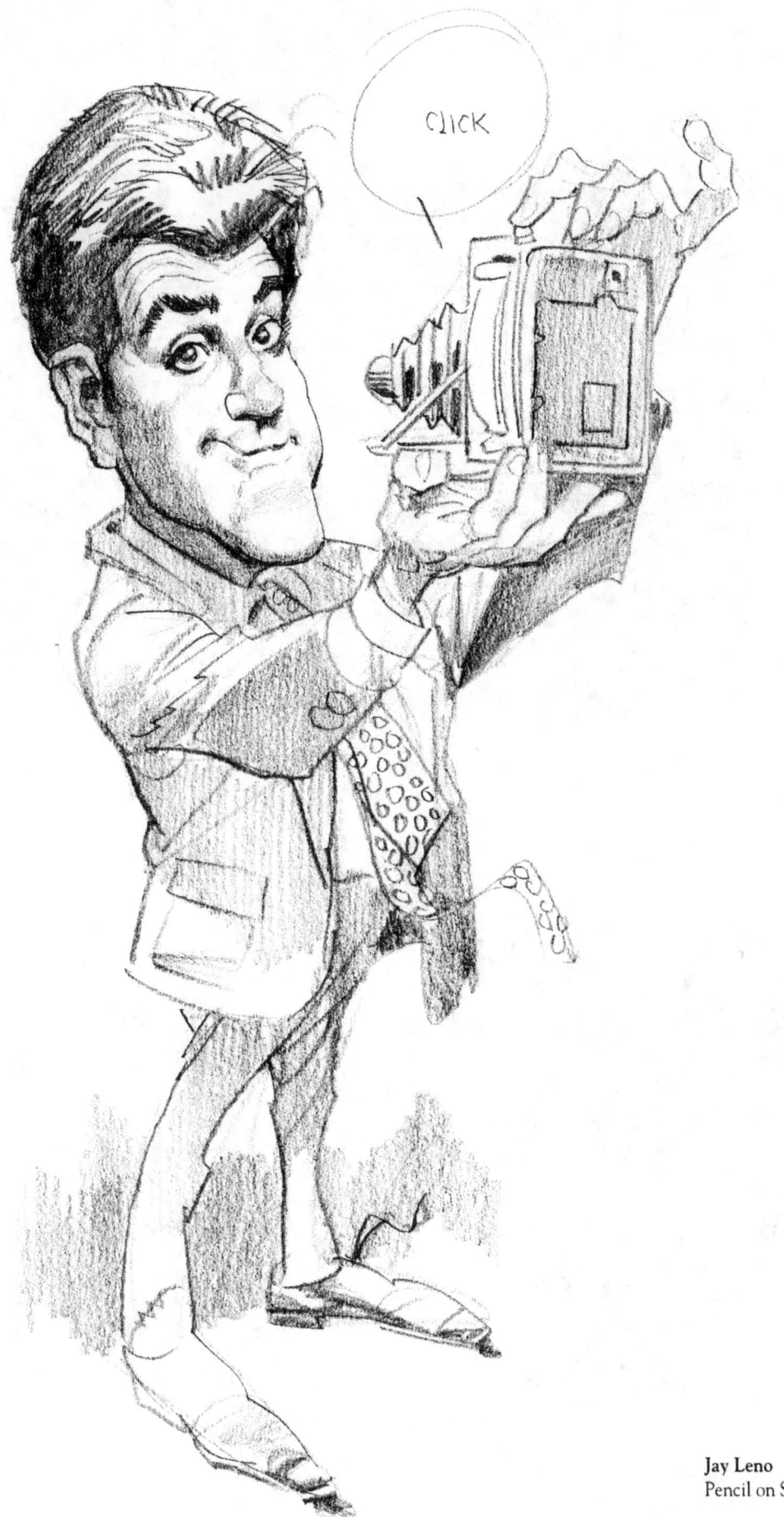

Jay Leno
Pencil on Strathmore

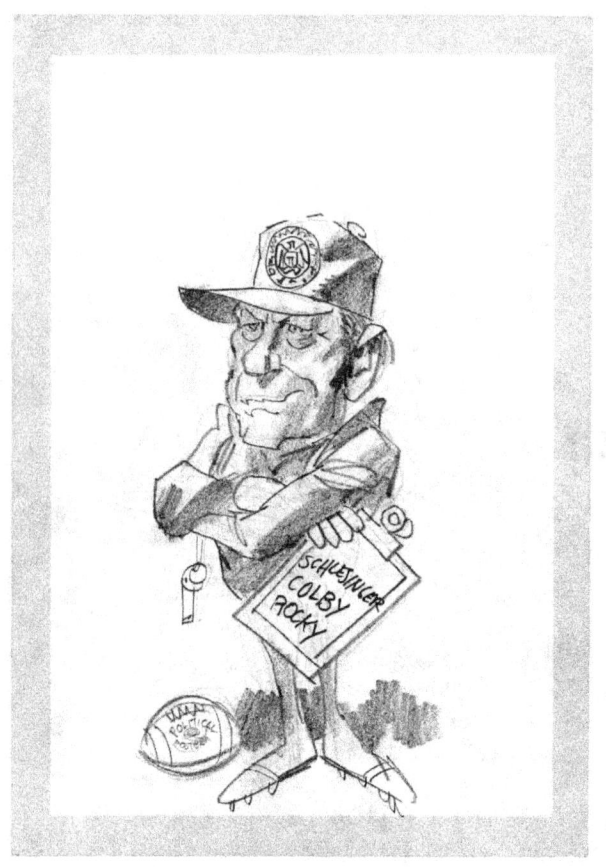

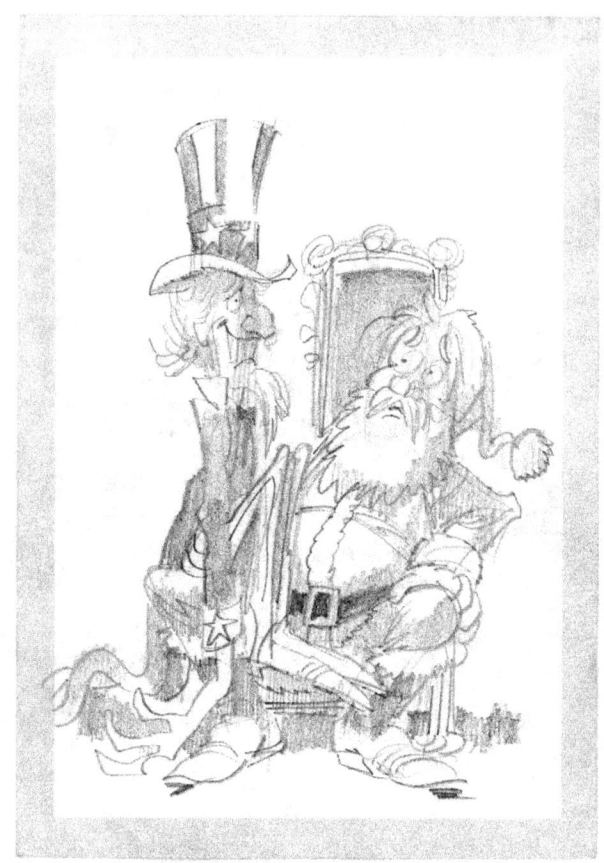

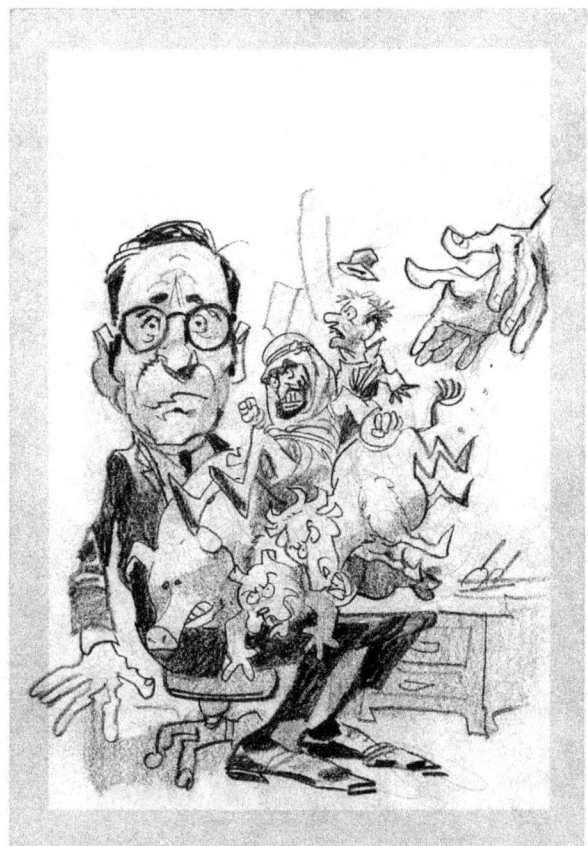

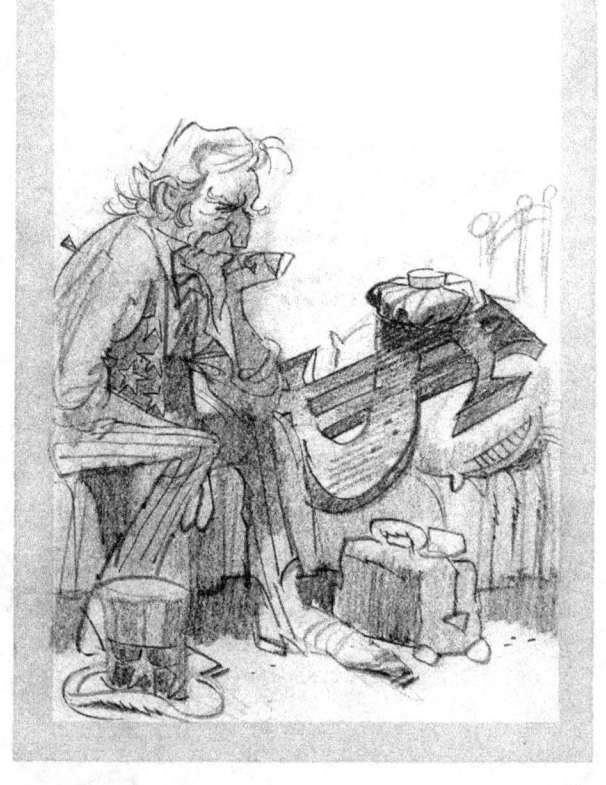

TIME *Magazine* **Cover Ideas**
Pencil on prepared sketch pad

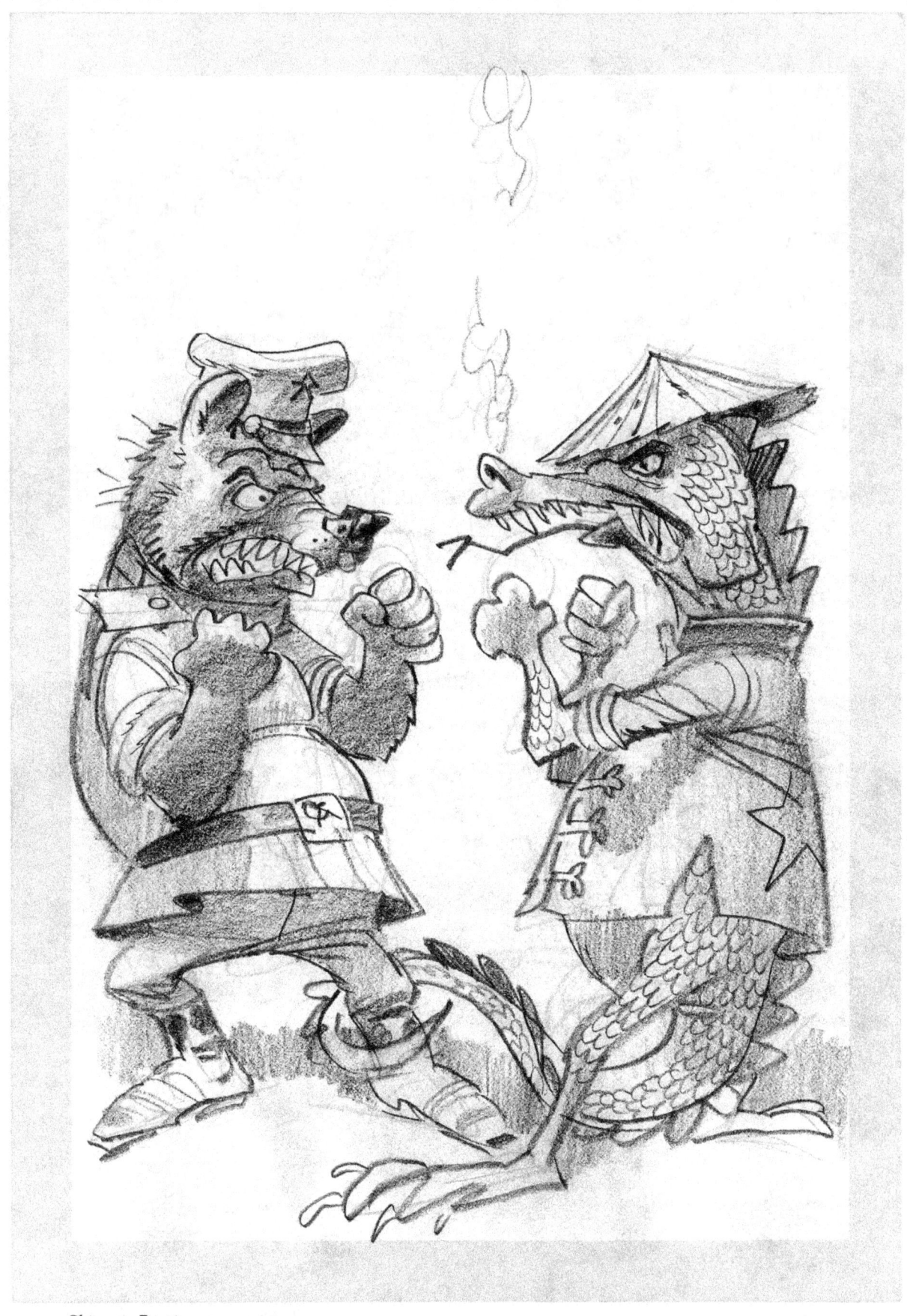

China vs. Russia
Pencil on prepared sketch pad
TIME Magazine cover idea

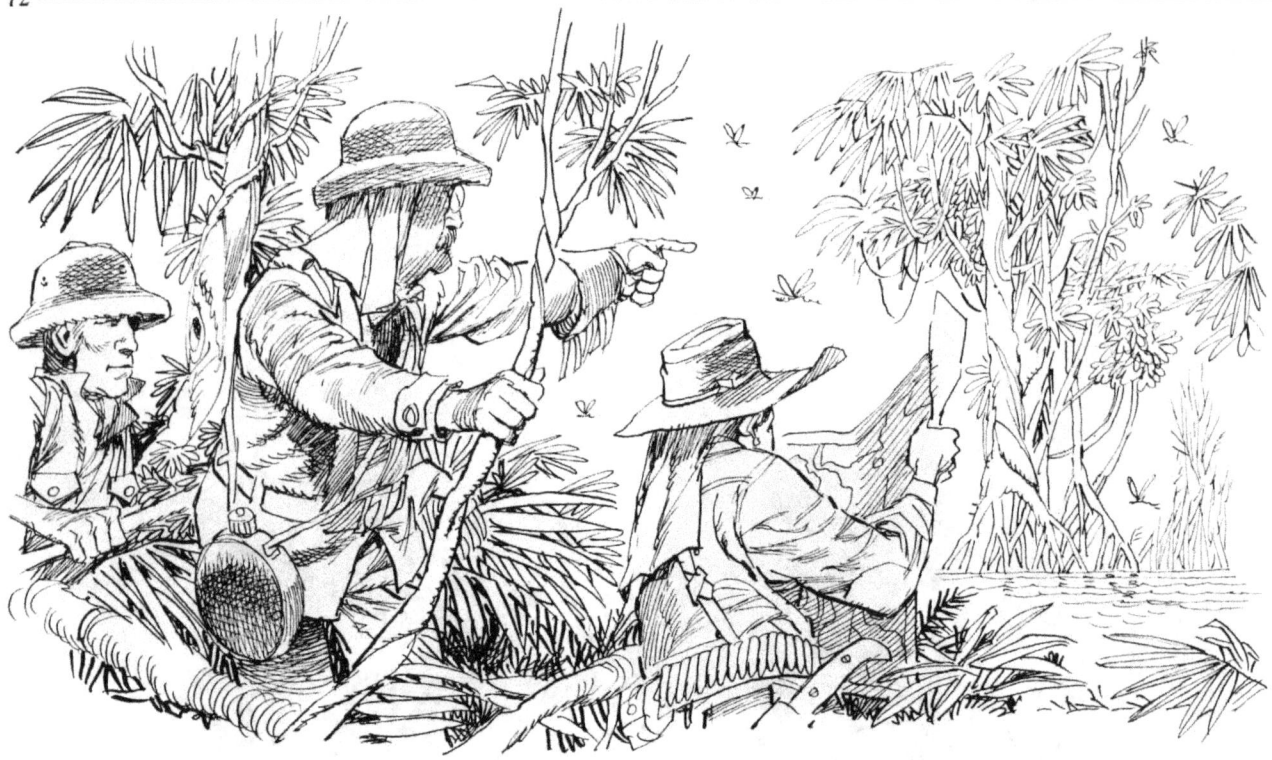

Teddy Roosevelt, Explorer
Pen & ink on illustration board
Meet Theodore Roosevelt children's book, 1966

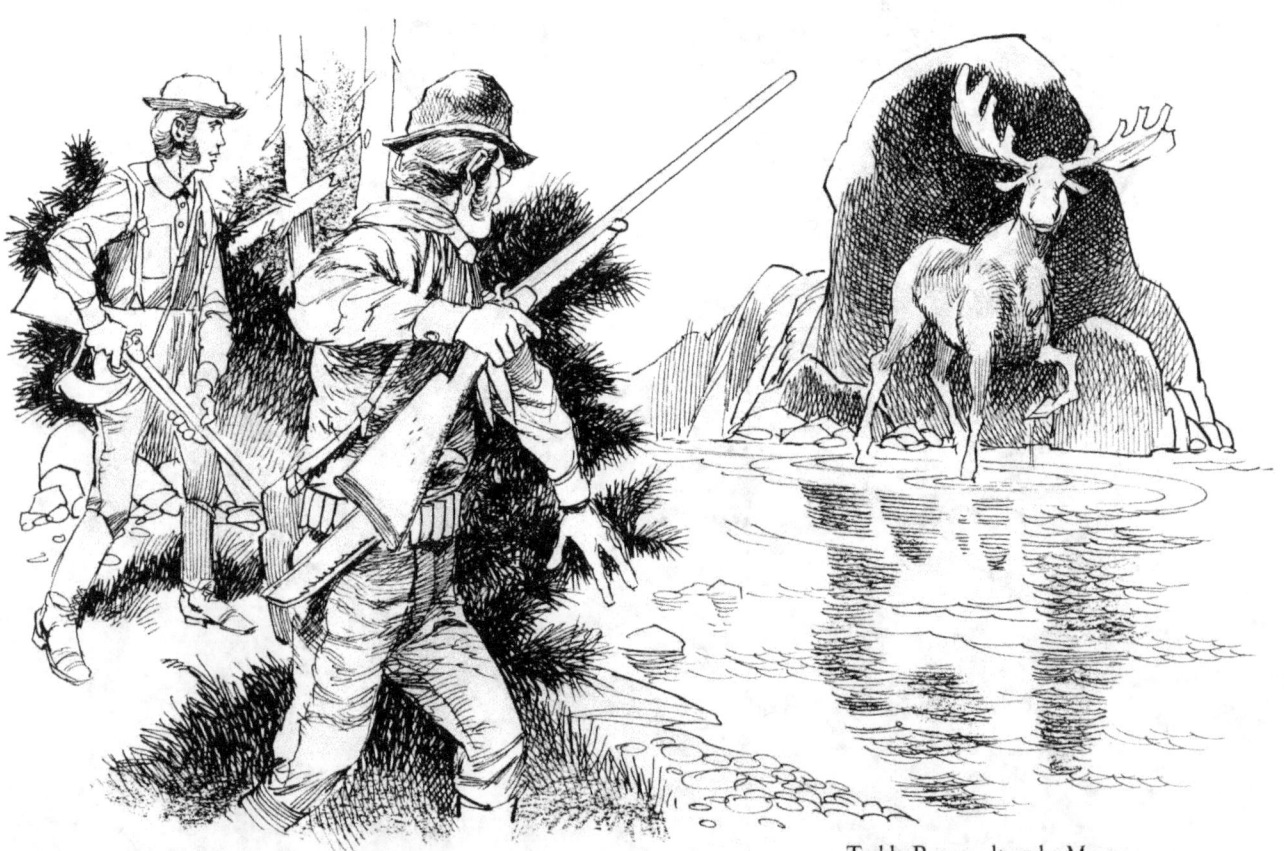

Teddy Roosevelt and a Moose
Pen & ink on illustration board
Meet Theodore Roosevelt children's book, 1966

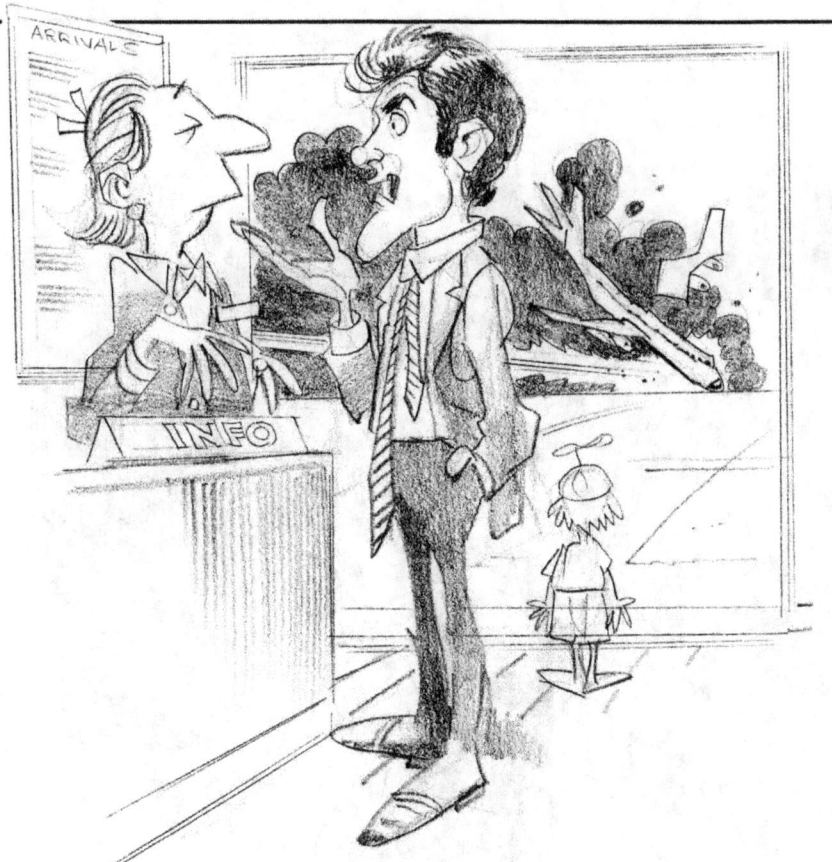

Jay Leno in Line
Pencil on Strathmore

Jay Leno Up a Creek
Pencil on Strathmore

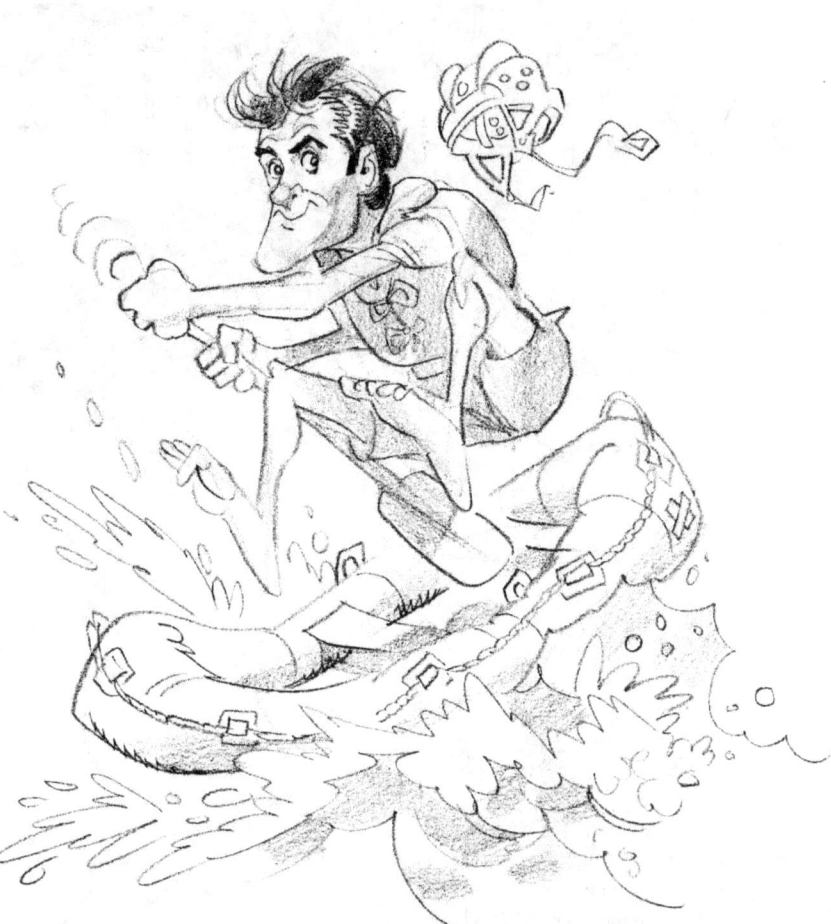

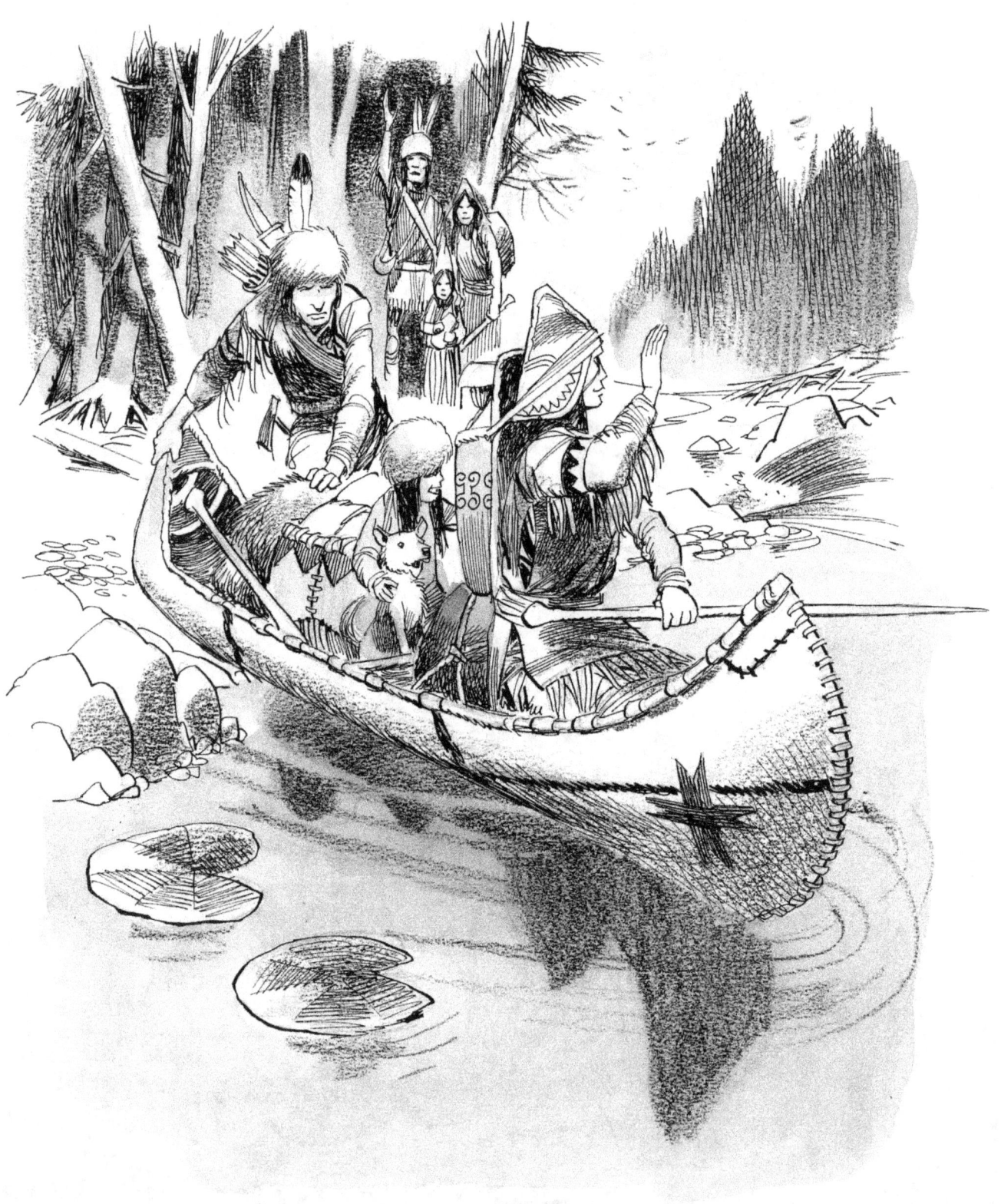

Canoe Trip
Mixed media on illustration board
Meet the North American Indians children's book, 1967

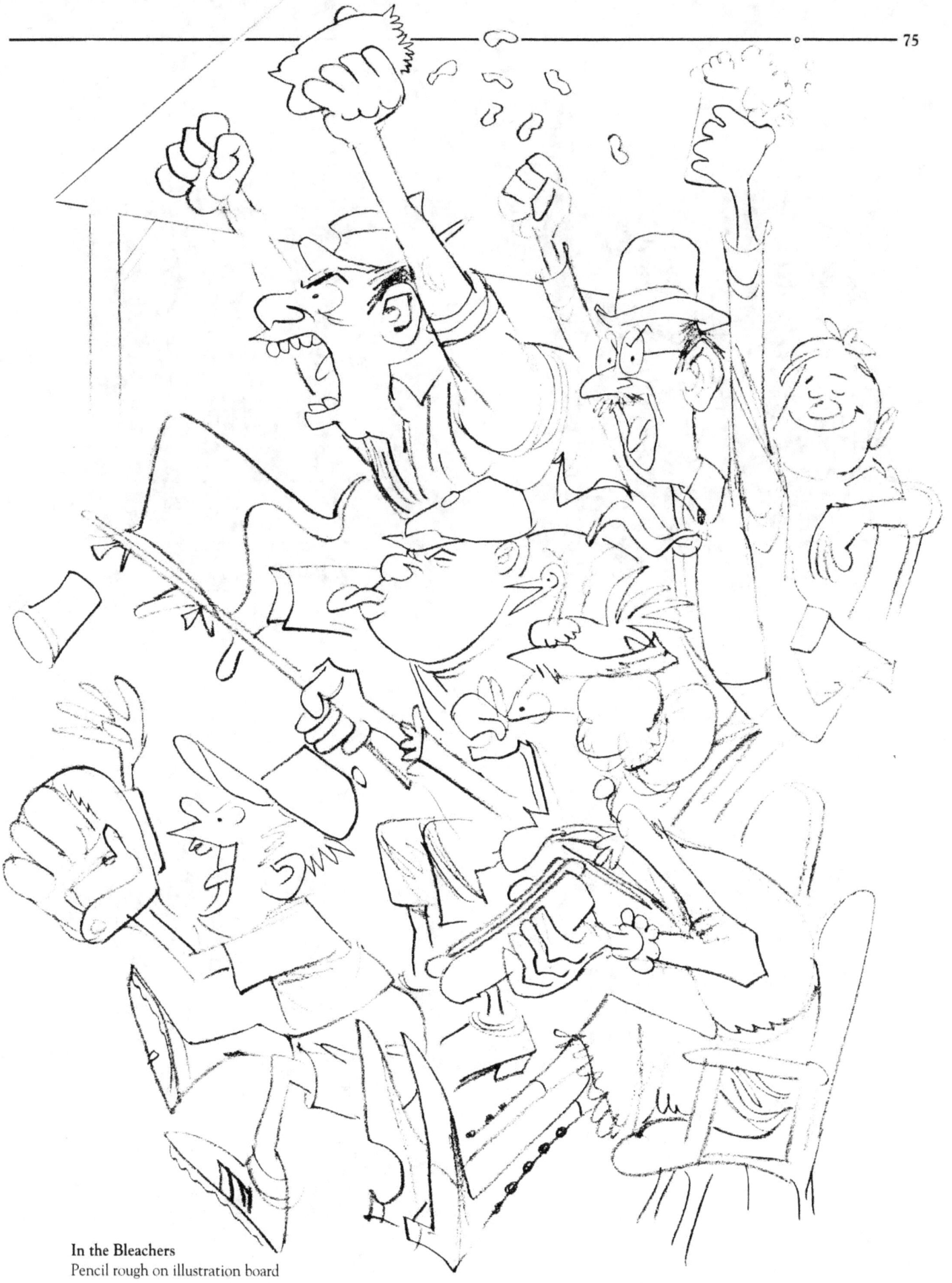

In the Bleachers
Pencil rough on illustration board

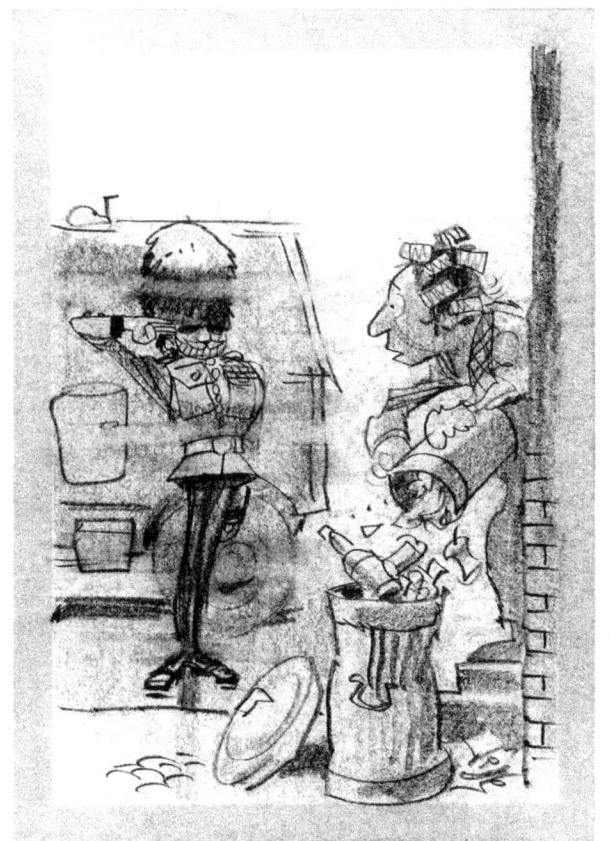
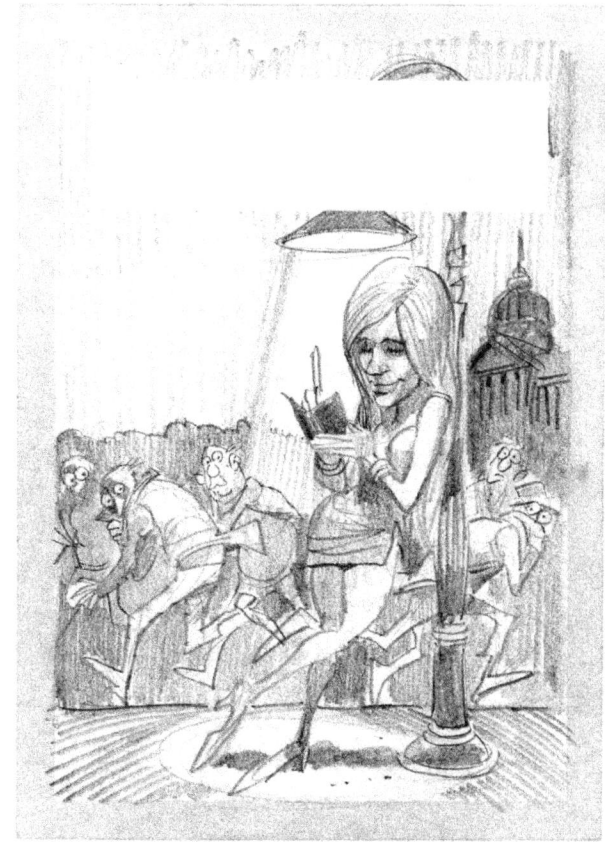
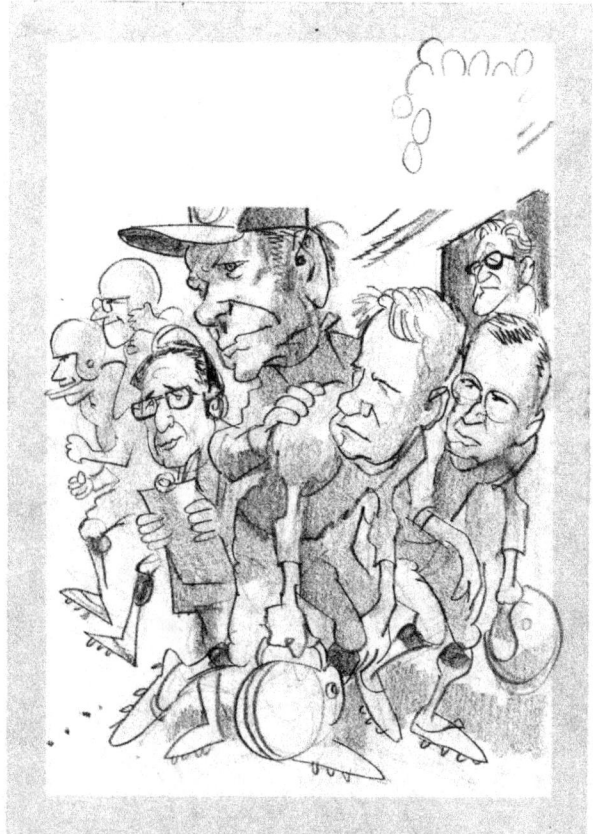
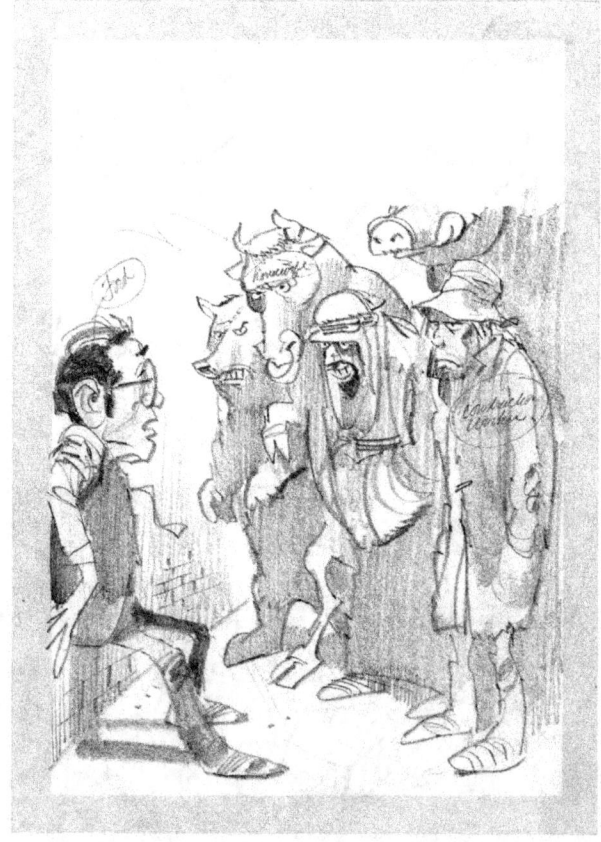

TIME *Magazine* **Cover Ideas**
Pencil on prepared sketch pad

Fast Nerves
Pen & ink on illustration board
Southern Fried book illustration, 1962

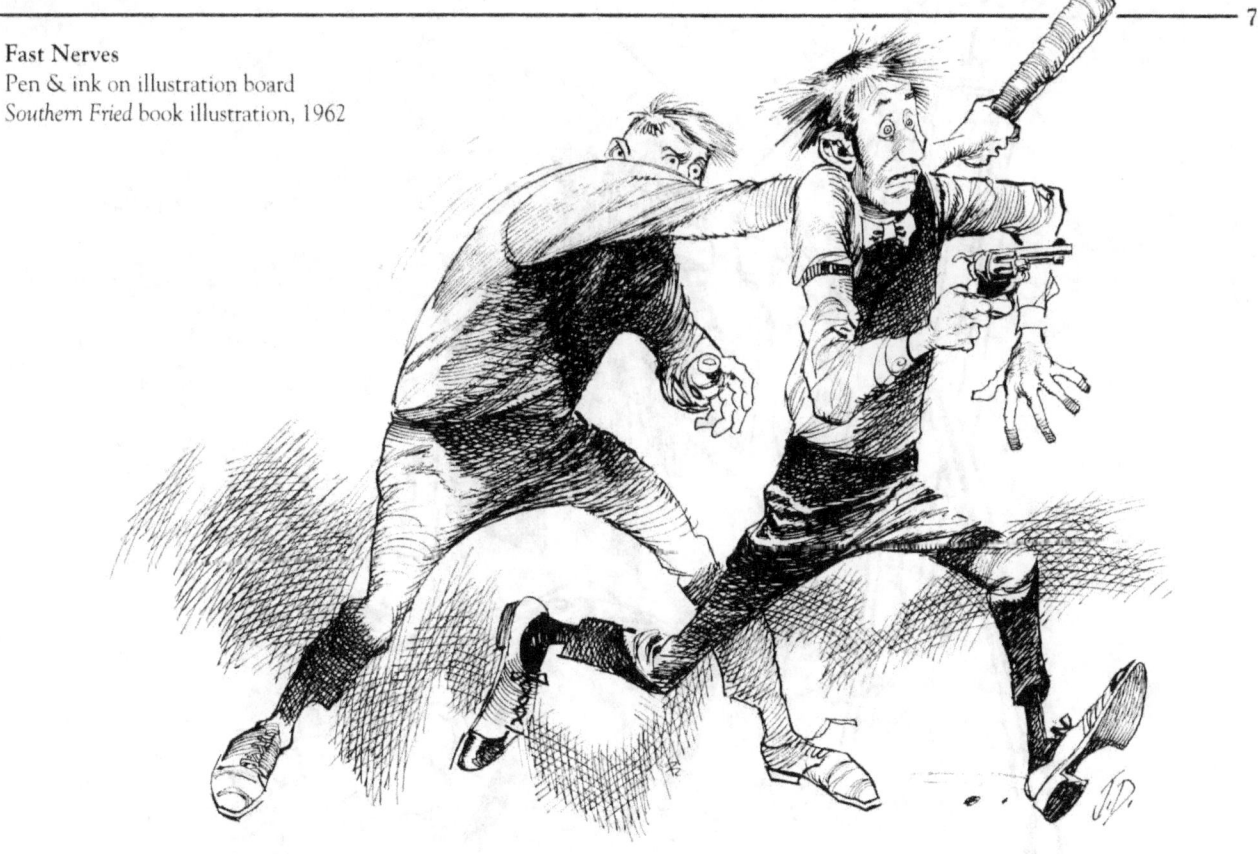

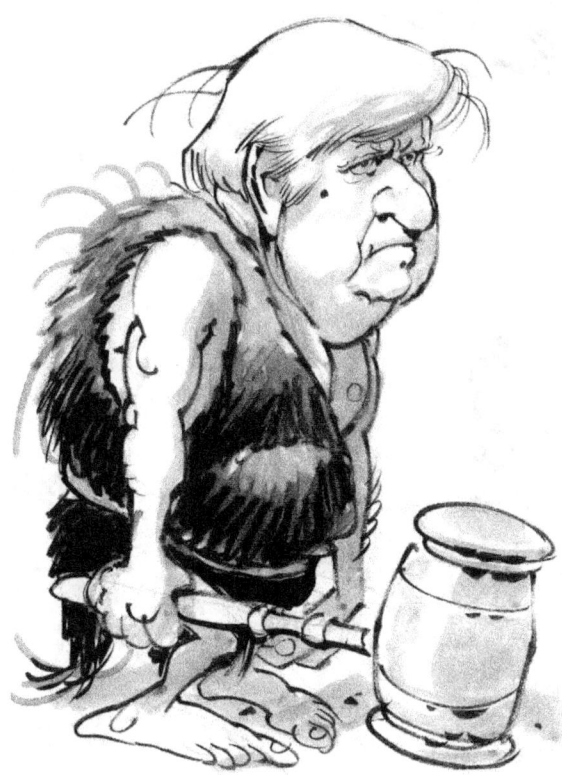

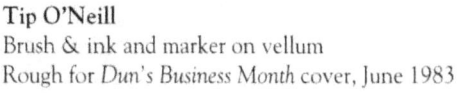

Tip O'Neill
Brush & ink and marker on vellum
Rough for *Dun's Business Month* cover, June 1983

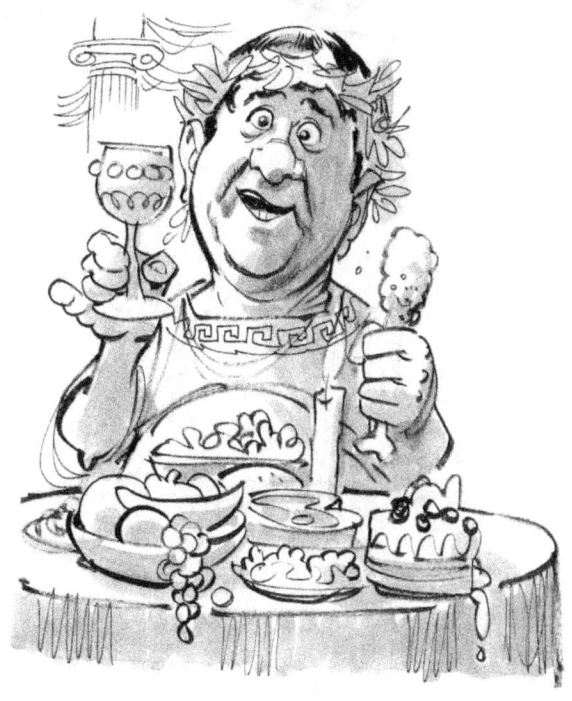

Buddy Hackett
Brush & ink, pen & ink and marker on vellum
Advertising rough

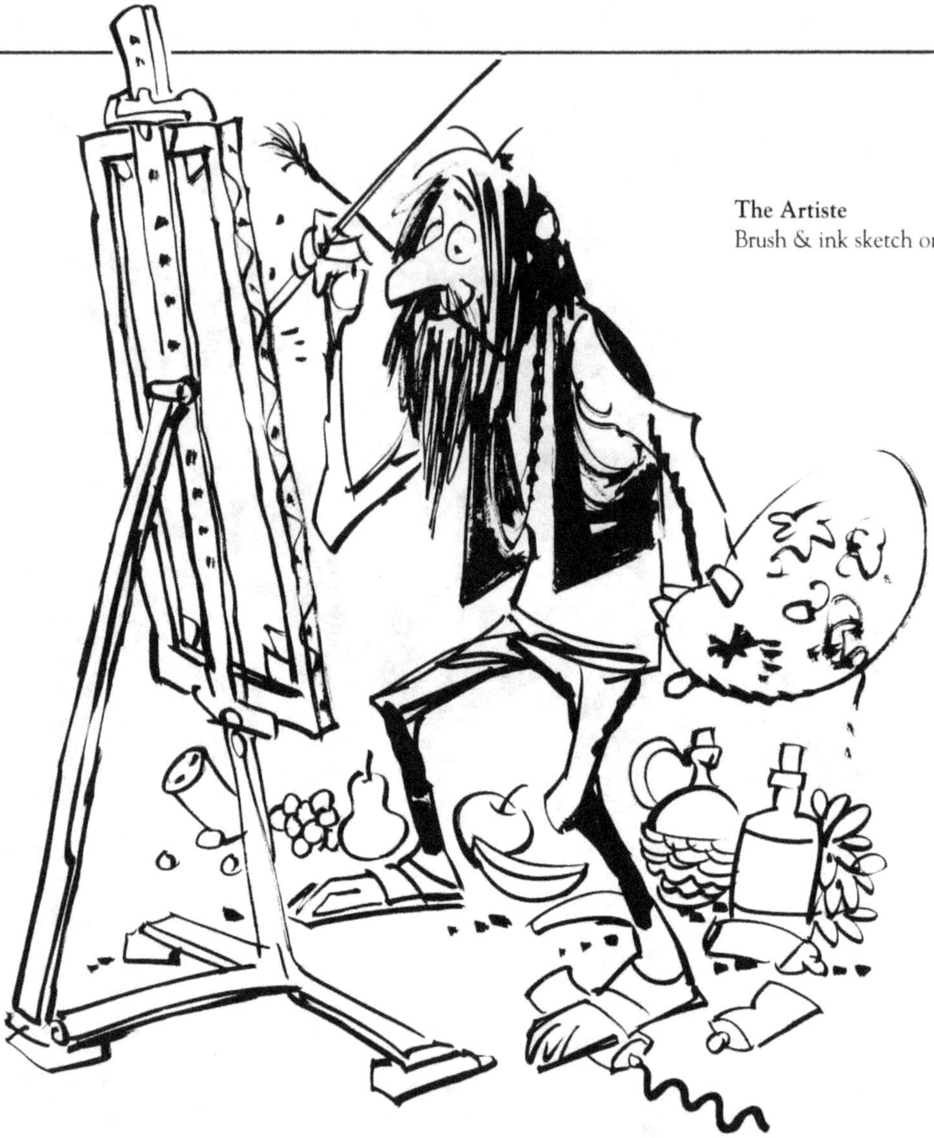

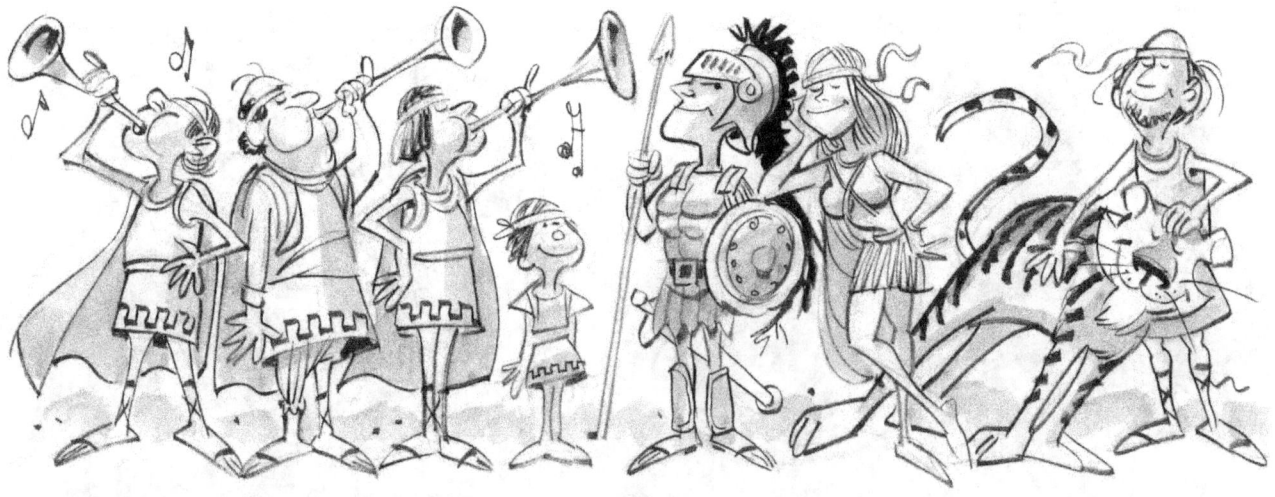

The Artiste
Brush & ink sketch on vellum

Romans
Brush & ink and marker on vellum
Advertising rough

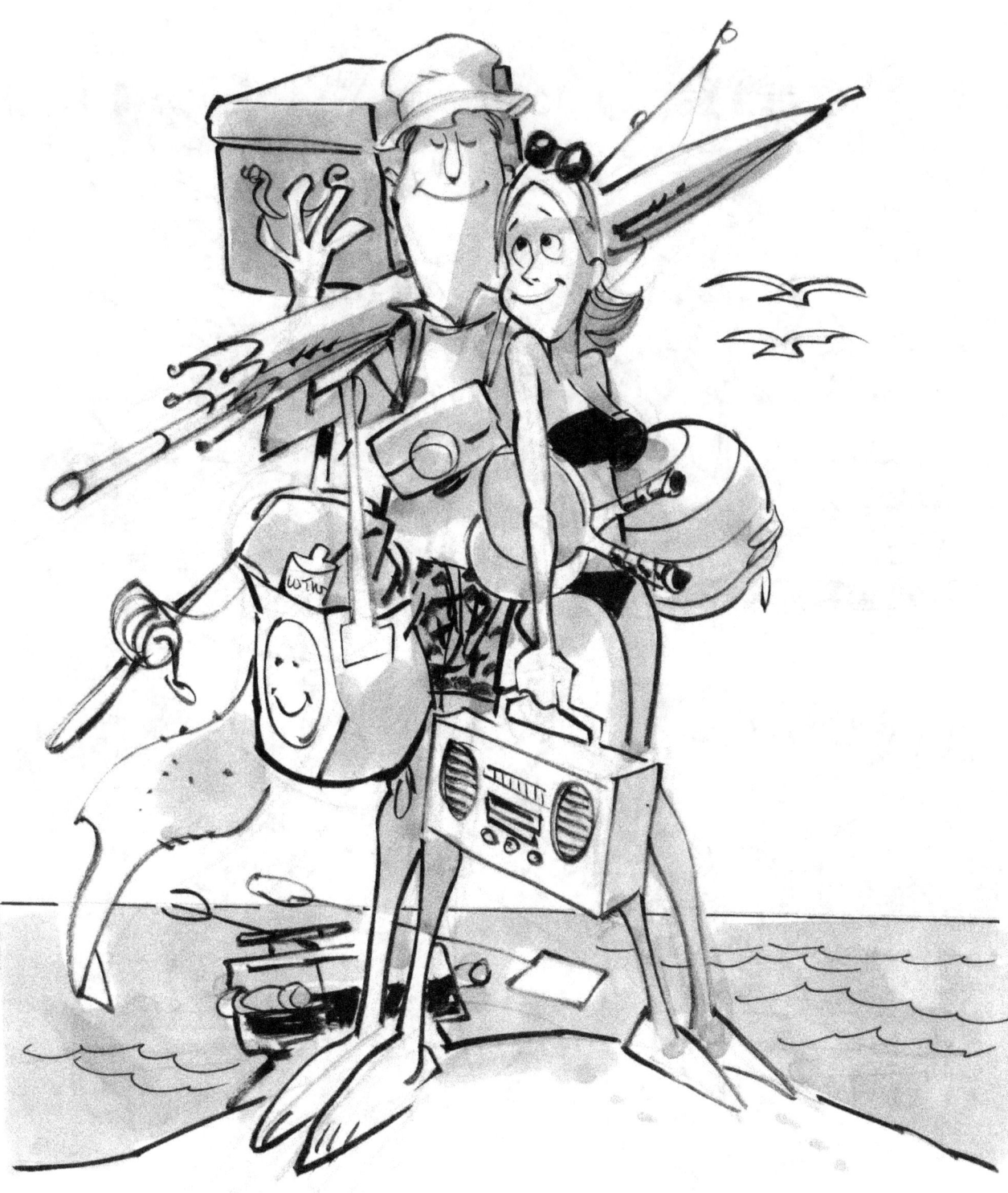

At the Beach
Brush & ink and marker rough on vellum

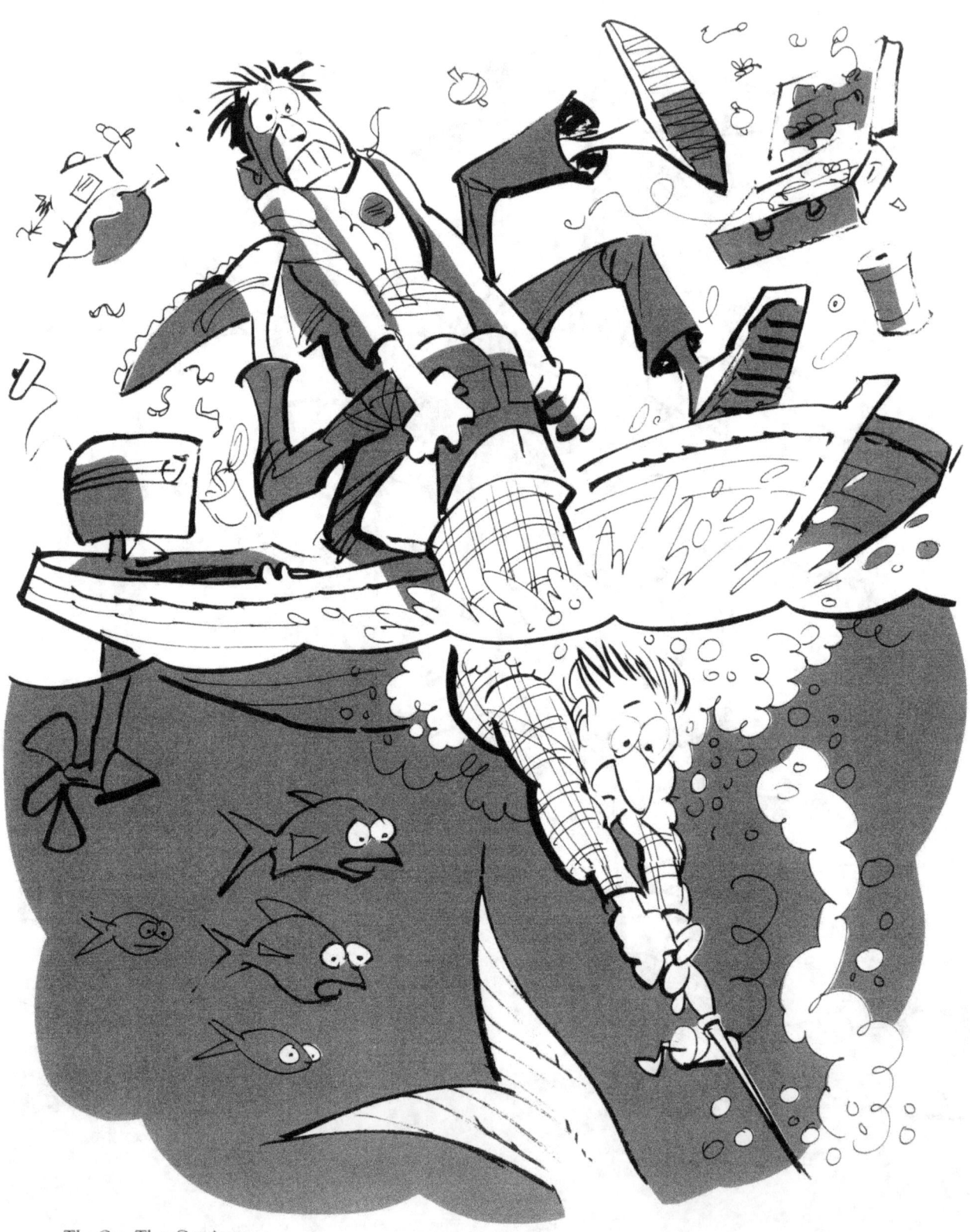

The One That Got Away
Brush & ink and marker rough on vellum

Agnew hangin' on by a thread
Pencil sketch on paper

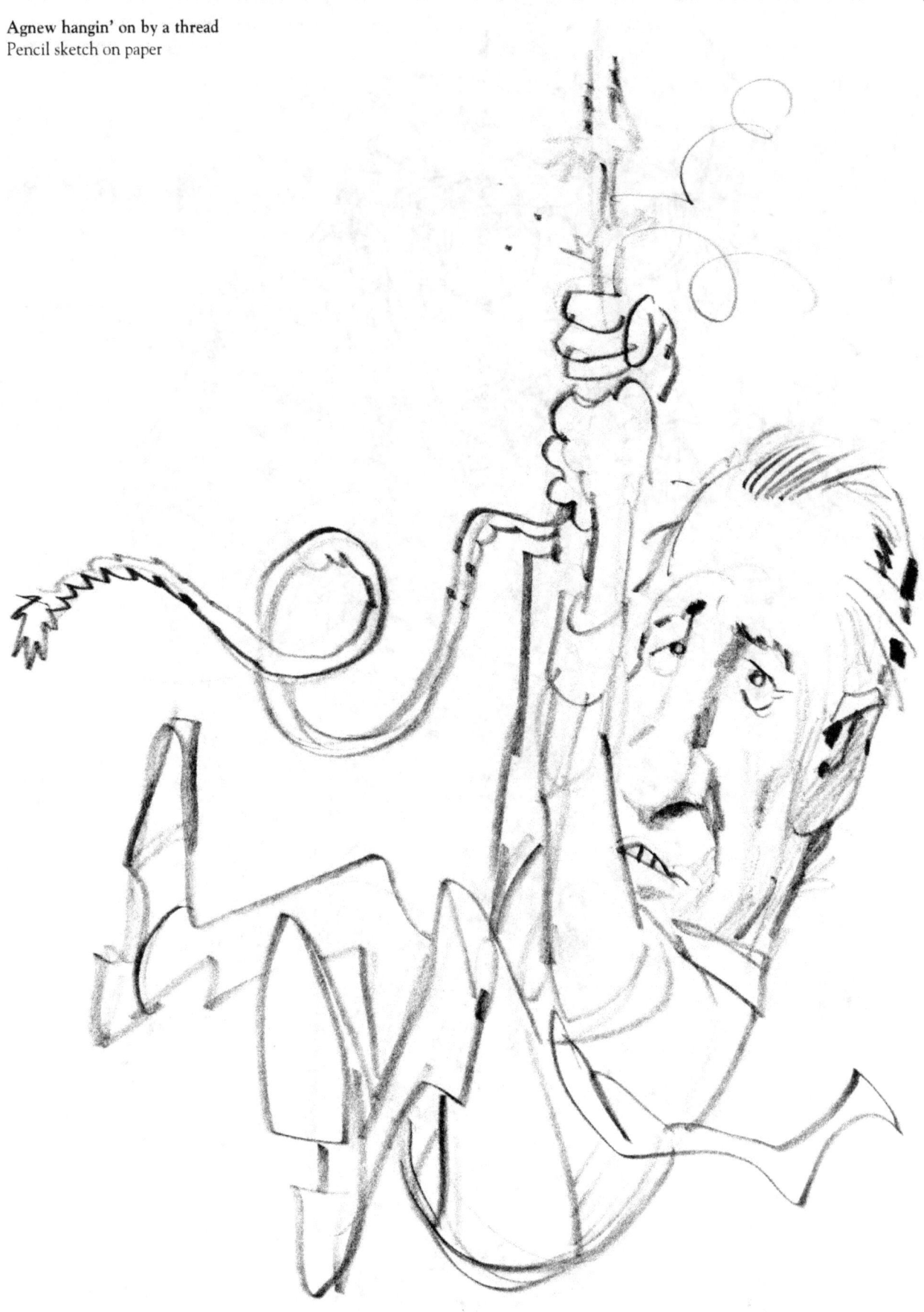

Kite flyin' days
Brush & ink and marker rough on vellum

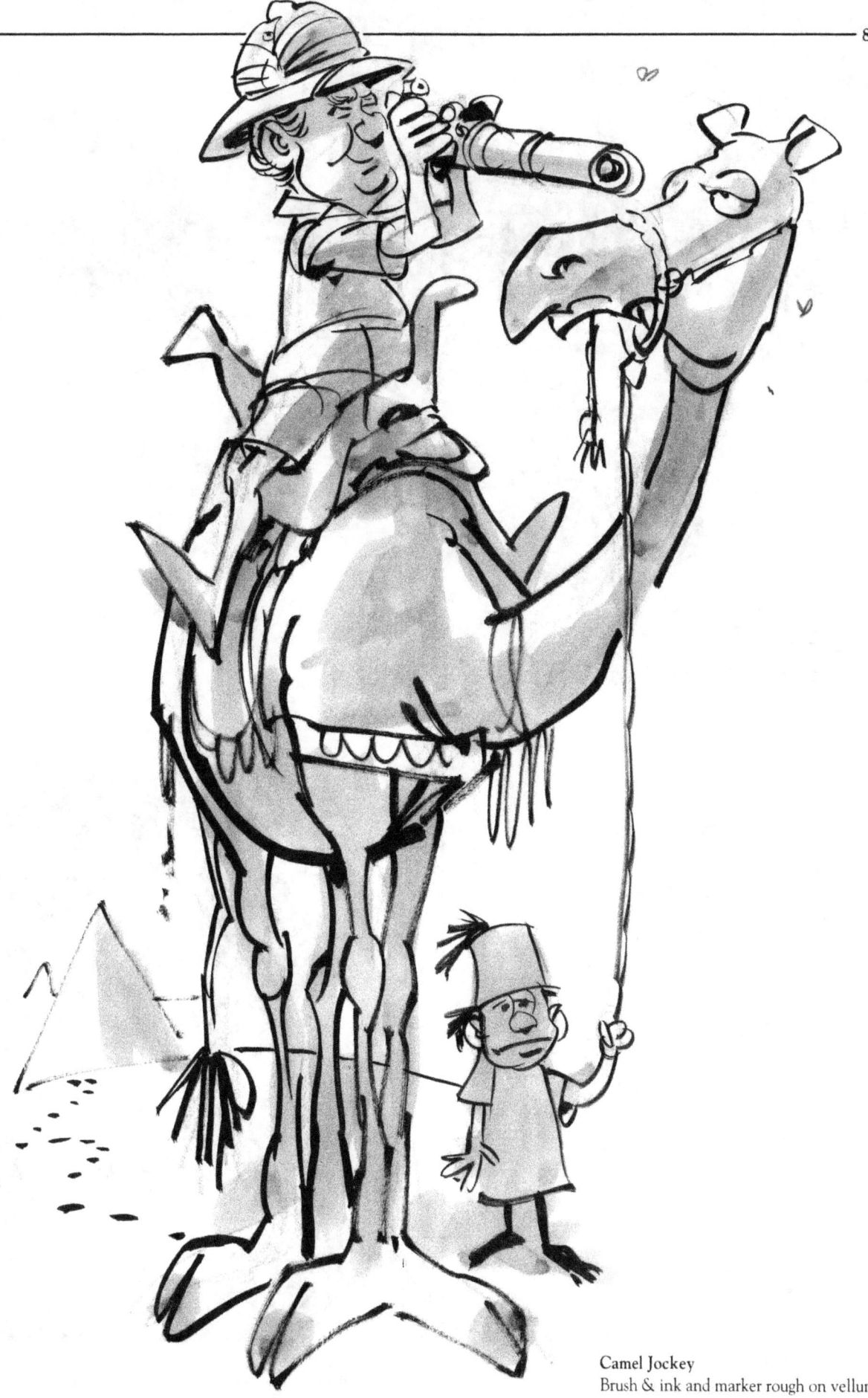

Camel Jockey
Brush & ink and marker rough on vellum

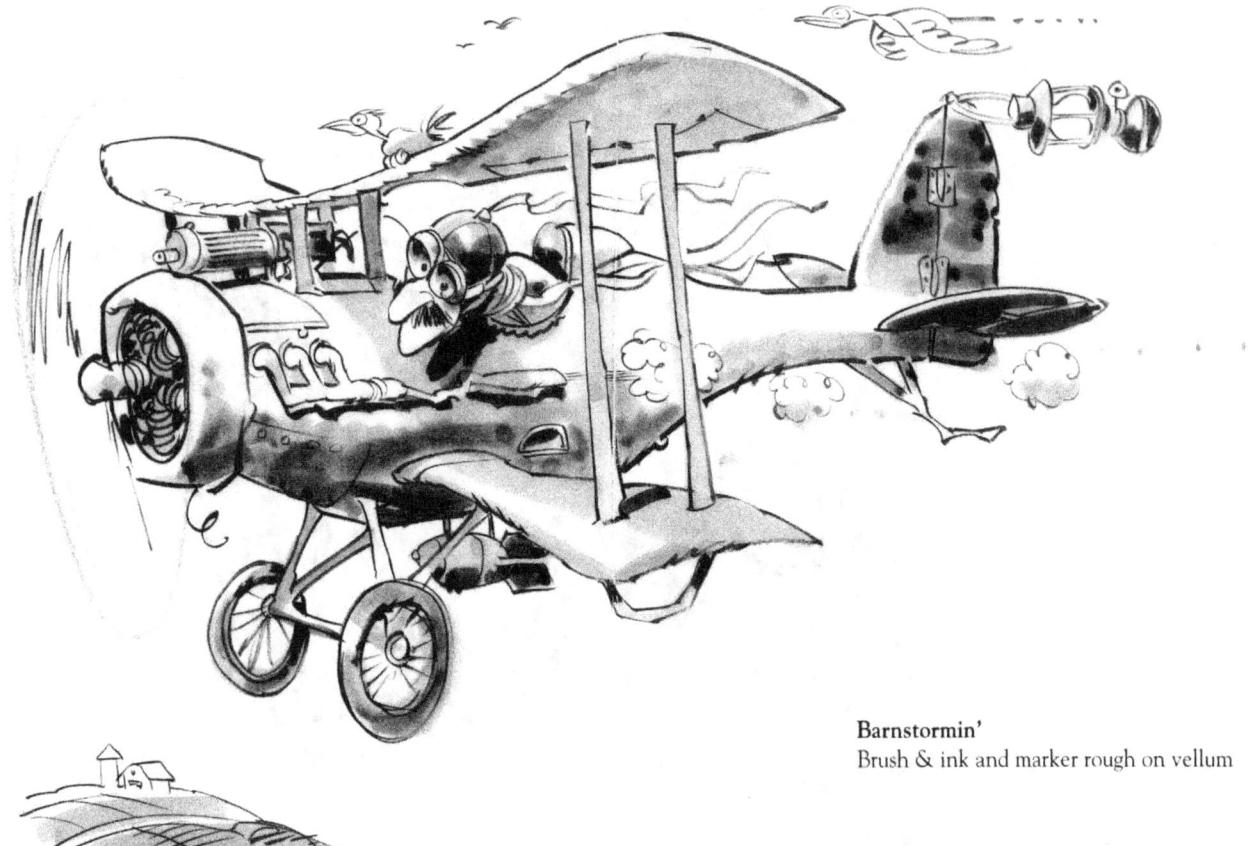

Barnstormin'
Brush & ink and marker rough on vellum

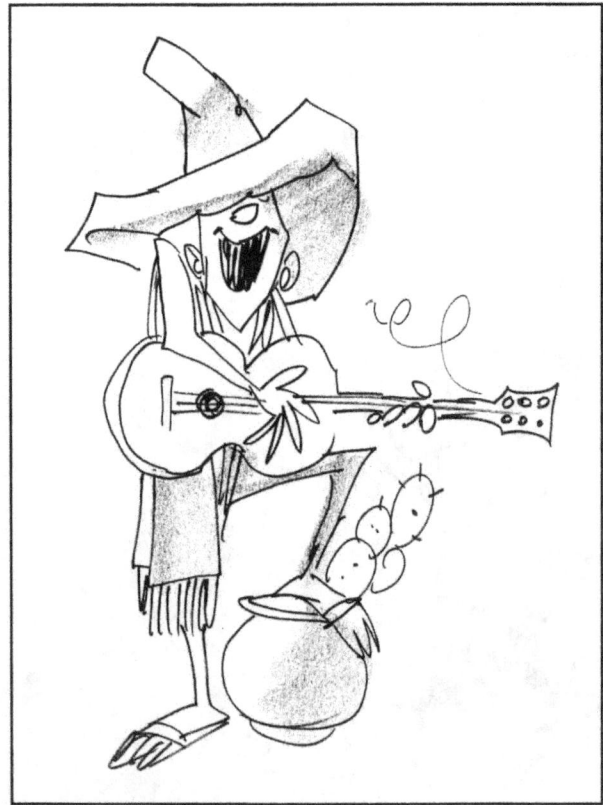

South of the Border
Felt-tip and pencil sketch on vellum

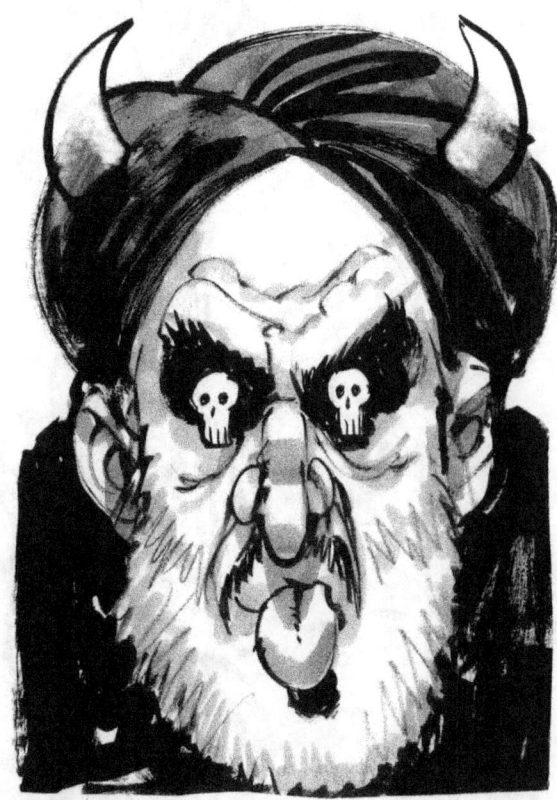

Ayatollah
Brush & ink and marker rough on vellum

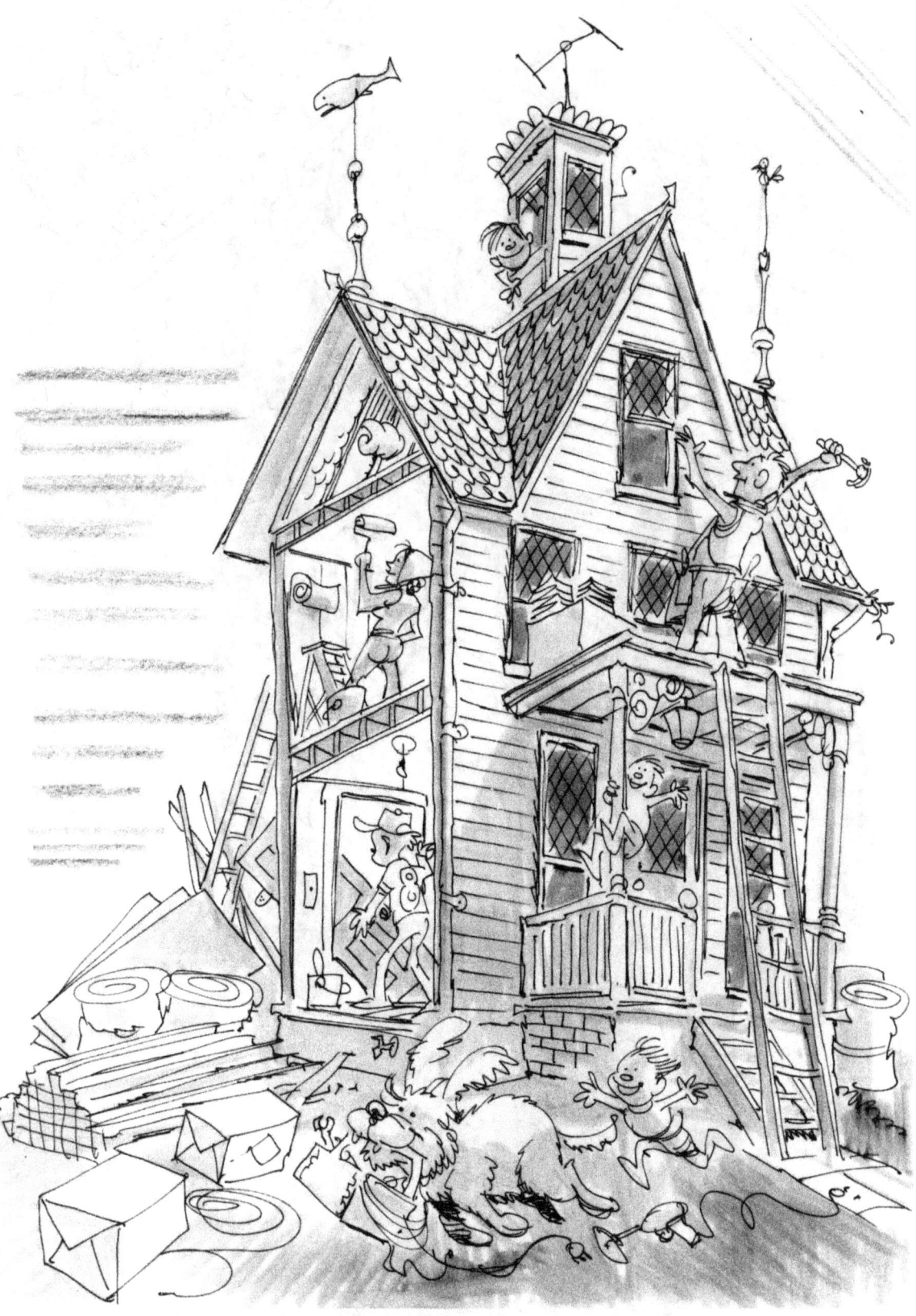

Home Improvement
Pen & ink and marker rough on vellum

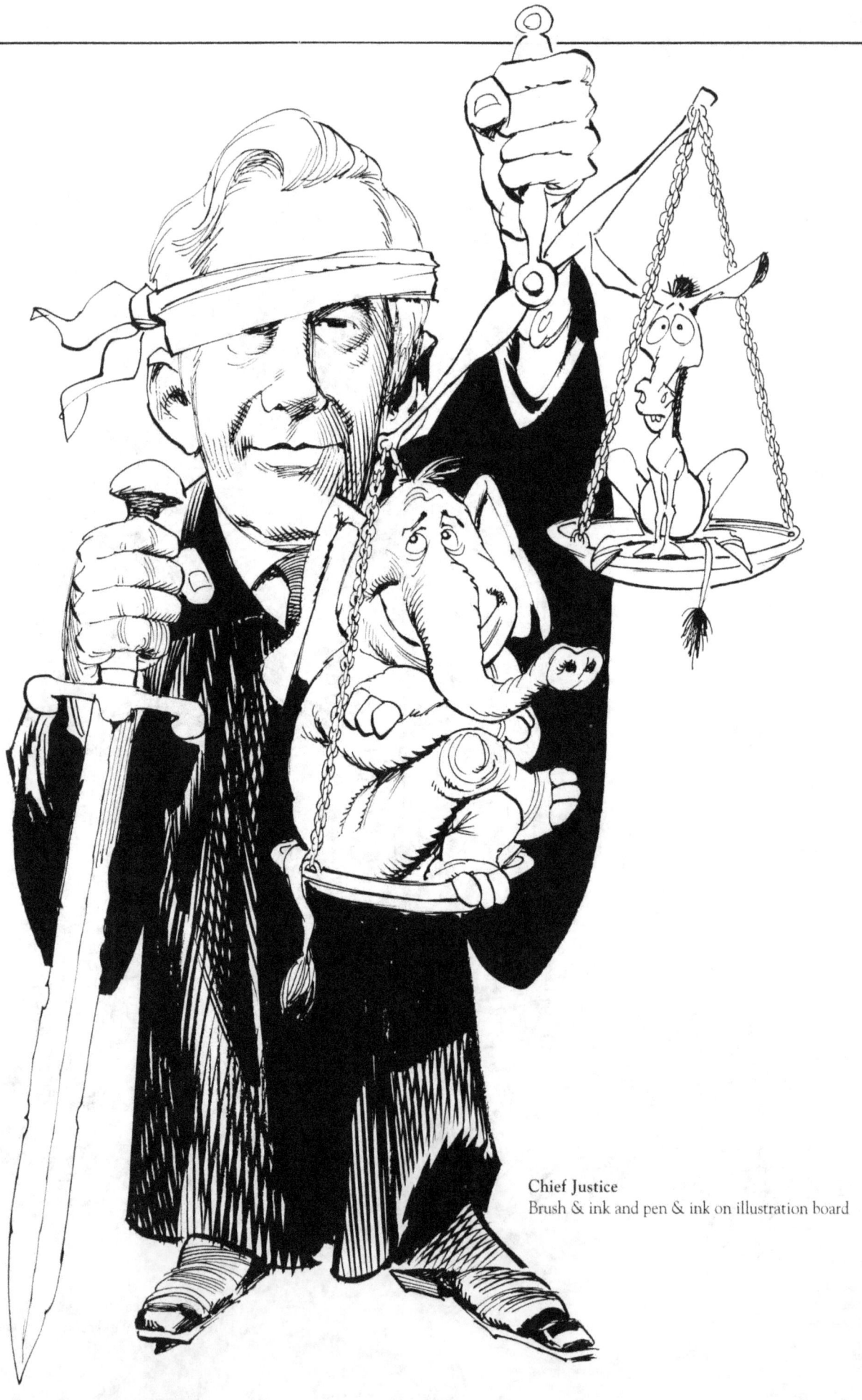

Chief Justice
Brush & ink and pen & ink on illustration board

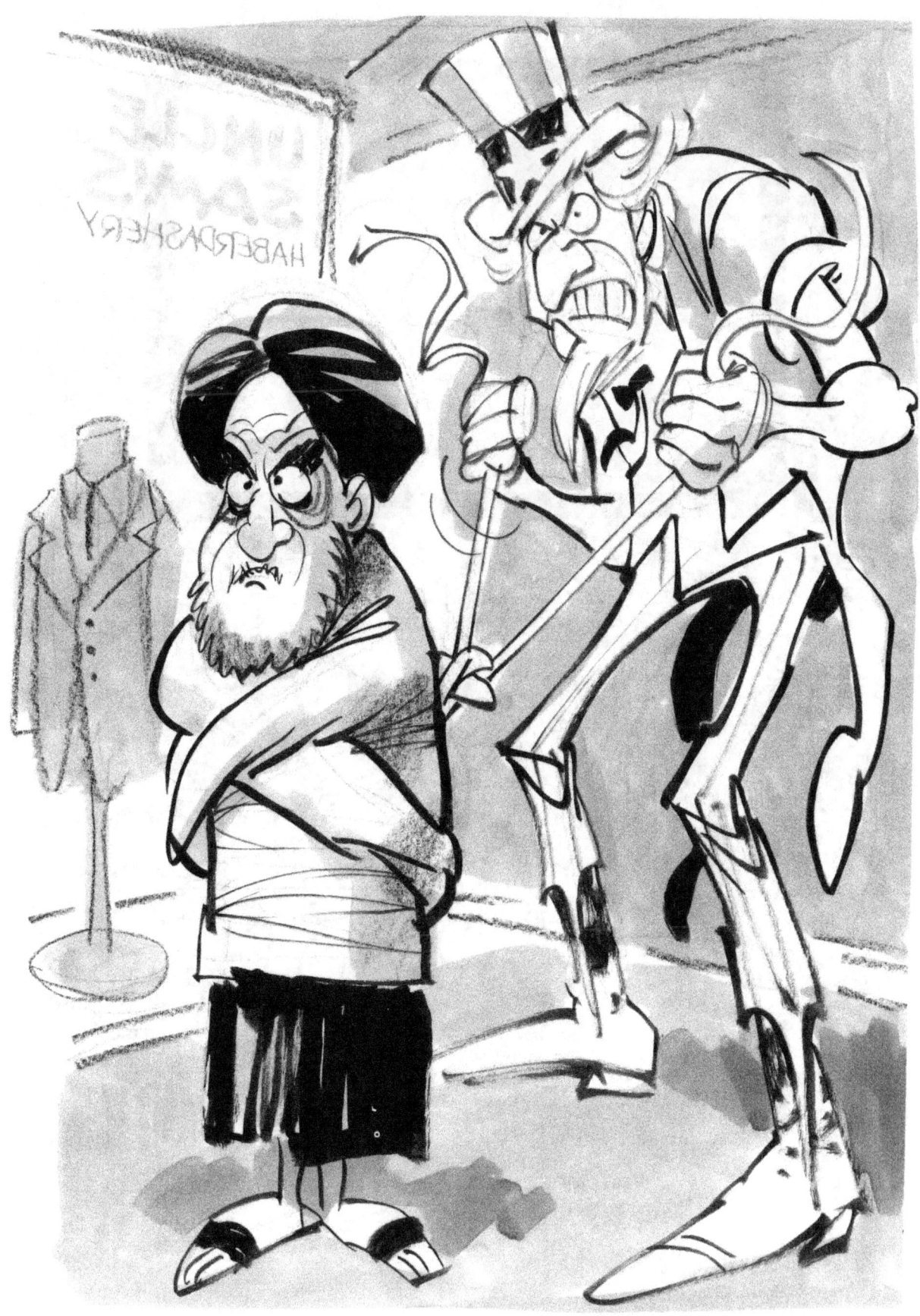

Uncle Sam's Haberdashery
Brush & ink and marker rough on vellum

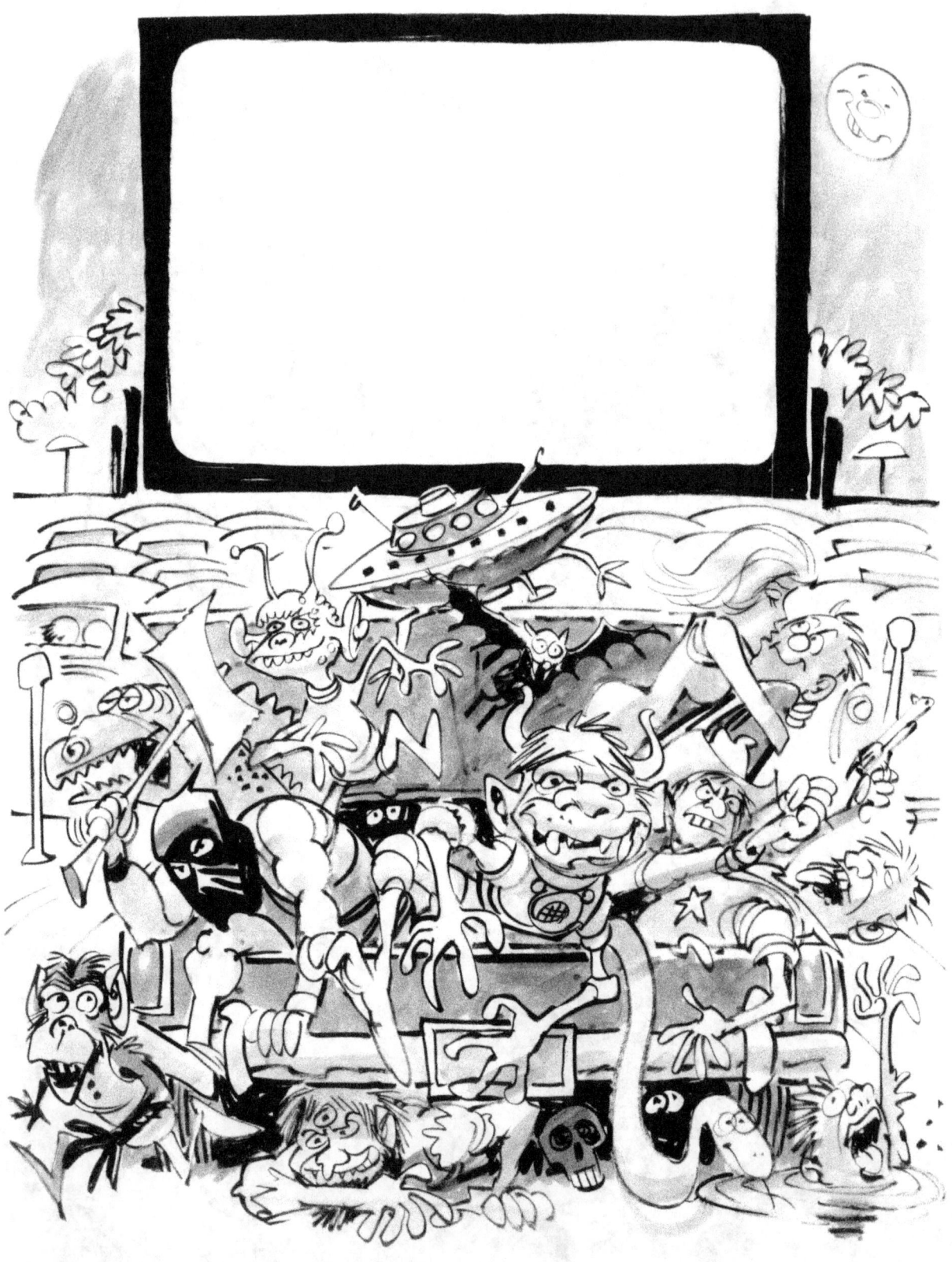

Drive-In Movies
Brush & ink and marker rough on vellum

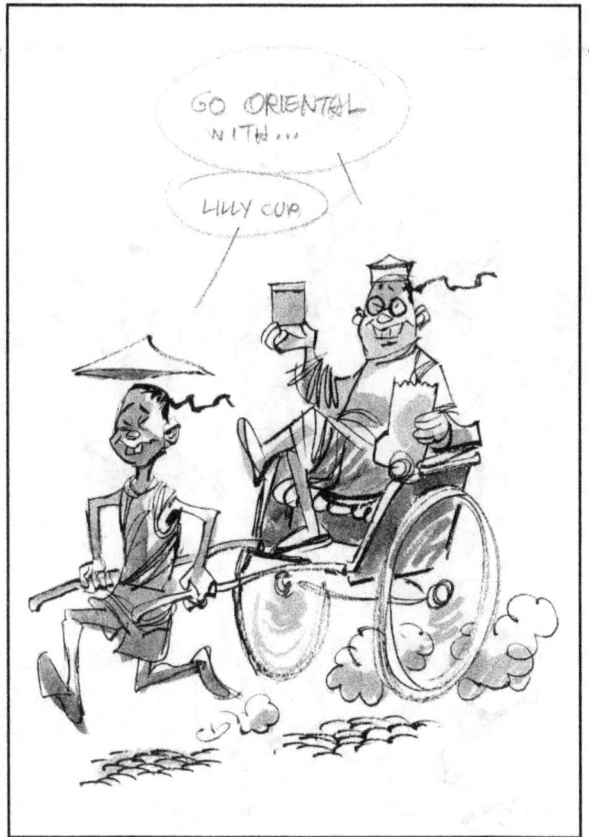

Go Oriental
Brush & ink and marker rough on paper

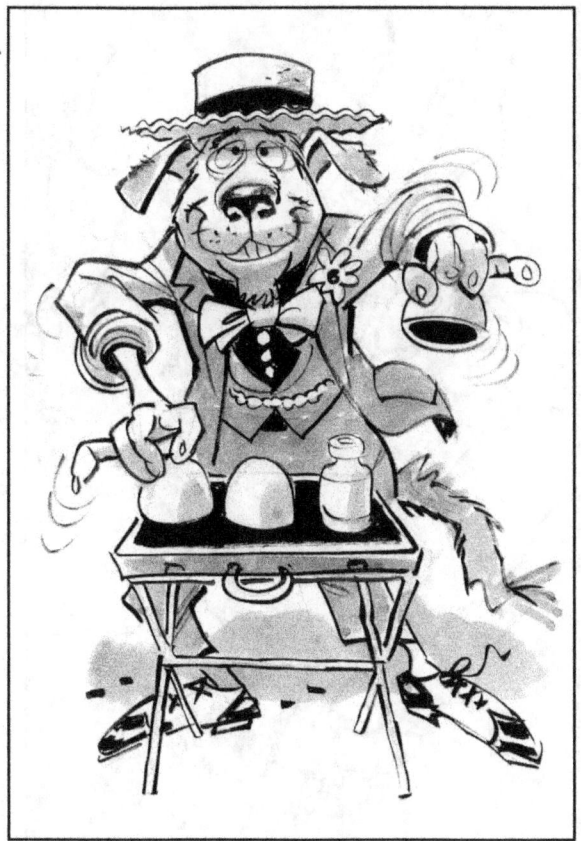

Shell Game
Brush & ink and marker rough on vellum

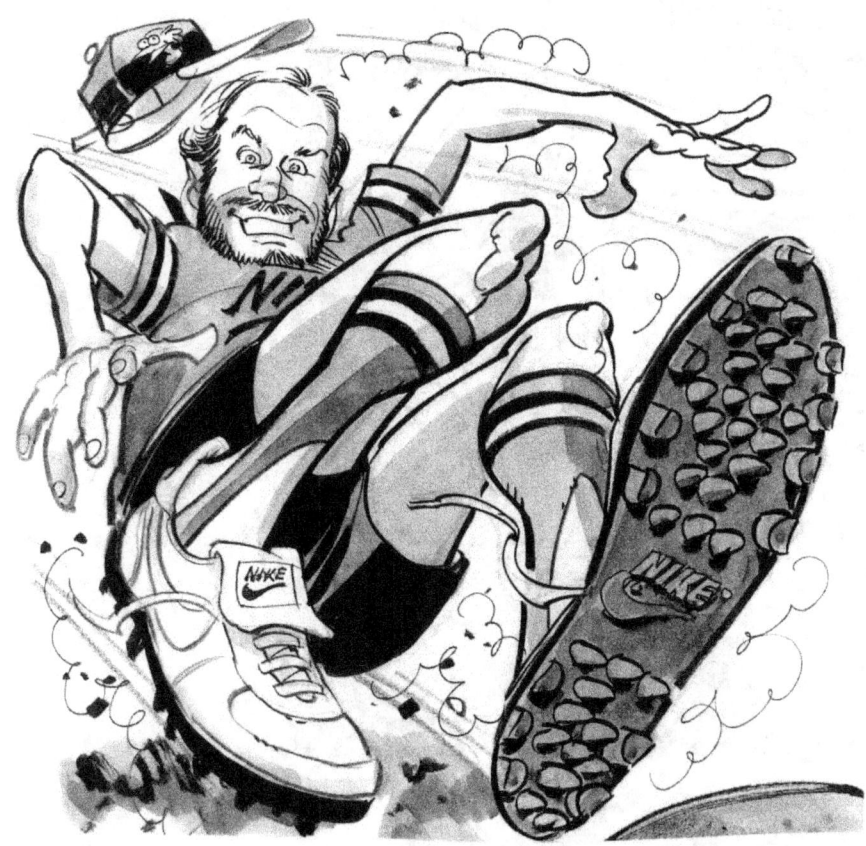

Sliding into Second
Brush & ink and marker on vellum
Advertising rough

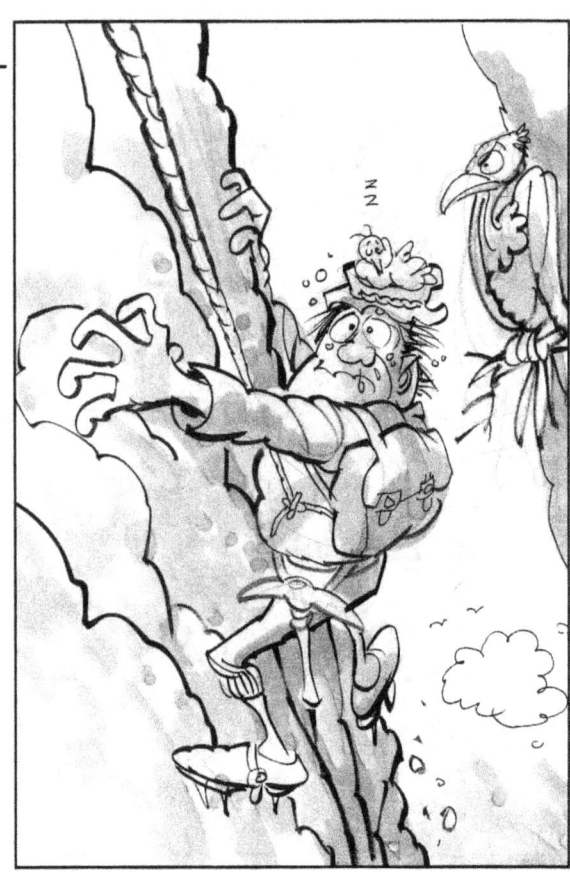

Mountain Climbing
Brush & ink and marker rough on vellum

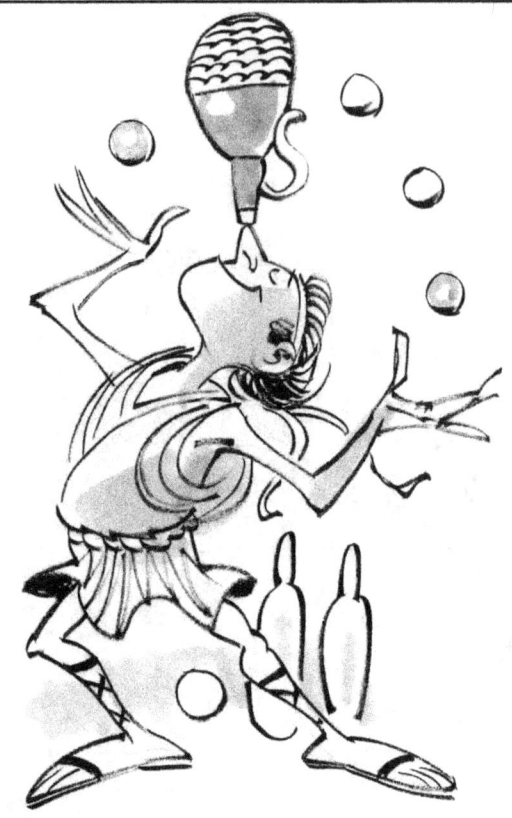

Juggler
Brush & ink and marker rough on vellum

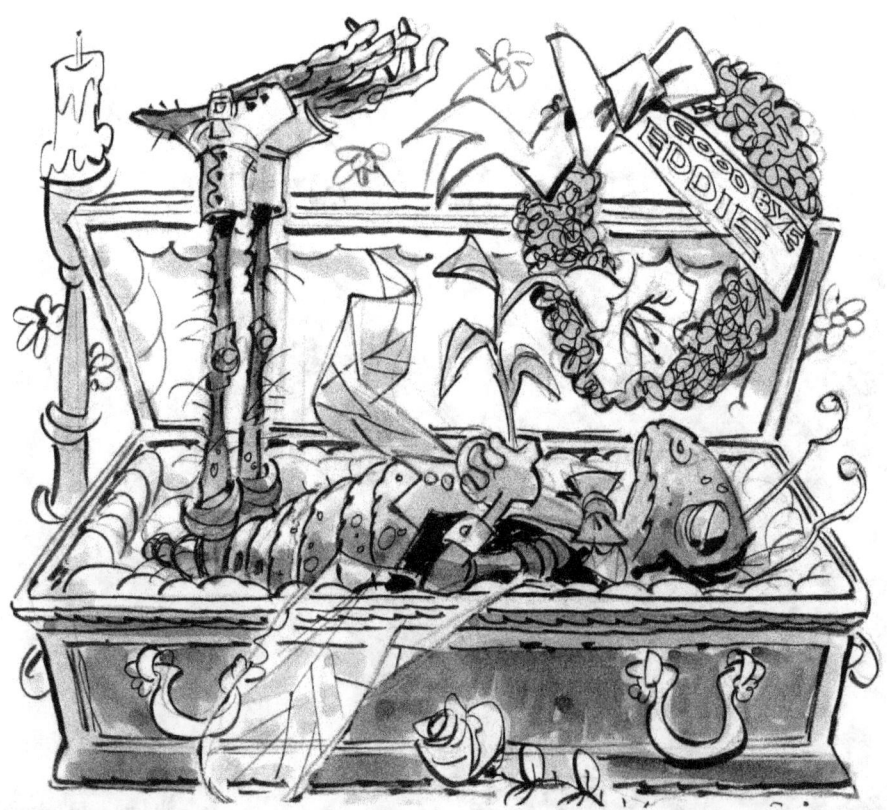

Goodbye, Eddie
Brush & ink and marker rough on vellum

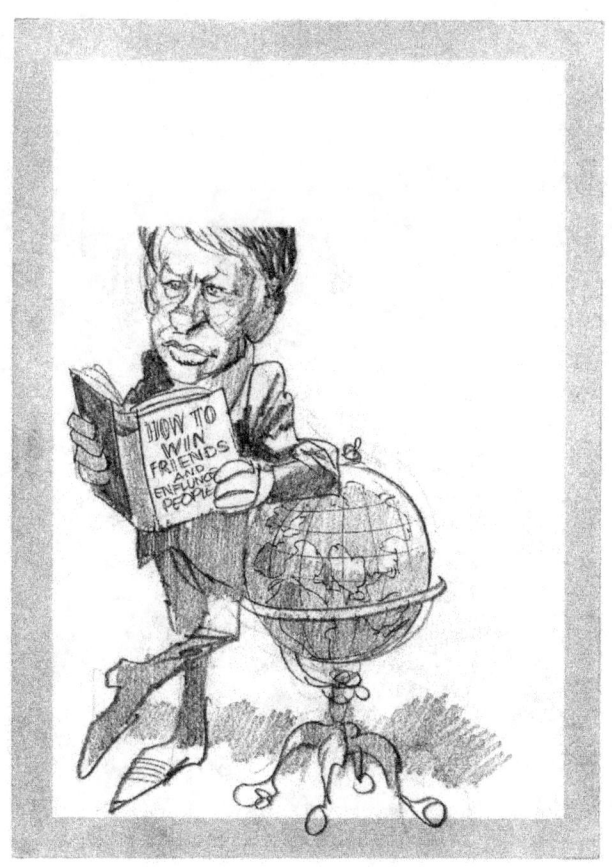
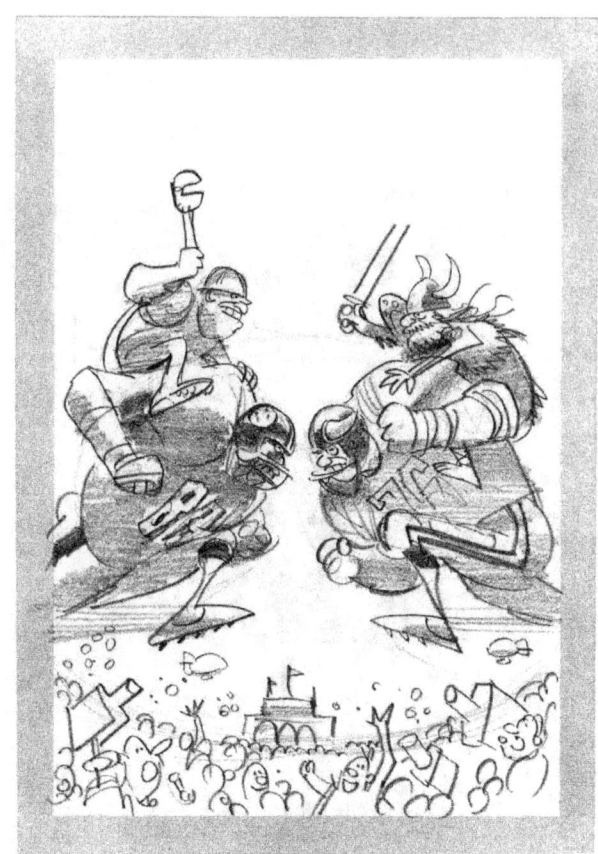
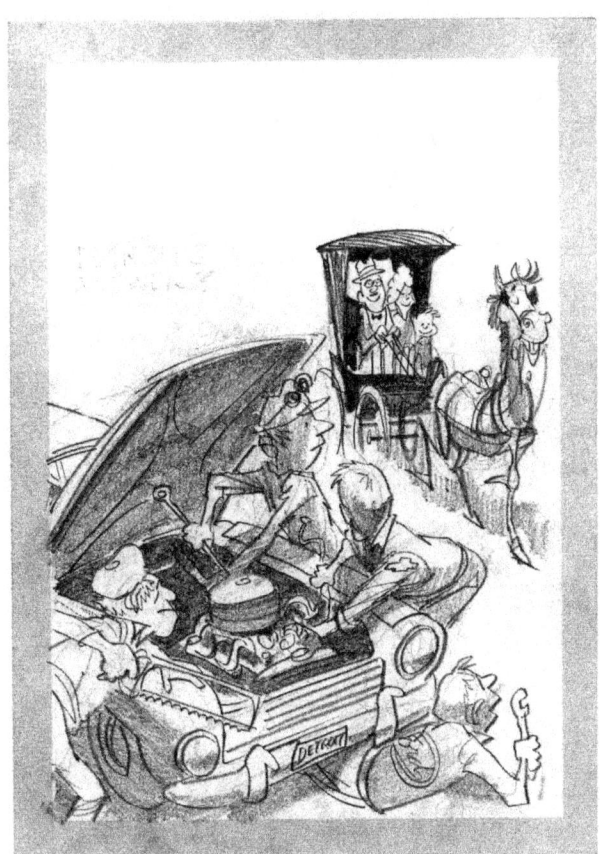
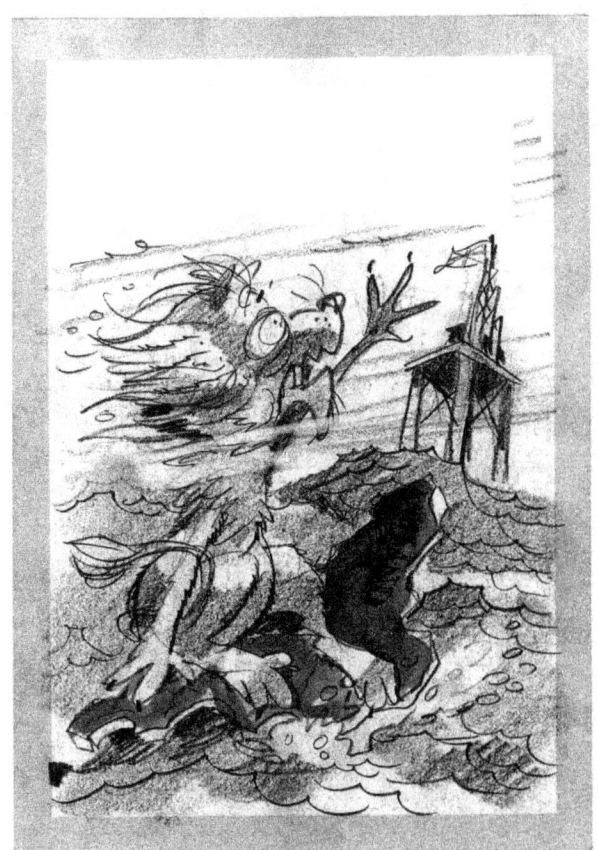

TIME *Magazine* **Cover Ideas**
Pencil on prepared sketch pad

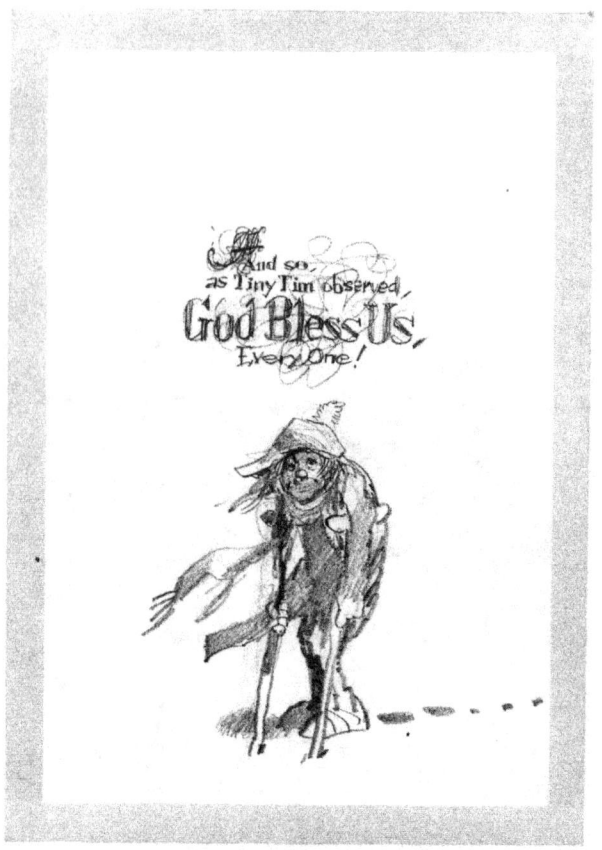

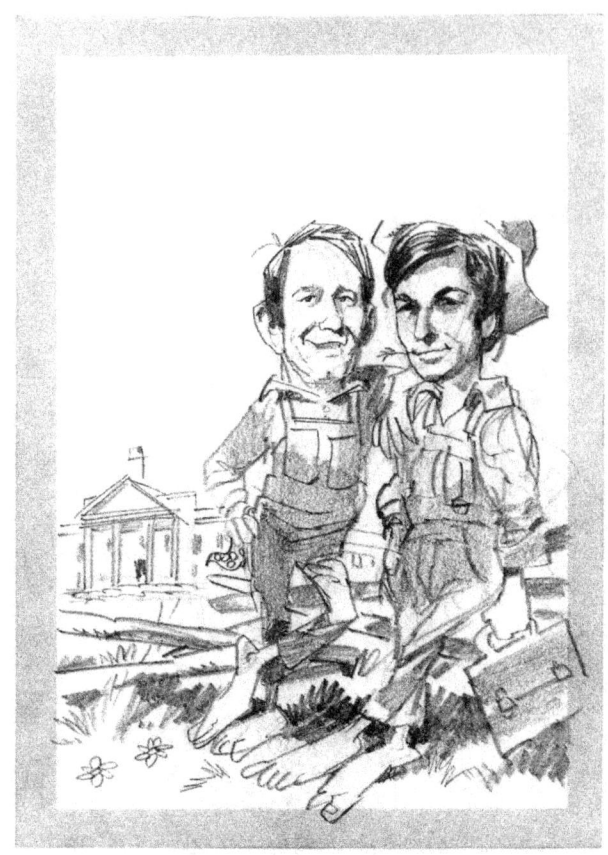

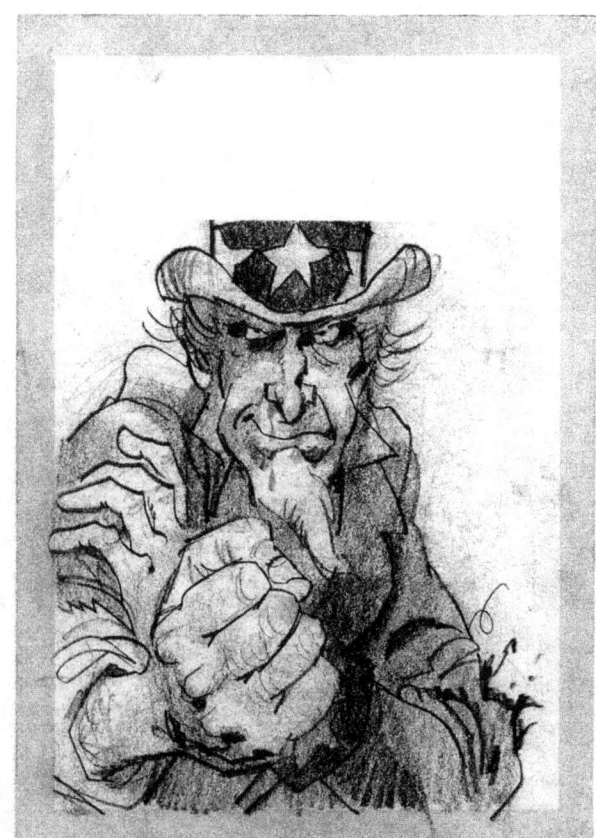

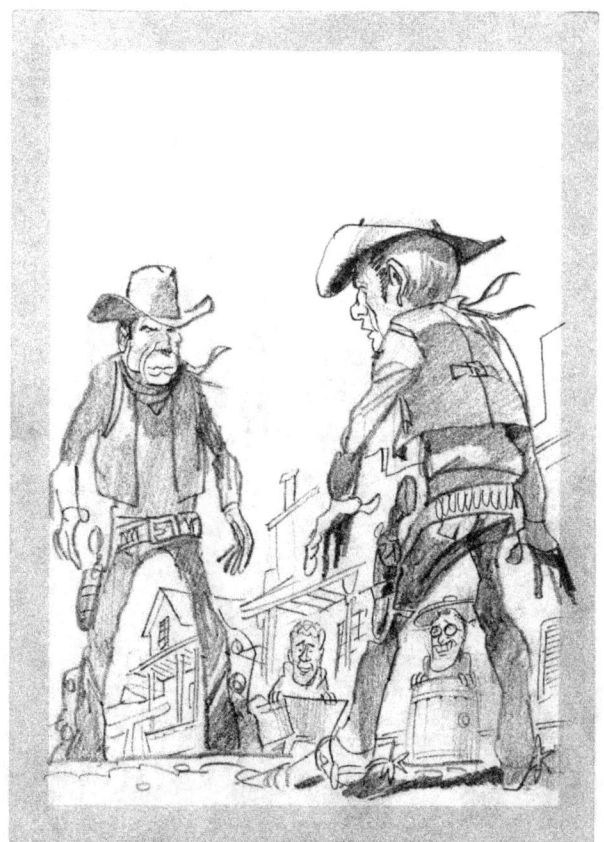

TIME *Magazine* Cover Ideas
Pencil on prepared sketch pad

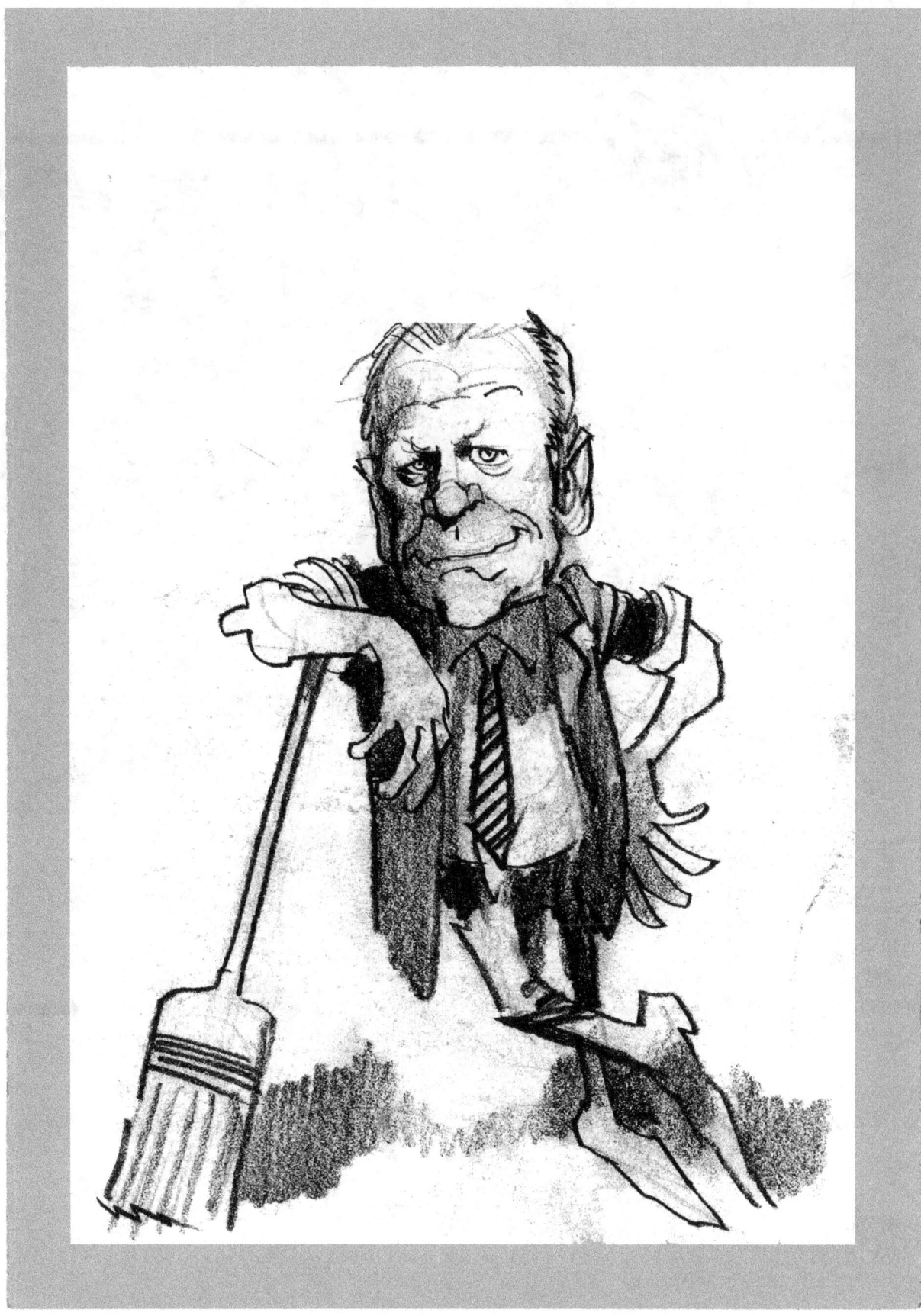

TIME *Magazine* Cover Idea
Pencil on prepared sketch pad

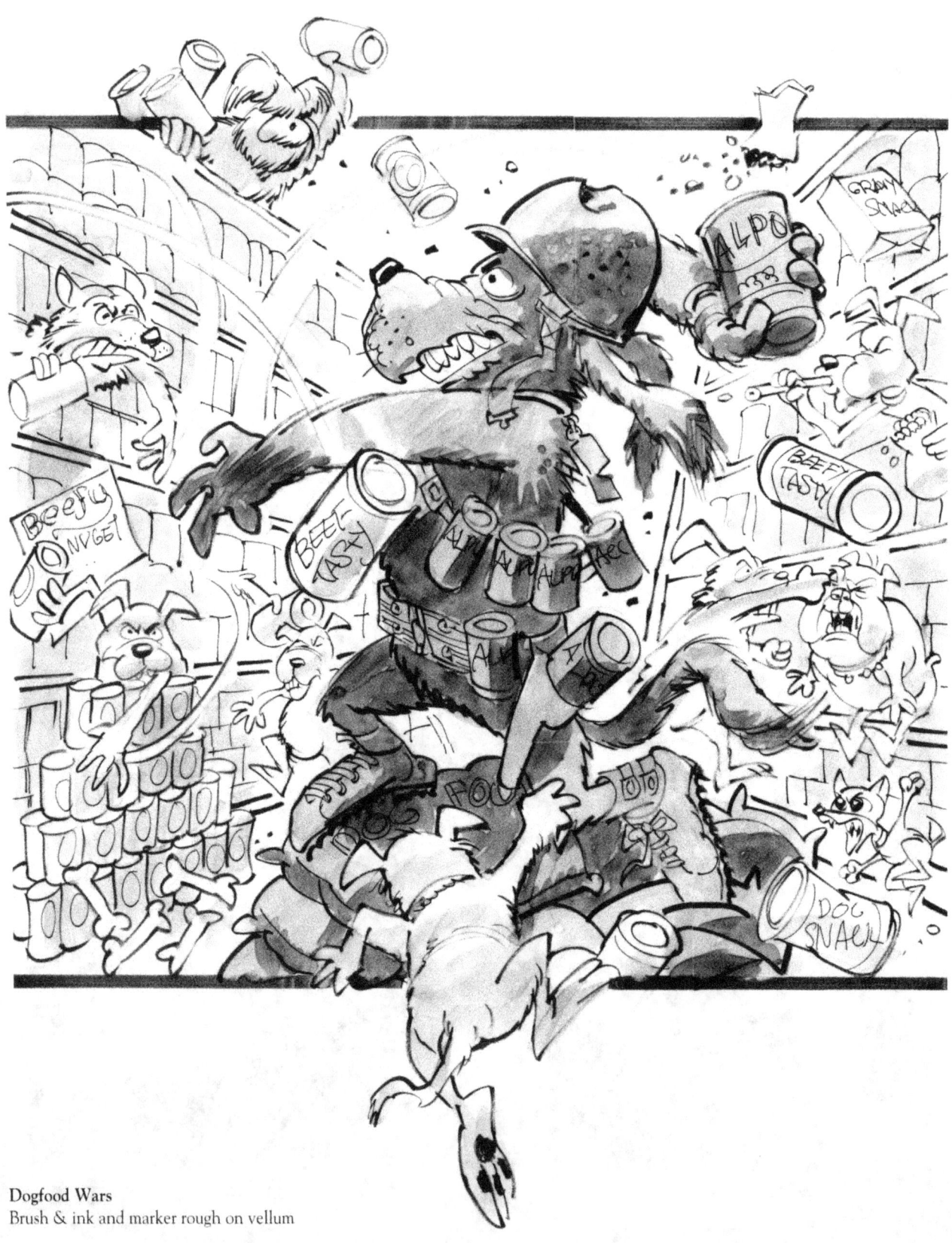

Dogfood Wars
Brush & ink and marker rough on vellum

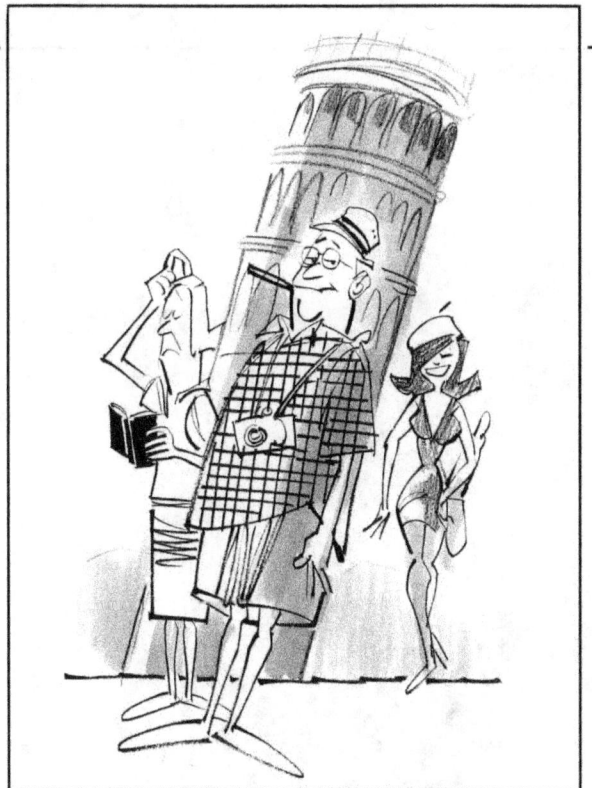

Leaning Tower of Pisa
Mixed media rough on Strathmore

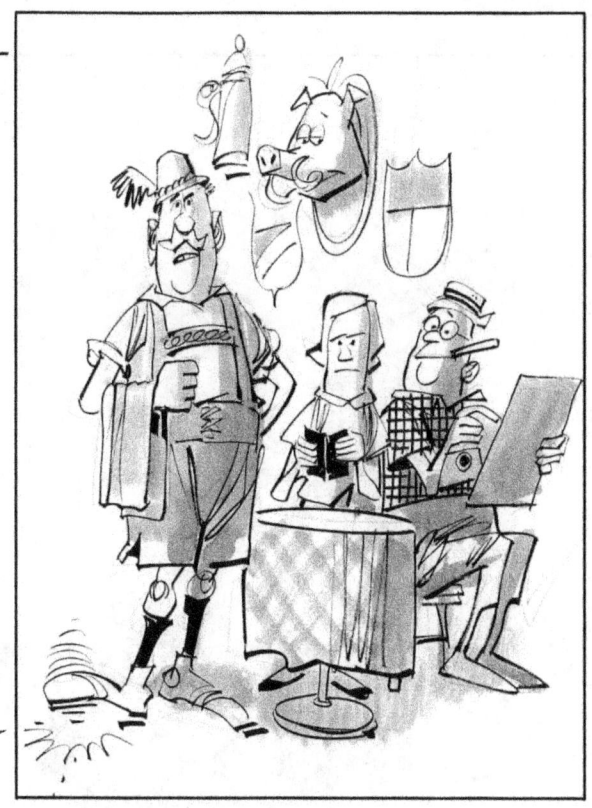

German Restaurant
Brush & ink and marker rough on Strathmore

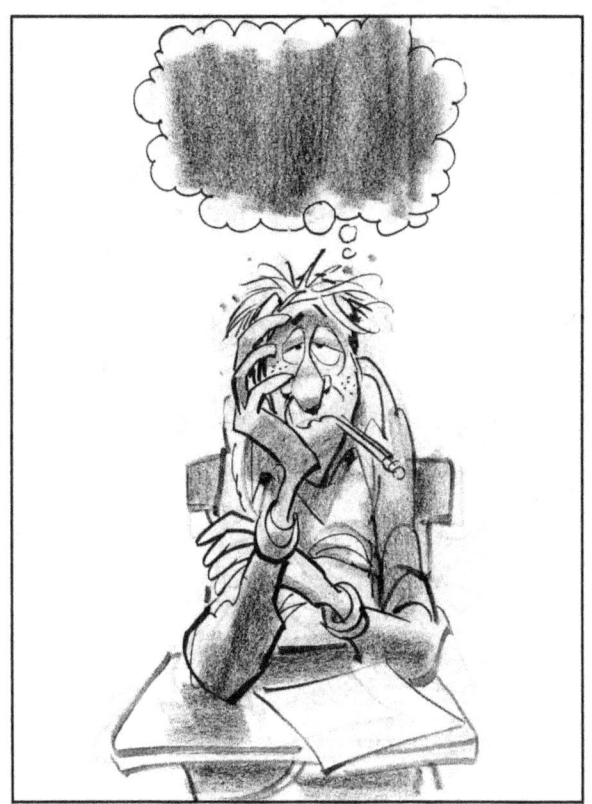

School Daze
Brush & ink and pencil rough on vellum

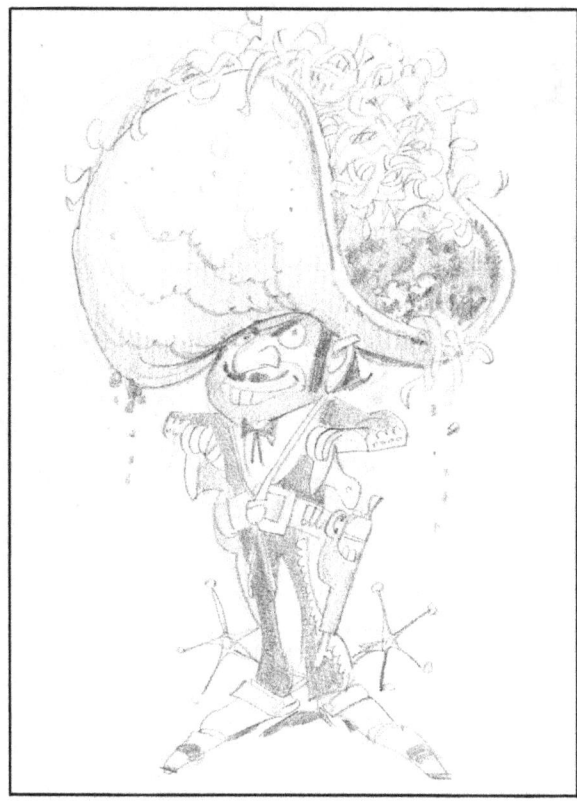

Chalupa Bandito
Pencil on illustration board
Advertising rough

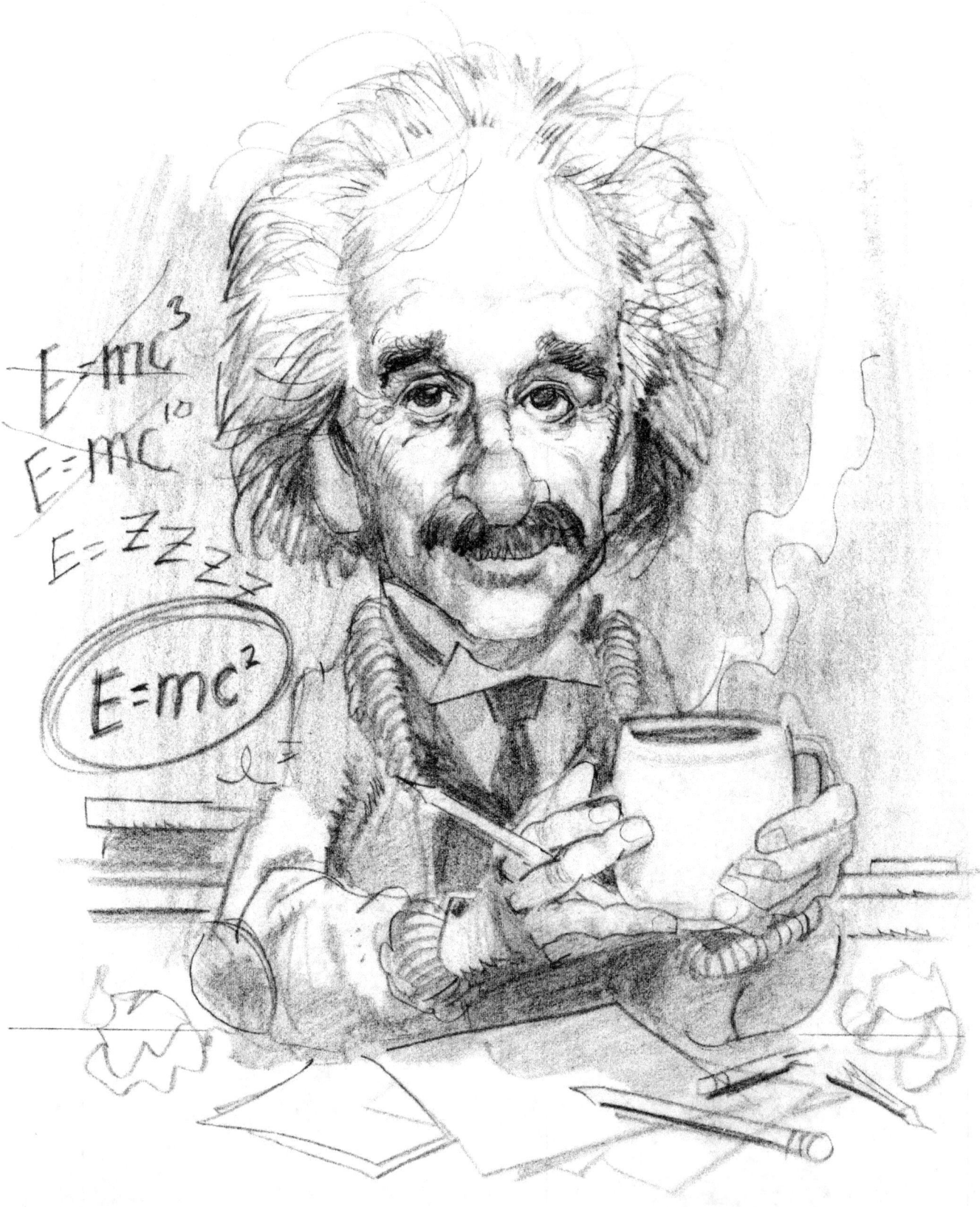

Albert Einstein
Pencil sketch on illustration board

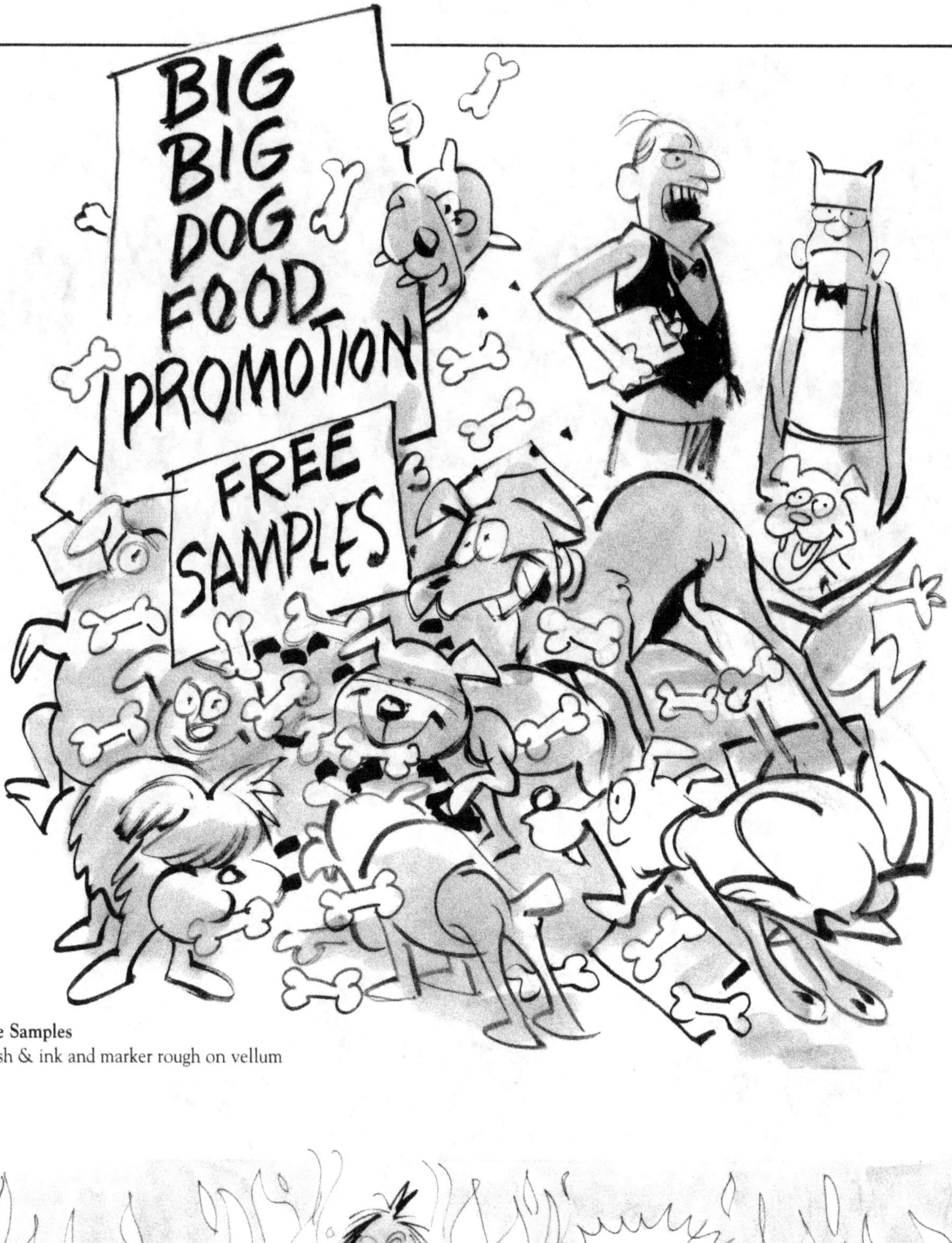

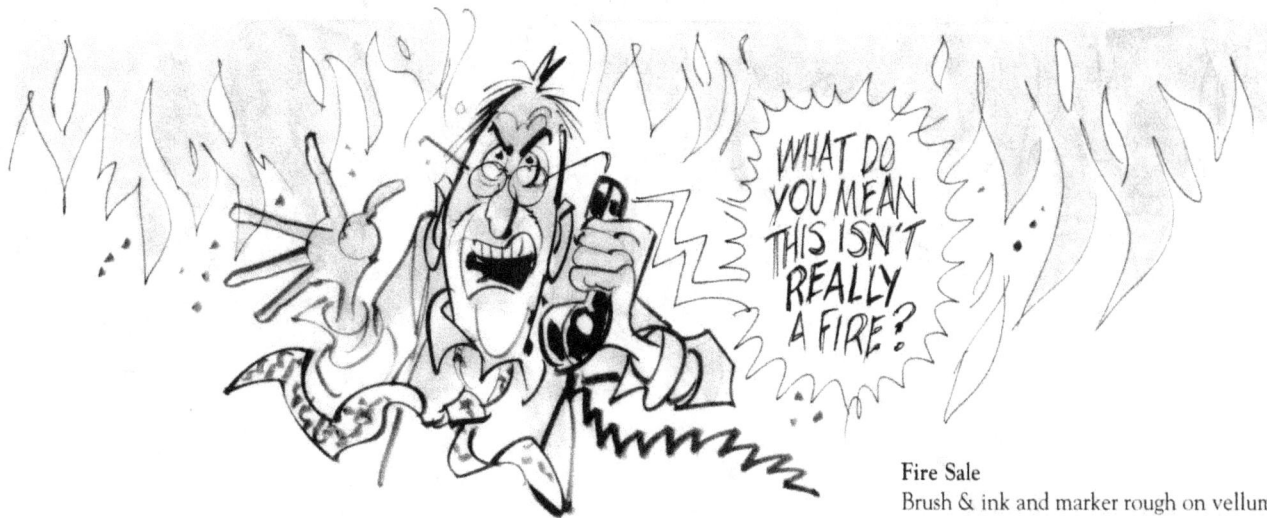

Free Samples
Brush & ink and marker rough on vellum

Fire Sale
Brush & ink and marker rough on vellum

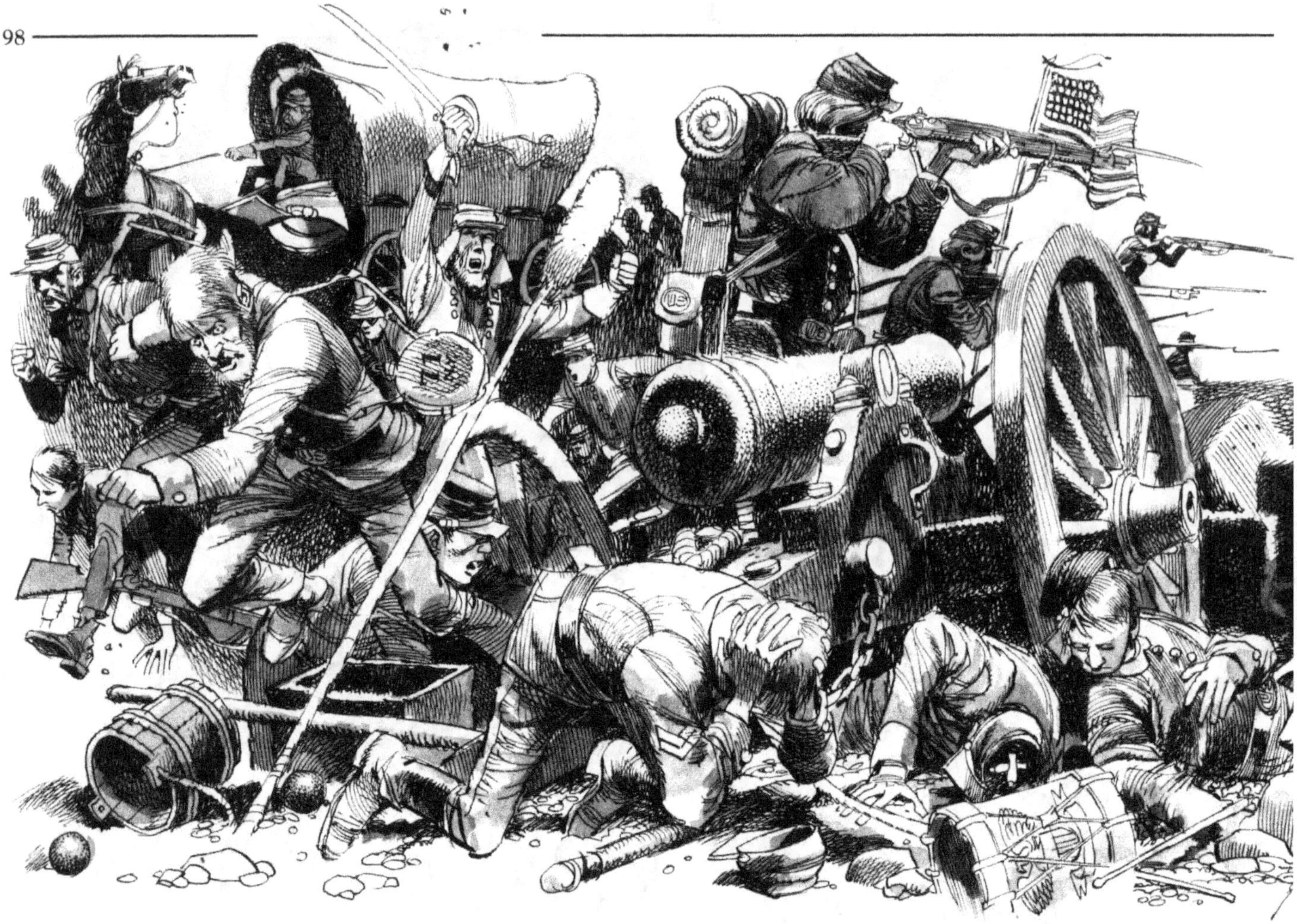

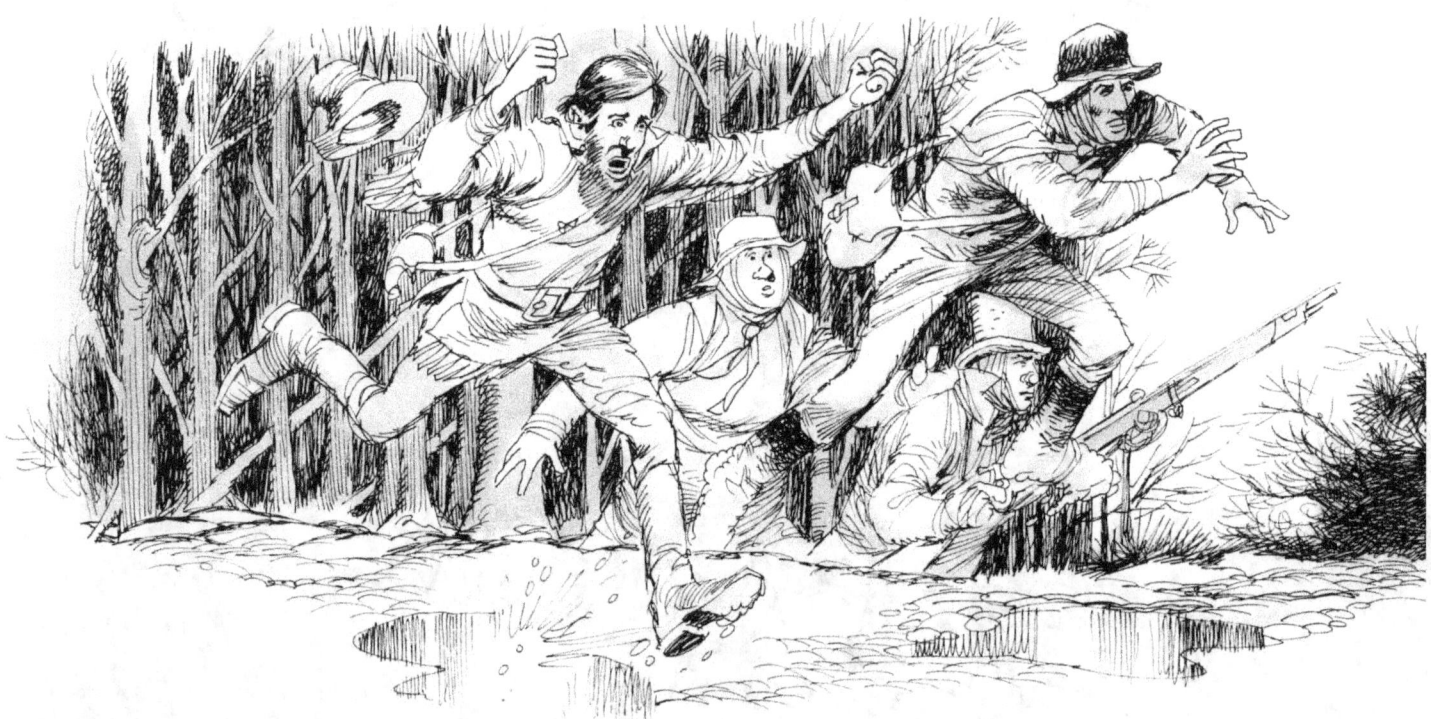

Chasin' Chickens
Pen & ink on illustration board
Meet Abraham Lincoln children's book, 1965

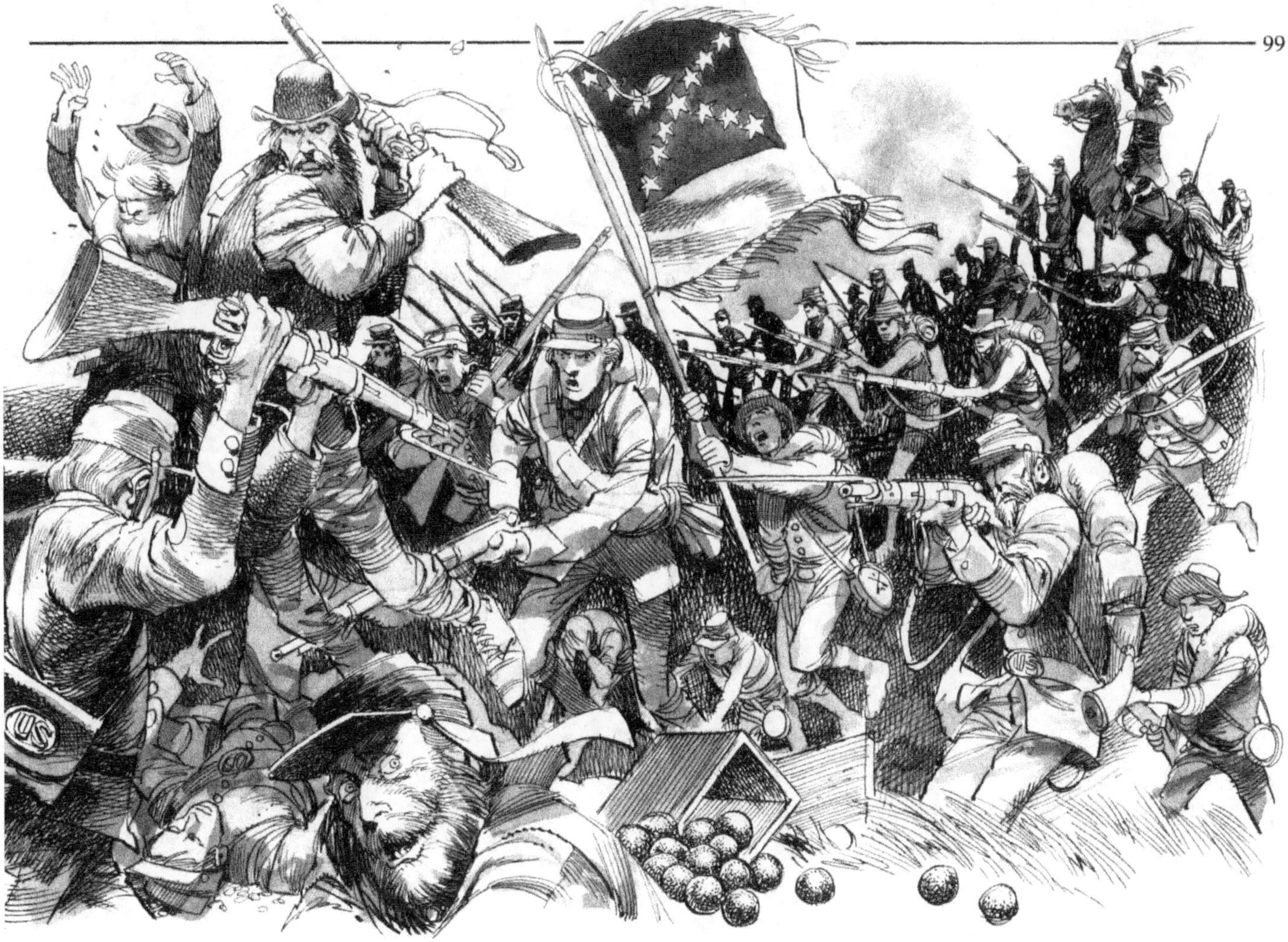

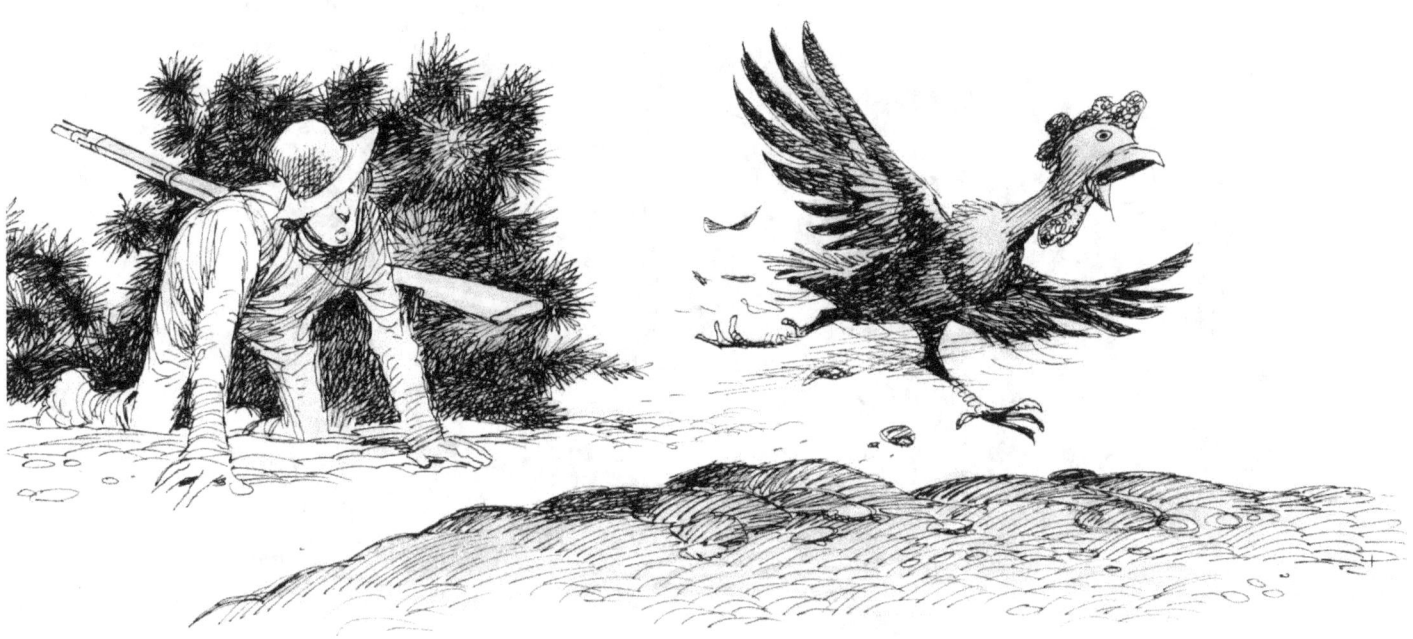

Civil War Battle
Pen & ink and wash on illustration board
Meet Abraham Lincoln children's book, 1965

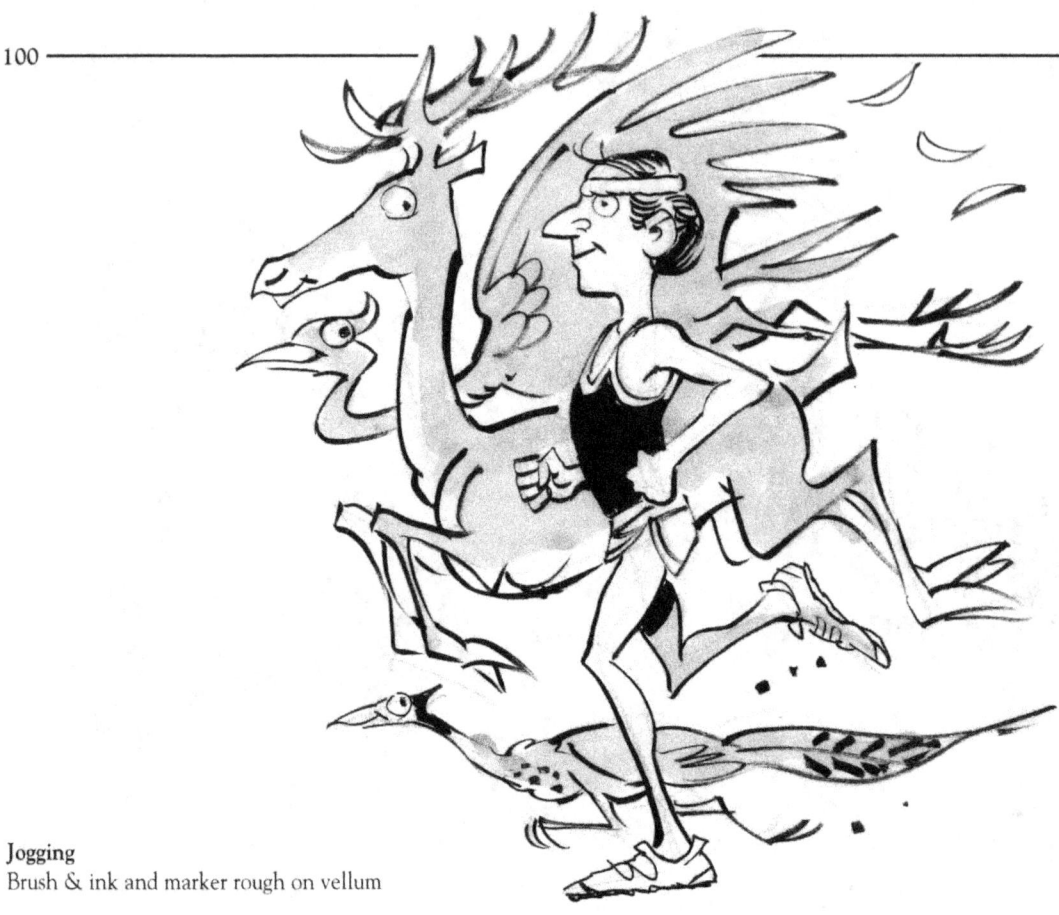

Jogging
Brush & ink and marker rough on vellum

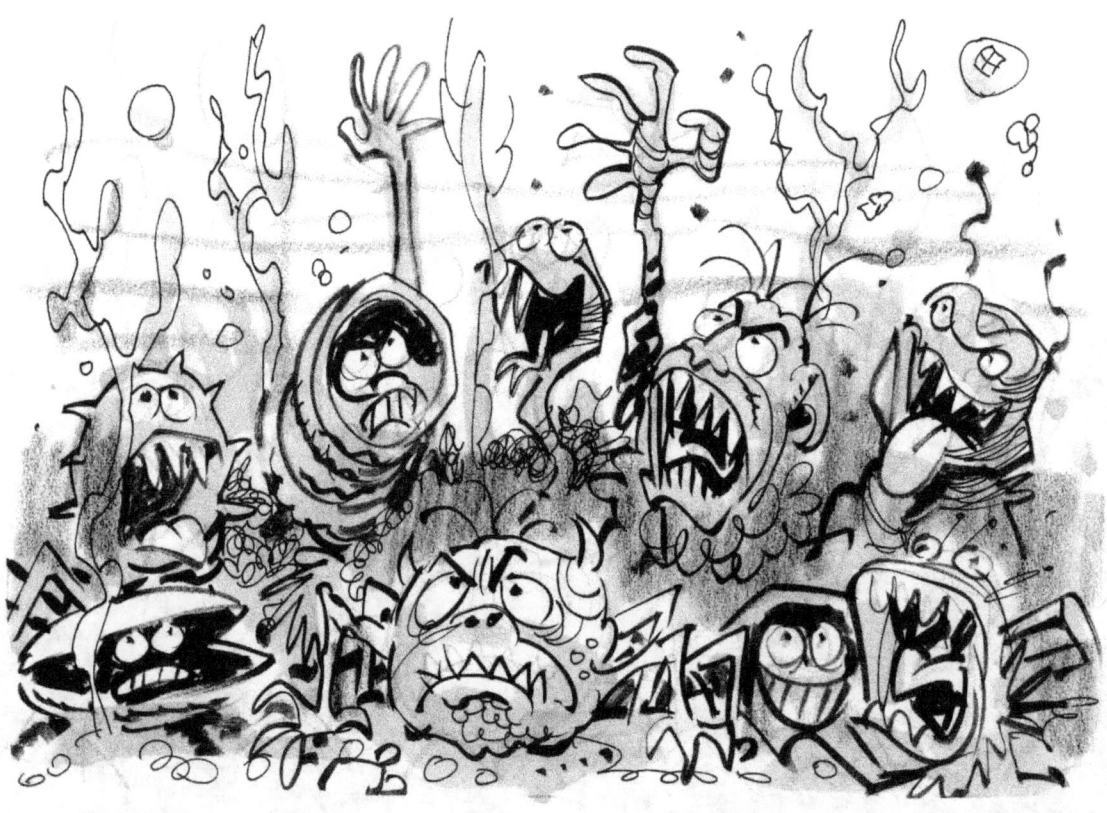

Barnacles
Mixed media rough on vellum

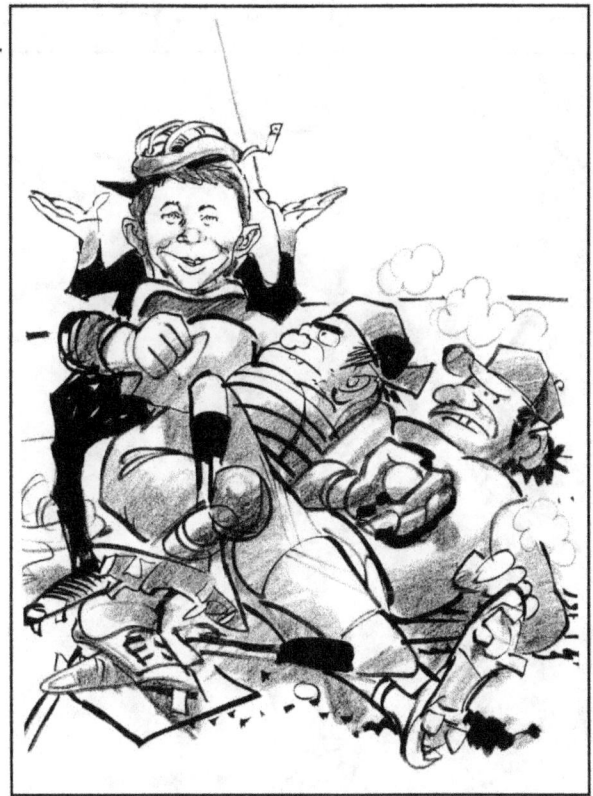

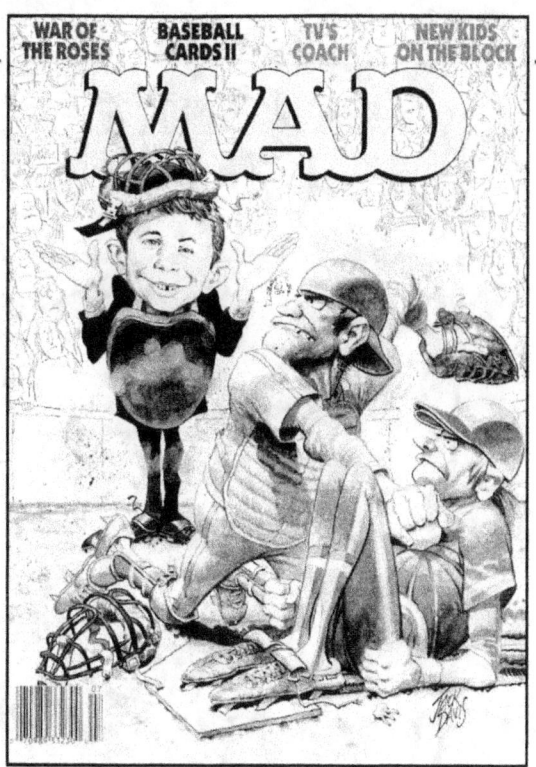

What — Me Out?
Brush & ink and marker rough on vellum

Mad Magazine, July 1990
Mixed media
© 1990 E.C. Publications Inc.

Snake Charmer
Brush & ink and marker rough on vellum

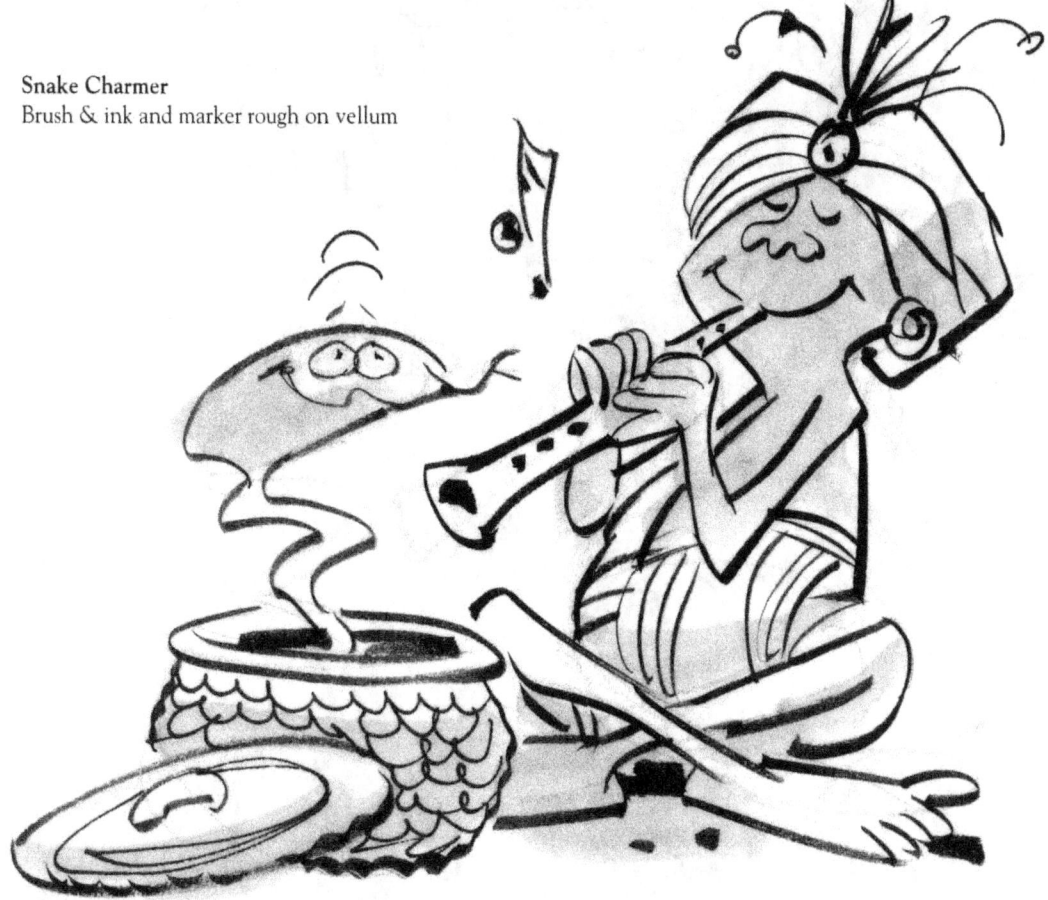

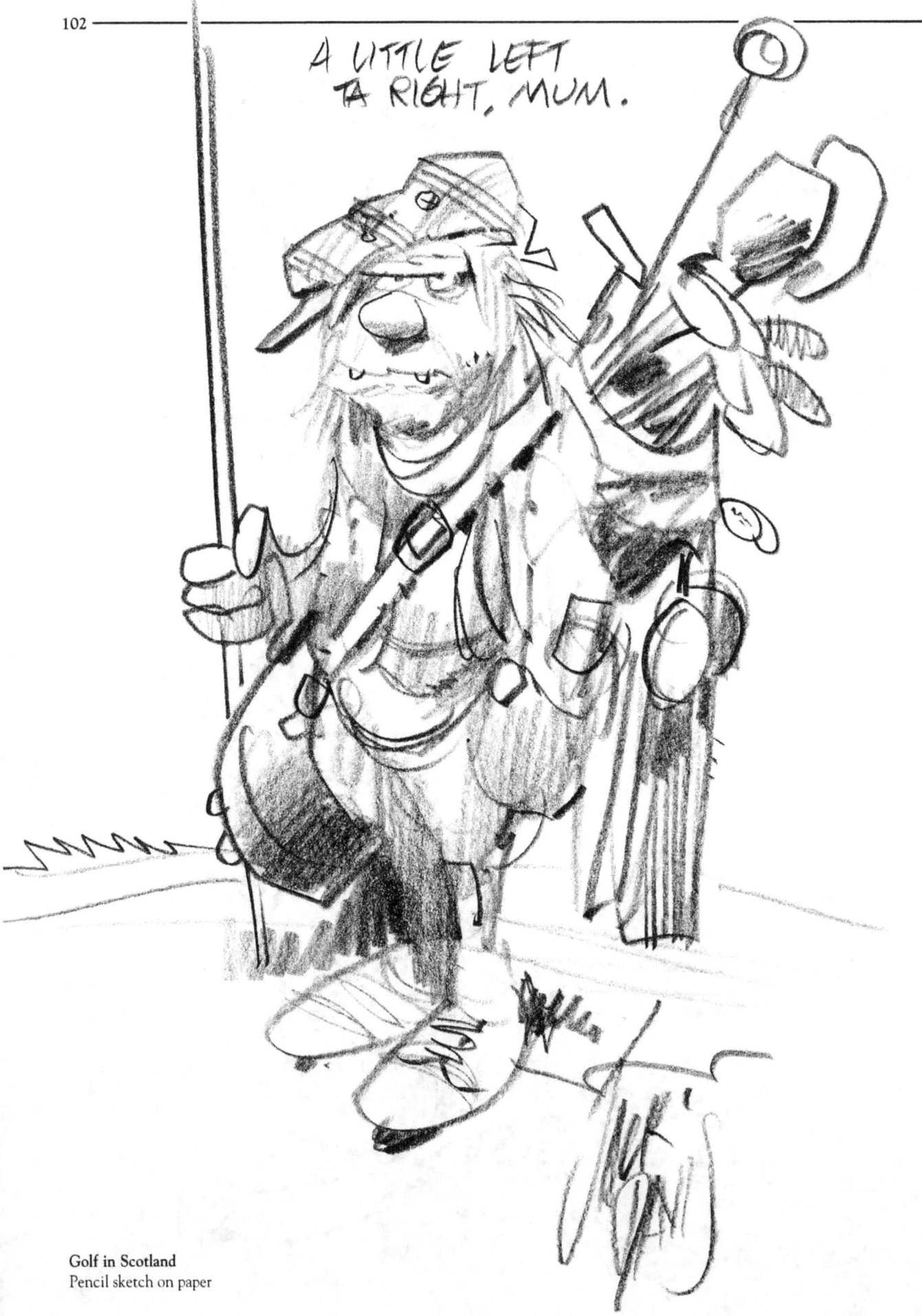

Golf in Scotland
Pencil sketch on paper

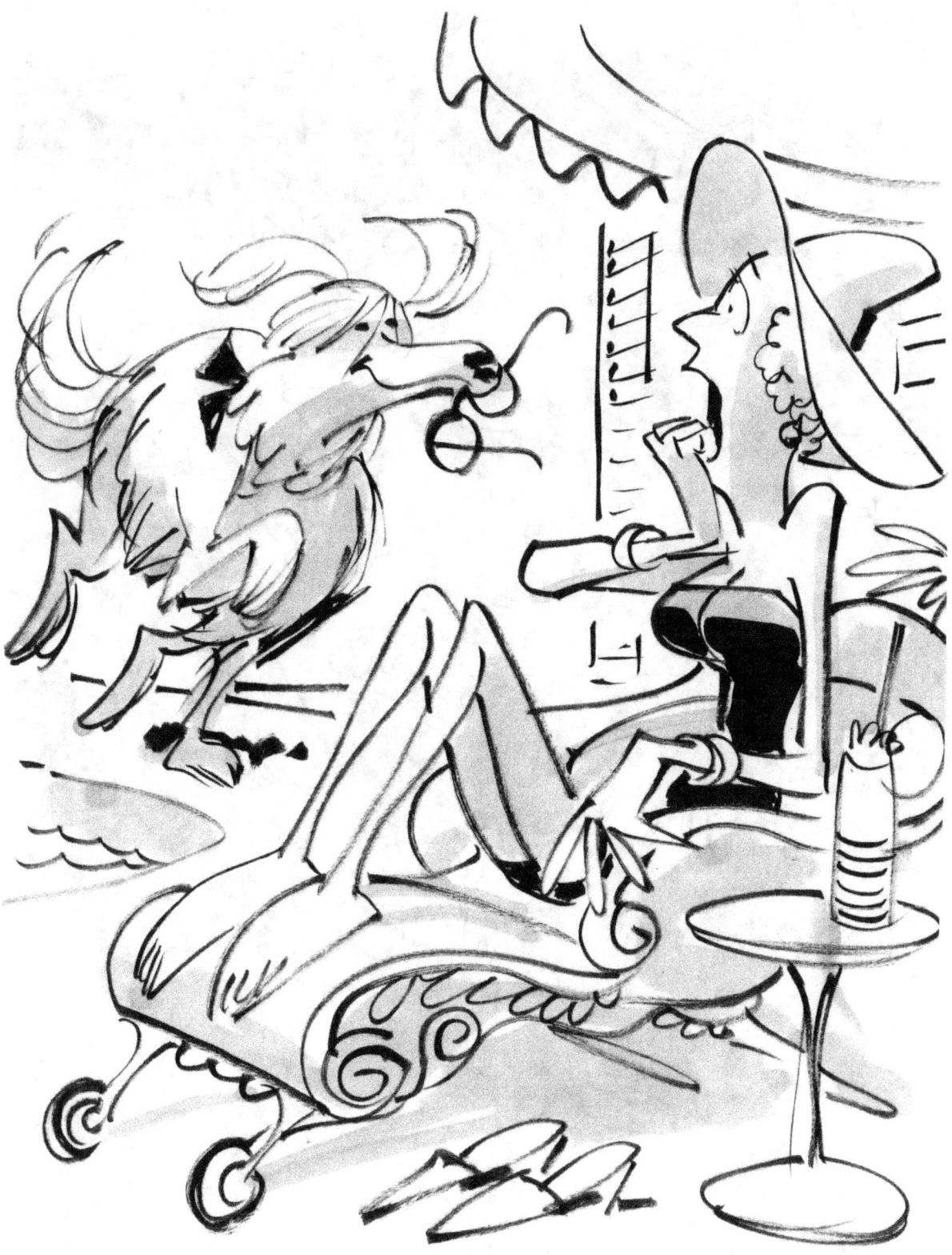

Fetch
Brush & ink and marker rough on vellum

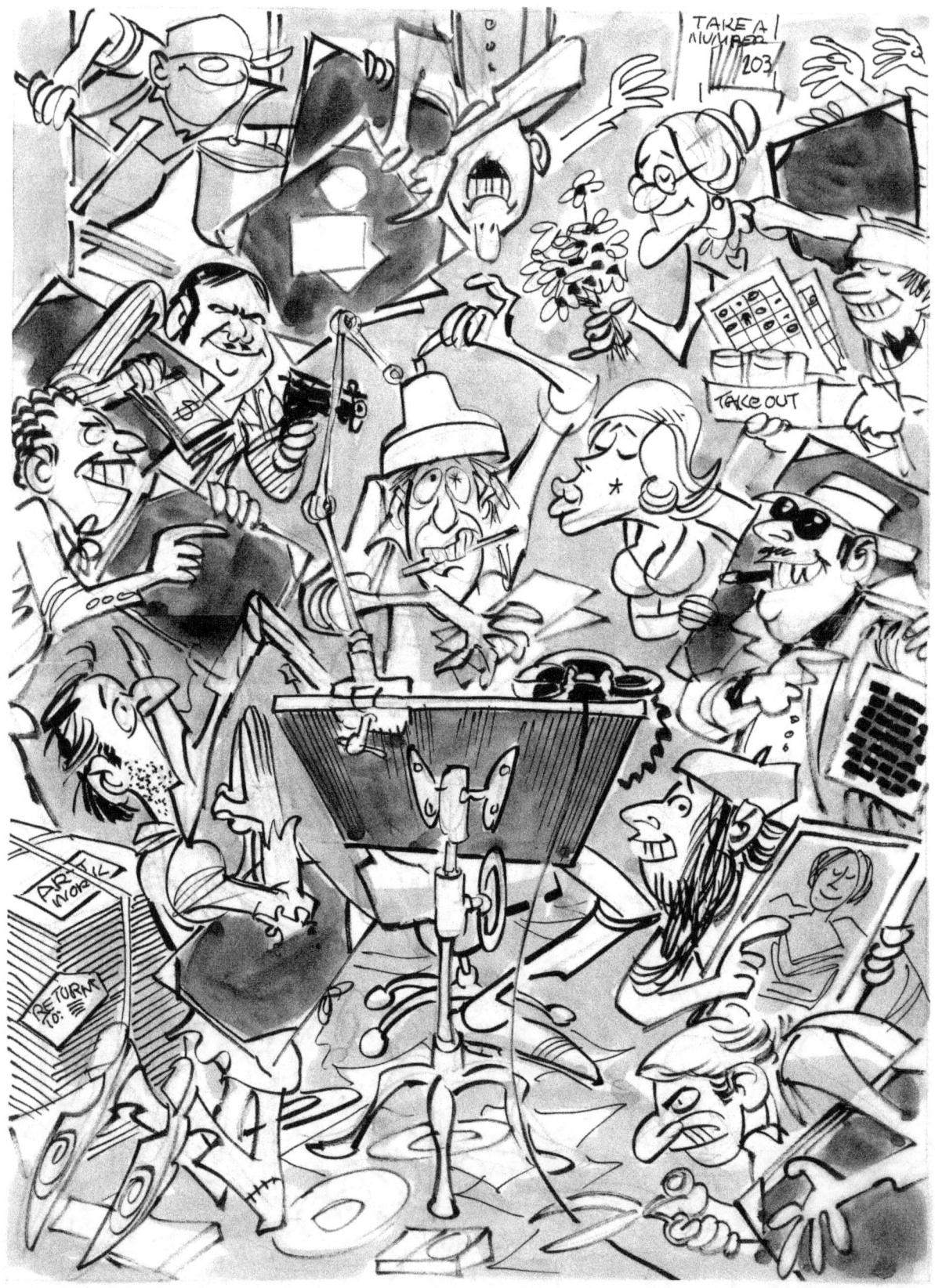

Deadlines!
Brush & ink and marker rough on vellum

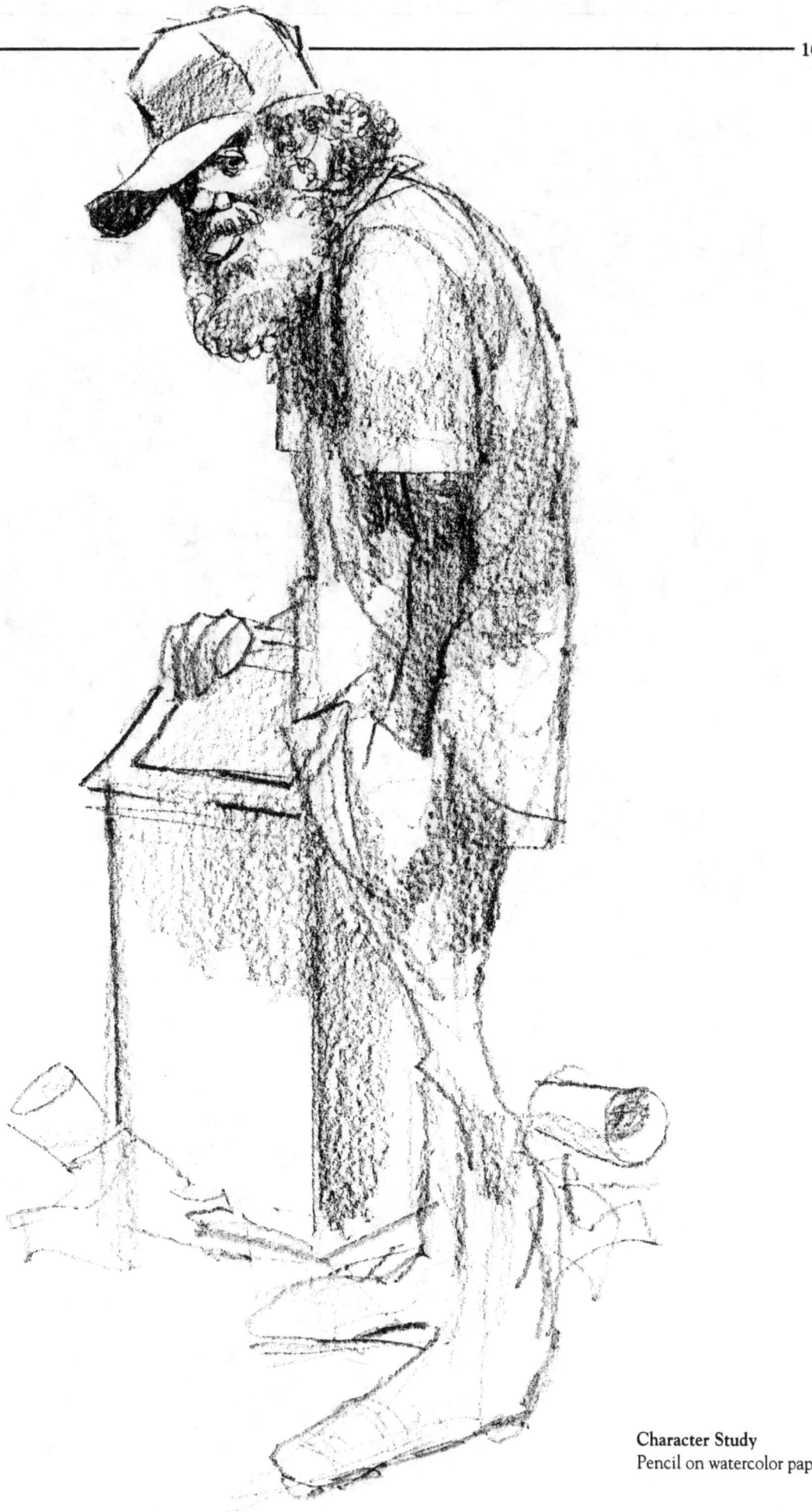

Character Study
Pencil on watercolor paper

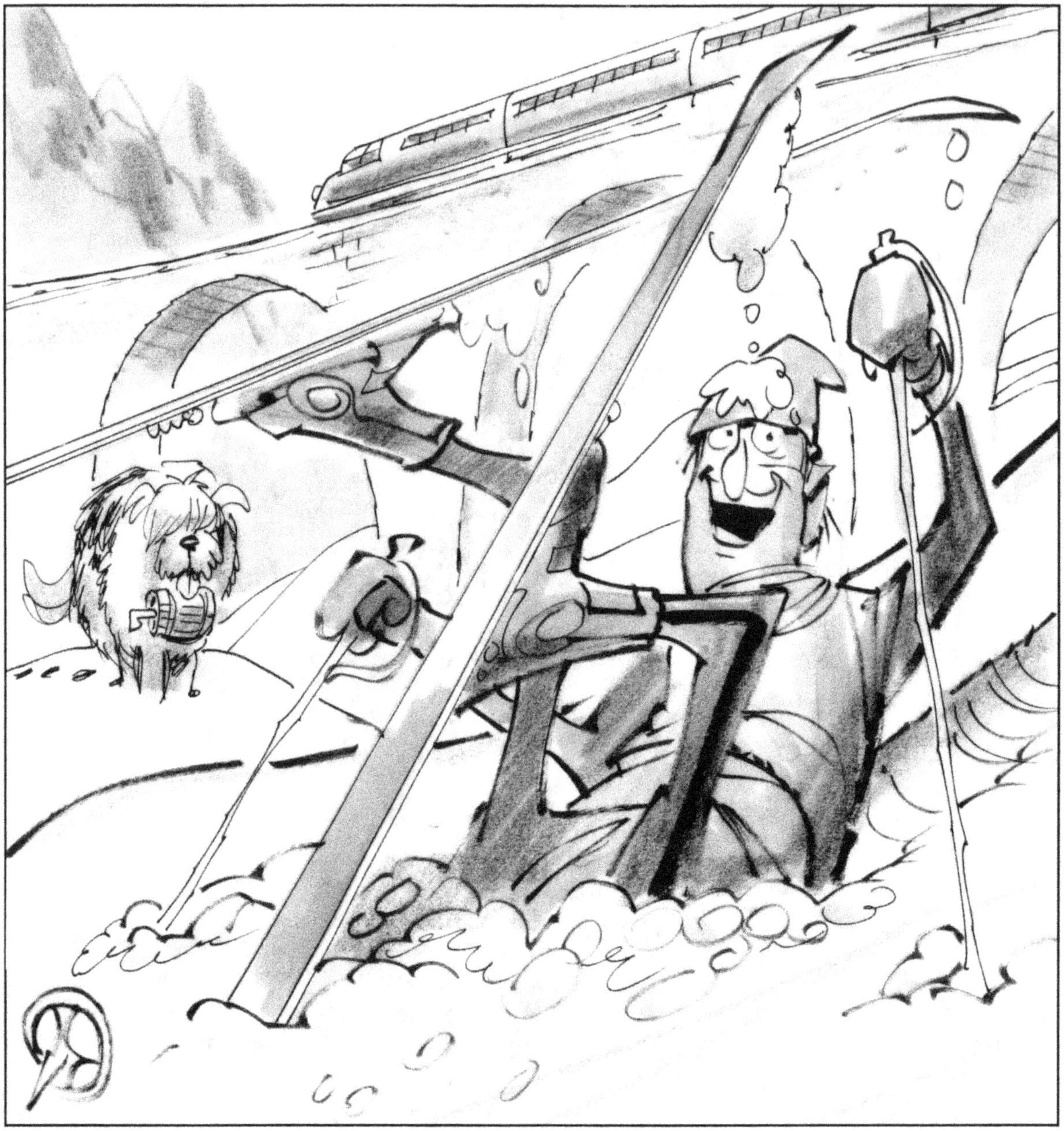

Skiing Trip
Mixed media rough on vellum

Frog
Brush & ink on Strathmore

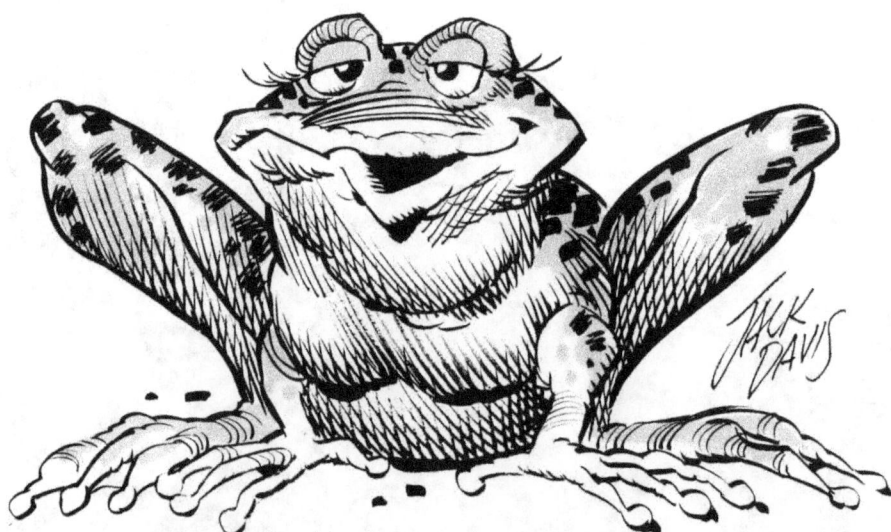

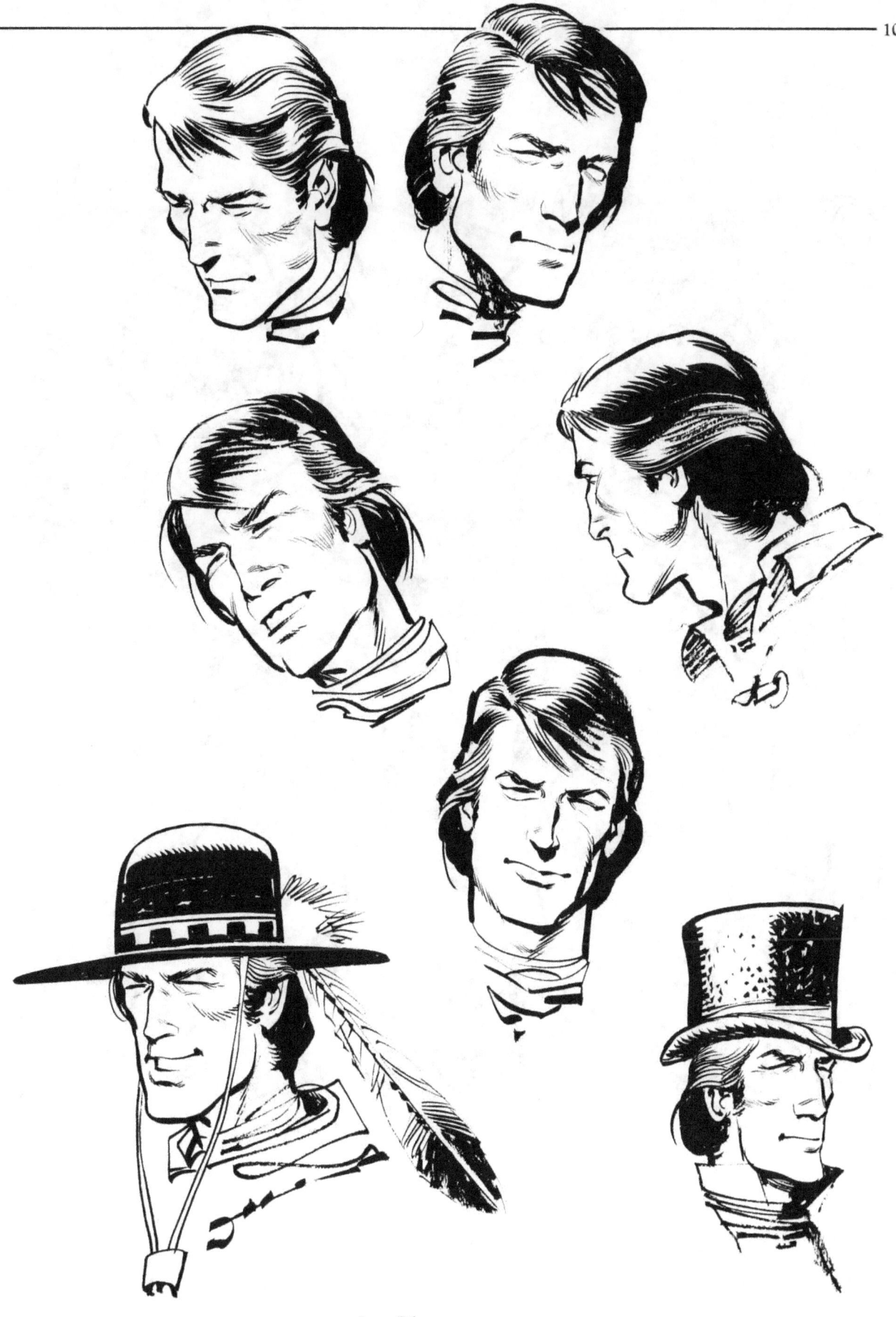

Jesse Pike
Brush & ink on Strathmore
Model sheet for proposed 50's comic strip

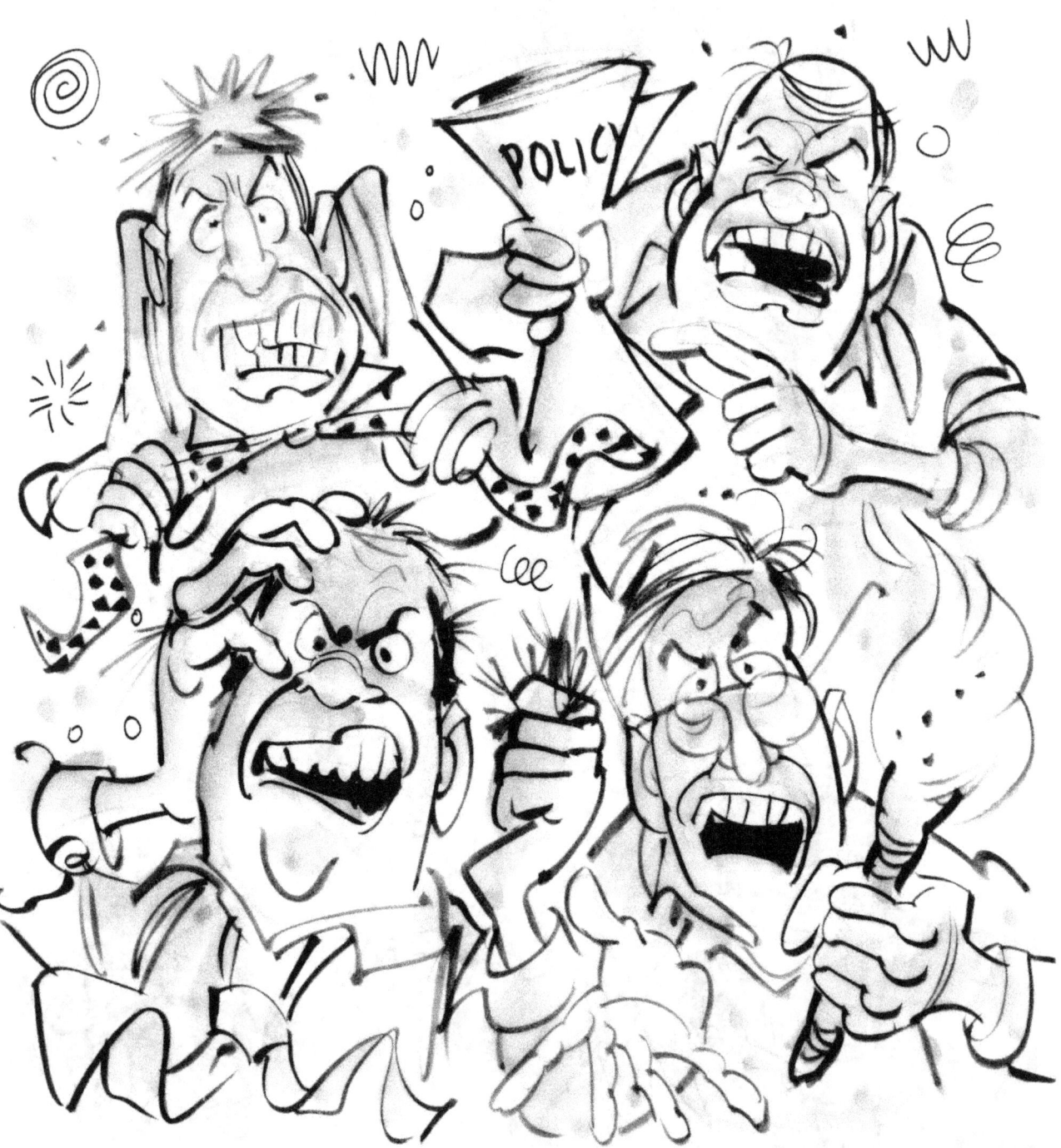

Irate Customers
Brush & ink and marker rough on vellum

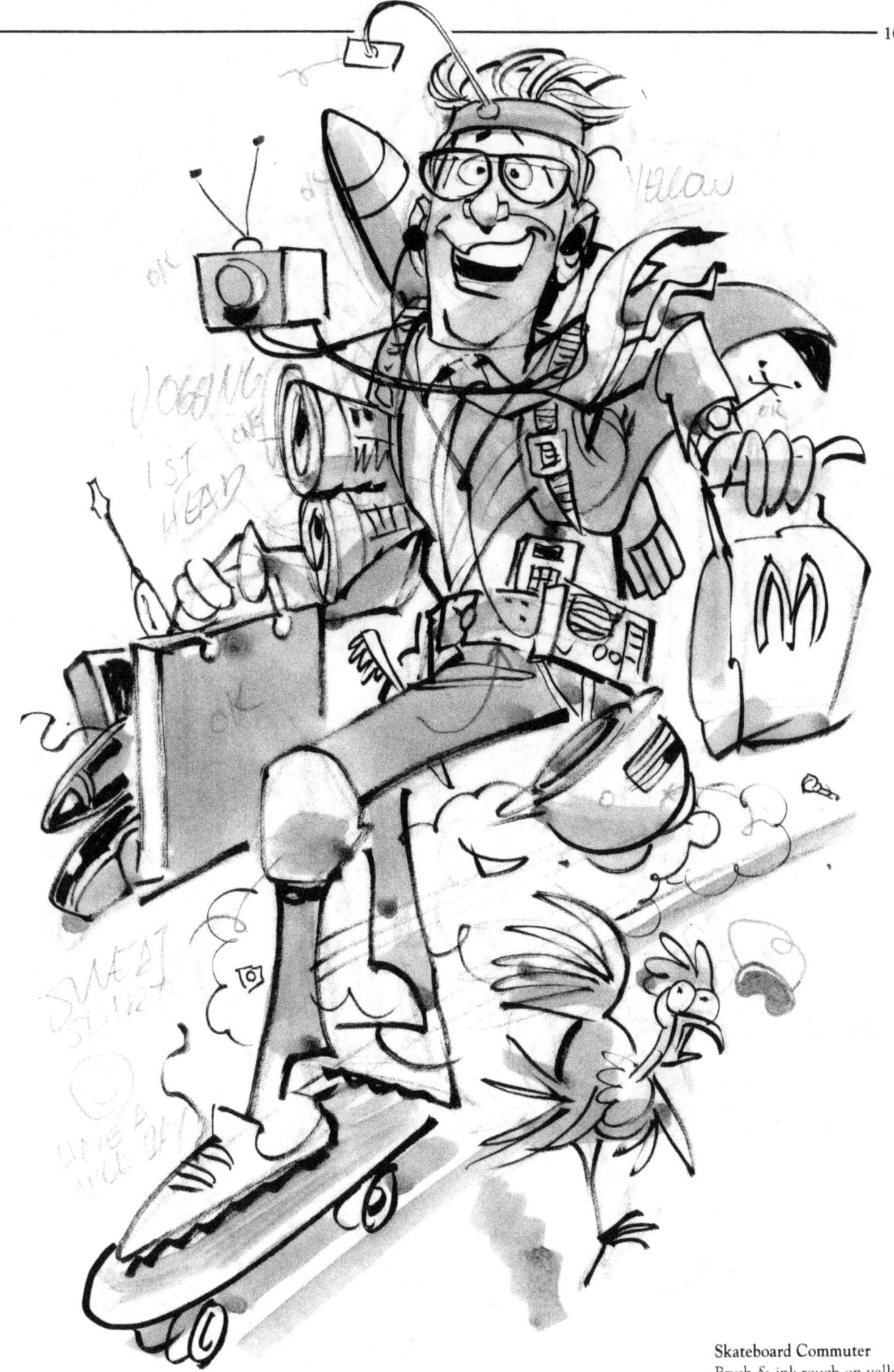

Skateboard Commuter
Brush & ink rough on vellum

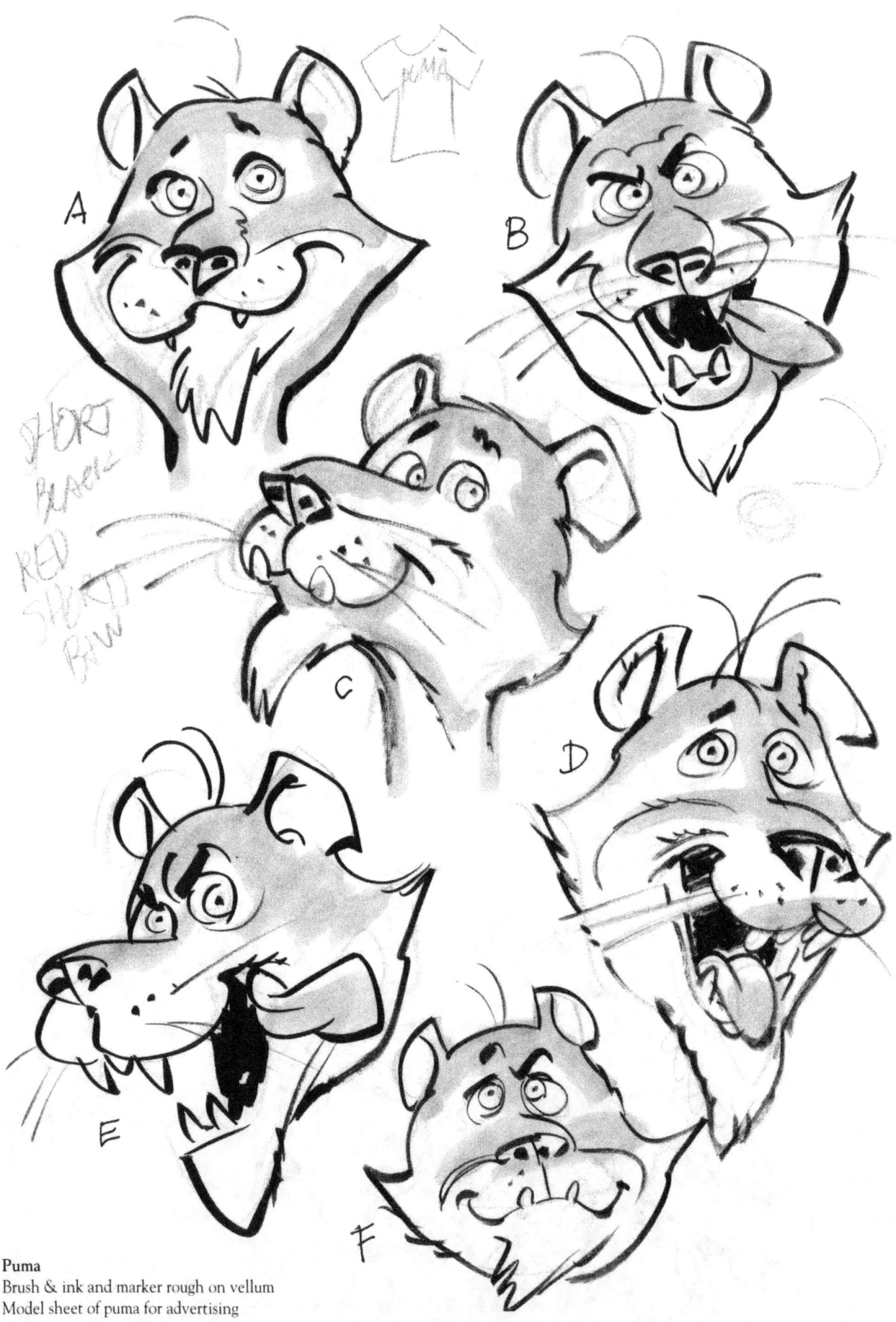

Puma
Brush & ink and marker rough on vellum
Model sheet of puma for advertising

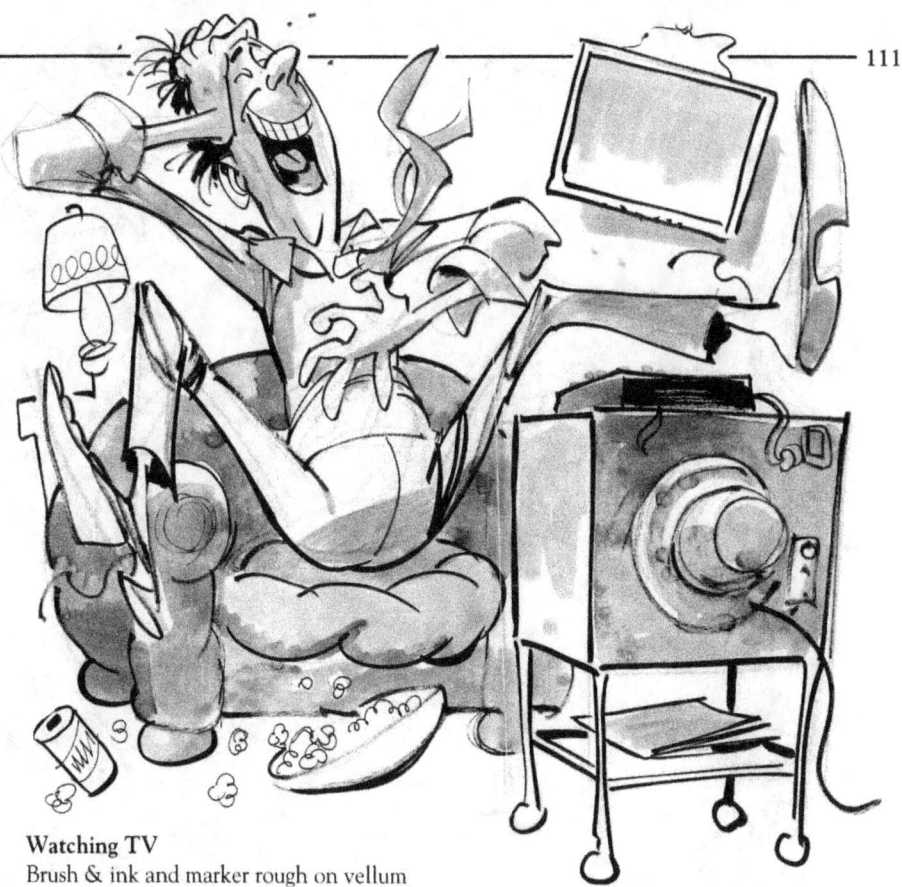

Watching TV
Brush & ink and marker rough on vellum

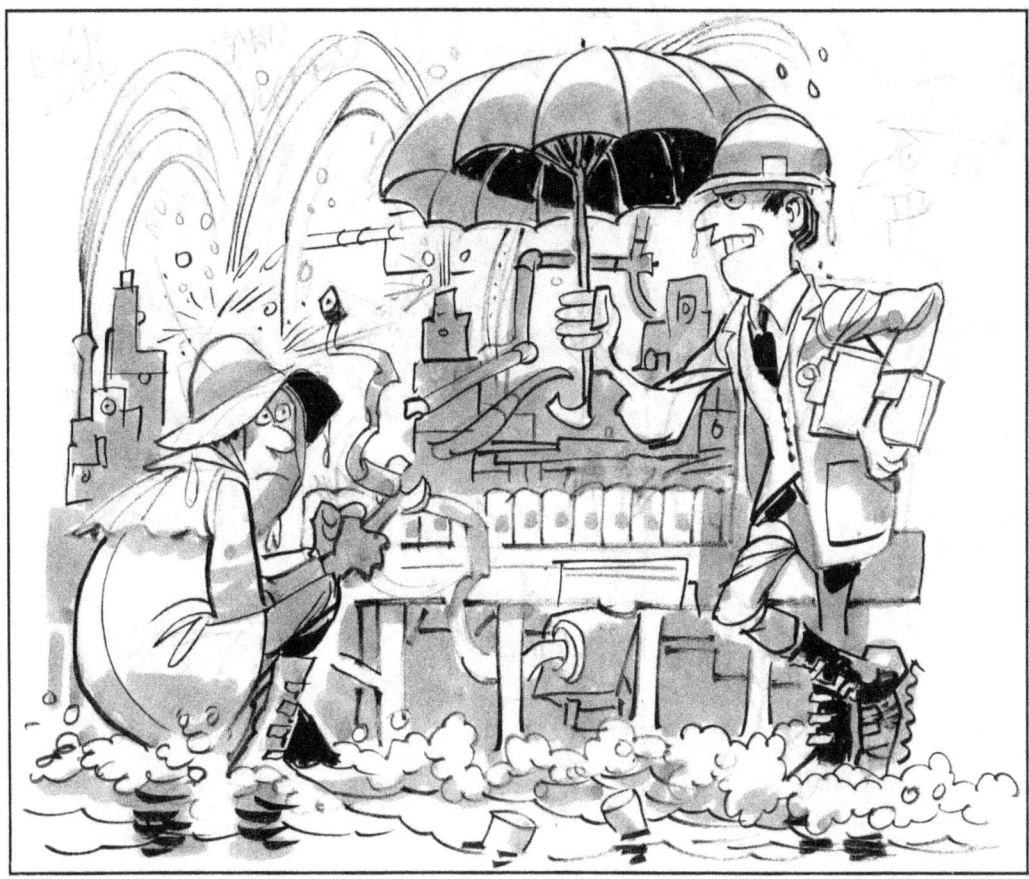

Repair Problems
Brush & ink and marker rough on vellum

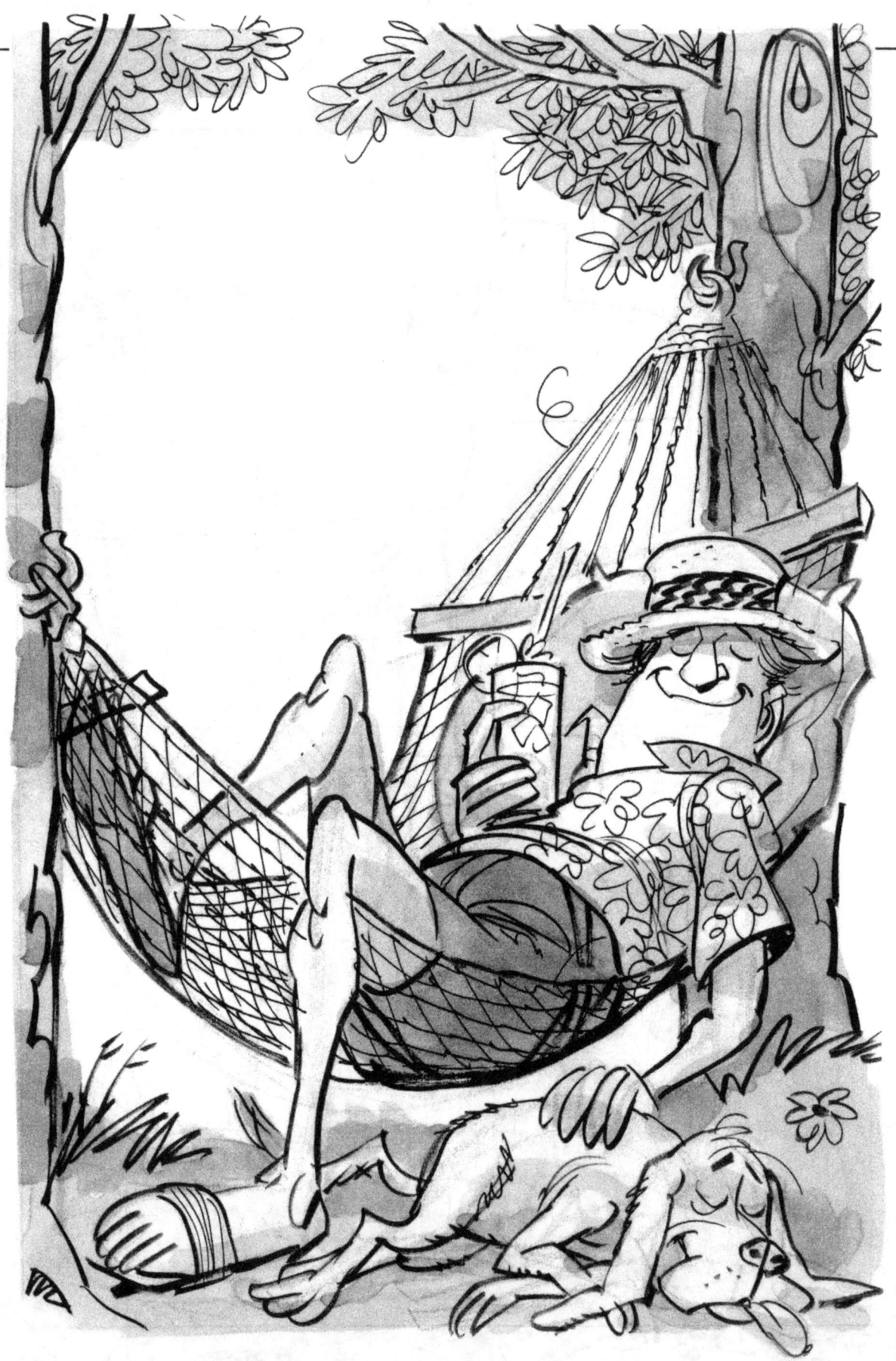

Relaxin'
Mixed media on vellum
Advertising rough

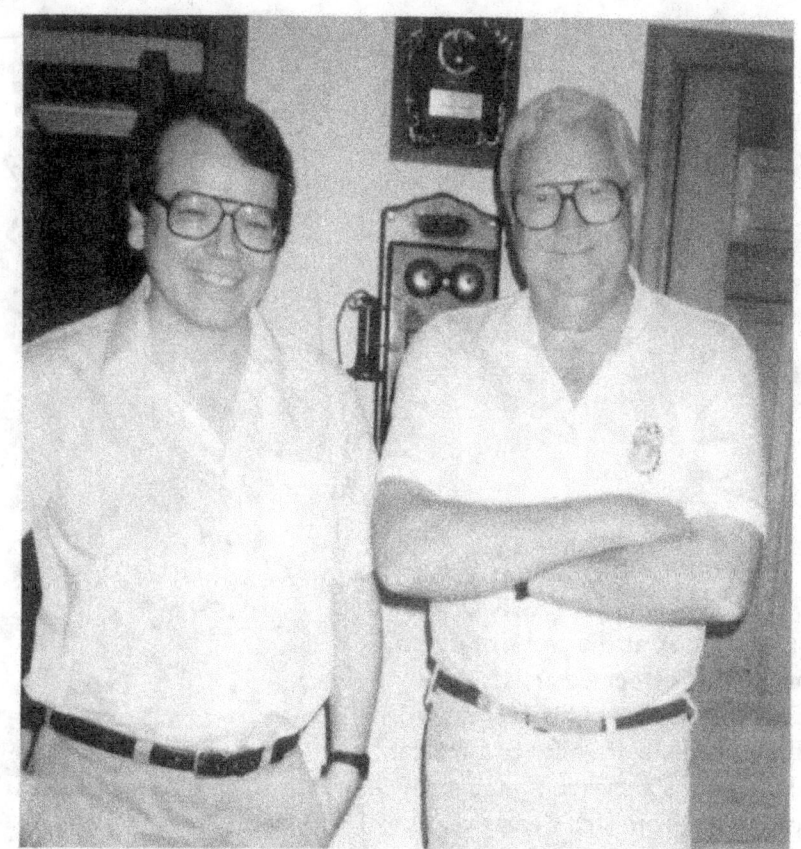

Hank Harrison and Jack Davis in Davis' studio.

A native Texan, Hank Harrison is an exhibit designer at The Witte Museum in San Antonio. Member of an entire family of commercial artists and musicians, Harrison is a veteran advertising agency art director. He is also a second-generation Davis fan. "My dad had a collection of E.C.'s and Humbugs, and we always had a subscription to Mad Magazine," he recalls. Hank and his brother Jeff became enthusiastic fans of Jack Davis' advertising work even as both young men began their advertising careers. Having amassed a large collection of Davis' artwork, Harrison began the research which led to the 1987 book, *The Art of Jack Davis*. Davis generously allowed Harrison access to his archives. It was quickly apparent that Davis' files contained material for more than just one book. So here is a second richly deserved tribute to the king of humorous illustration, Jack Davis.

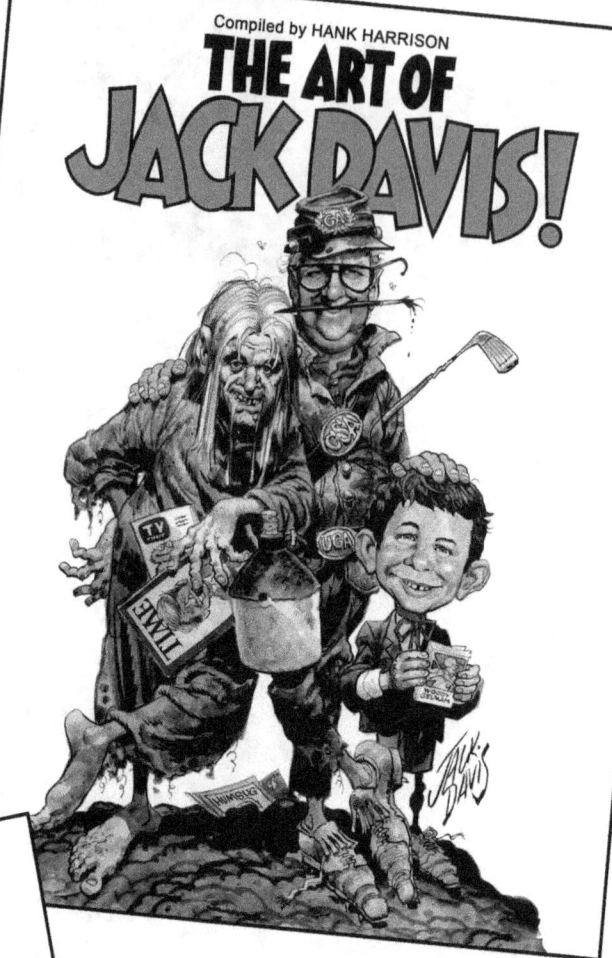
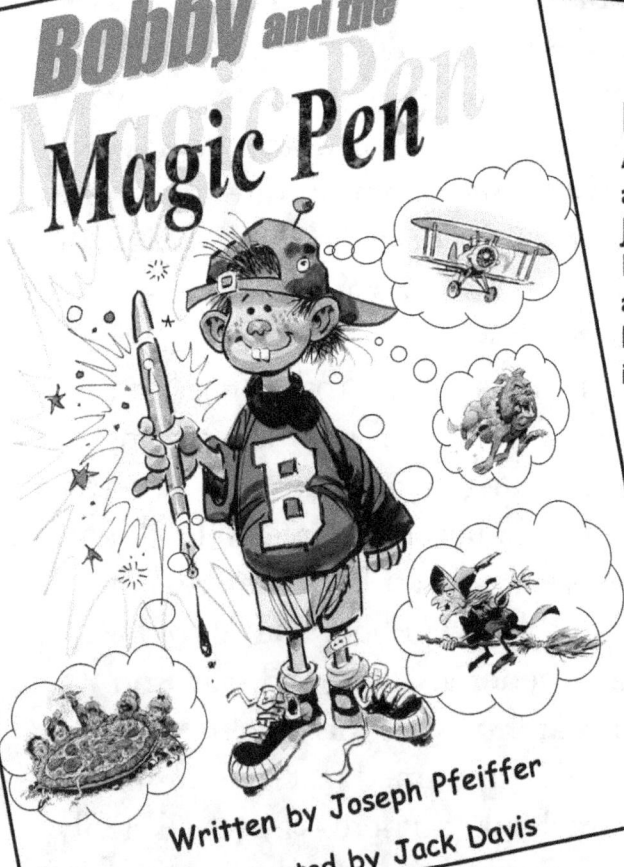
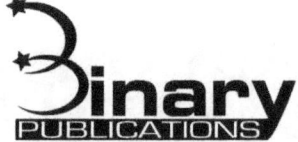

www.ingramcontent.com/pod-product-compliance
Lightning Source LLC
Chambersburg PA
CBHW080930170526
45158CB00008B/2239